WHO'S
WHO IN
BLOOMSBURY

WHO'S WHO IN BLOOMSBURY

ALAN & VERONICA PALMER

THE HARVESTER PRESS

First published in Great Britain in 1987 by
THE HARVESTER PRESS LIMITED
Publisher: John Spiers
16 Ship Street, Brighton, Sussex

© Alan and Veronica Palmer, 1987

British Library Cataloguing in Publication Data
Palmer, Alan
  Who's who in Bloomsbury.
  1. Bloomsbury group   2. Intellectuals—
  England—London—Biography   3. London
  (England)—Biography   4. London (England)
  —Intellectual life
  I. Title   II. Palmer, Veronica
  700'.92'2   DA688

  ISBN 0-7108-0312-5

Typeset in 11 on 12 point Plantin by
Eager Typesetting Co, Hove, East Sussex

Printed in Great Britain by Mackays of Chatham Ltd, Kent

THE HARVESTER PRESS PUBLISHING GROUP

The Harvester Group comprises The Harvester Press Limited (chiefly publishing literature, fiction, women's studies, philosophy, psychology, history and science and trade books), and Wheatsheaf Books Limited (chiefly publishing economics, international politics, women's studies, sociology, and related social sciences).

Contents

v

Preface

Bloomsbury is a district in central London, slightly over a mile north-east of Piccadilly Circus; the name is derived from the mediaeval manor of Blemundsbury, the family of Blemund having held the land in the early thirteenth century. Today the place name is associated with the British Museum and the long line of educational institutions to the north of it, the Senate House of London University, the Courtauld Institute Galleries, and the Royal Academy of Dramatic Art among them. Geographically, however, the district has never been clearly defined. It certainly includes the Russell estate—Bedford Square, Russell Square, Woburn Square, Tavistock Square, etc.—and it goes as far east as the Grays Inn Road and south to Bloomsbury Way, while the Euston Road forms a boundary to the north. But in the west does it cross Tottenham Court Road? Not historically, perhaps, yet there is no doubt that the vestigial Adam elegance of Fitzroy Square, Lilliputian beside today's telecommunications tower, matches in character the façades of Gordon Square and what remains of traditional Bloomsbury architecture after the bombing and hotel-building. It was here, where terraced houses around open squares recalled the courts and quadrangles of older universities, that a cultured circle of writers and artists flourished from the last years of Edwardian England until the Second World War.

This Bloomsbury group, which was never a formally organised body, came into being in October 1905 with evening gatherings of friends at 46 Gordon Square, the home of the sons and daughters of the late Sir Leslie Stephen. To some extent Gordon Square—and, after Thoby Stephen's death in 1906, Fitzroy Square—served as a London outpost for intellectuals recently expatriated from Cambridge, although the group was always less exclusive than the all-male societies of Trinity College and King's College. Over the

nine years before the First World War the surviving Stephens—
Vanessa, Virginia and Adrian—were gradually joined by more than
a dozen friends whose talk and ideas constituted what Virginia
Woolf was to call "Old Bloomsbury".

Doubt remains over who really belonged to this select circle. All
agree that among these friends, by 1914, were three Stracheys
(Lytton, James and Marjorie), Clive Bell, Leonard Woolf,
Maynard Keynes, Duncan Grant, E. M. Forster, Roger Fry,
Desmond and Molly McCarthy, Saxon Sydney-Turner, and
H. T. J. Norton. But there were others, too, on the fringe; several
of them, like Francis Birrell and David Garnett, became closer to
the original Bloomsbury group during and after the war. At the
same time younger writers and artists brought a new and
challenging vitality to stimulate the nuclei, gathered in 1920 in
membership of a Memoir Club.

So varied were the interests, achievements and disappointments
of this gifted circle that it has seemed worthwhile to us to collect
summary biographies of them in the present book. We have added
entries for men and women never at the heart of affairs but
associated with the group, both before the coming of the war and
later, when Bloomsbury expanded and conclaves would gather, as
often as not, in Sussex or Wiltshire and sometimes in France.
Certain familiar names may seem more "Chelsea", "Kensington",
"Cambridge", or "Garsington" than "Bloomsbury", and we
recognise that to some readers our reasons for including or rejecting
such fringe figures must appear arbitrary. Our criterion has been,
not so much a person's eminence, as his or her relevance to what
their friends were thinking and doing at any particular time.
Writers who knocked at Bloomsbury doors only to turn away in
repugnance from a narrow, brittle society are in; so, too, is a Nobel
Prize Winner who remained Bloomsbury's friend although his
beliefs rejected its assumptions on life and on death. But later
critics who complained that Bloomsbury was élitist—even a
seedbed of treason—are excluded. For it has seemed to us that
Bloomsbury art and Bloomsbury literature possess qualities of
resilience that leave the critics dated, not the originals. We have,
however, noticed an interesting continuity of families through three
centuries; for the names Strachey, Cecil and Garnett appear, not
only in *Who's Who in Bloomsbury*, but in our *Who's Who in
Shakespeare's England* too.

Collectively pre-1914 Bloomsbury was apolitical, irreverent, and
iconoclastic; it found a Socratic good in the contemplation of

beauty, and its sensitivities were exhilarated by the fiery afterglow of French Impressionism. Some of its daring thought was staler than Fitzroy Square assumed: Bloomsbury agnosticism retains a Late Victorian mustiness of disbelief. Occasionally there came a faint echo of the Pre-Raphaelites, for "Old Bloomsbury" too was in revolt against drabness; but it was never so homogeneous as the Brotherhood nor so self-conscious as the "greenery-yallery, Grosvenor Gallery" aesthetes mocked in *Patience*. If Roger Fry was Bloomsbury's Ruskin, he declined to function as an interpreter of artistic content; he preferred to shift away from pictorial reference and to teach the perception of a painting, as if it were music touching the eyes. For in those post-Edwardian years of opulence Bloomsbury observed and trained the senses rather than decreed what was culturally acceptable. Occasionally—as when the Diaghilev Ballet first came to London—Bloomsbury followed social fashion. But for the most part whatever sweetened the Blooms-berries remained sour to popular taste.

In the 1920s and 1930s Bloomsbury was primarily a literary movement, helping to shape and reflect a critical scepticism which recognised the validity of stylistic change. The publication of Holroyd's massive study of Strachey in 1967–8, the six annotated volumes of Virginia Woolf's letters in 1975–80 and the five volumes of her diaries in 1977–84, together with two complementary biographies of her by Quentin Bell (1972) and Lyndall Gordon (1984), have given fresh emphasis to this literary legacy at the expense of what was achieved by Bloomsbury's artists. Yet apart from Forster's earliest novels—which owe no inspiration to metropolitan London—the reputation of Old Bloomsbury before 1914 rested, if not on alleged innovations in sexual morality, then on success in the decorative arts and, above all, in painting. The collective noun "Bloomsbury" first appeared as a mild pejorative criticising, not a book or an article, but the selection of canvases to hang in the Post-Impressionist exhibition at the Grafton Gallery. Of the first two genuinely Bloomsbury books, Strachey's slim *Landmarks in French Literature* was underrated, and it was Clive Bell's *Art* which, in February 1914, caught the public eye. "Significant Form" was a cliché of the London intelligentsia a dozen years before "stream of consciousness" (although the phrase itself predates Bloomsbury). One of the most interesting developments of the mid-1980s has been the revived public attention given to Bloomsbury art and the Omega experiment. The careful work on restoring Charleston Farmhouse has ensured that Sussex nurtures a prize bloom, of native breeding and fertilised from France, which could never spread its beauty in today's academised Bloomsbury squares.

We would like to acknowledge our debt to the books which we have cited after some of the biographical entries. The sign * shows that there is an entry for the person, under his or her surname, in this book. A brief gazetteer, "Where's Where", a glossary, "What's What", explaining some of the less familiar terms, and a general bibliographical note have been added at the back of the book.

ALAN PALMER
VERONICA PALMER
Woodstock, Oxford; April 1987.

BLOOMSBURY IN THE 1920s

A

ANREP, Boris (1883–1969), mosaicist: son of Vassili von Anrep and a descendant of Baltic barons, born in St Petersburg, first visiting England as a schoolboy in 1899, to acquire his idiosyncratic English. He studied law in St Petersburg, where he became a professor, and taught art at the Académie Julian in Paris (1908) and Edinburgh College of Art (1910–11). Anrep came to London as a friend of Henry Lamb,★ through whom he met Lytton Strachey,★ and in 1912 he organised the Russian contribution to Fry's★ second Post-Impressionist exhibition. After fighting as an officer in Galicia in 1915–16 he returned to London as Military Secretary to the Russian Government Committee (1917).

After the war Anrep won recognition as Europe's leading mosaicist, with the Montparnasse studio he had rented in 1910 as his main workshop. He also had a home in London, where he was responsible for mosaics in the National and Tate Galleries, the Chapel of the Blessed Sacrament in Westminster Cathedral, and the Greek Orthodox Cathedral, as well as in the private houses of friends and colleagues. In seeking to portray the heads of the Twelve Apostles for the Orthodox Cathedral, Anrep wanted to use prominent members of the Greek community as models but their wives objected; they saw enough of their husbands at home, they said. Portraits of many of the Bloomsbury group appear in his most famous mosaics, in the vestibule floor of the National Gallery (1928–33). When the work was enlarged in 1952 he added other famous heads, Churchill's among them.

In 1918 Anrep married Helen Maitland (*infra*), who was the mother of his two children, Anastasia and Igor; she left him in 1926 to live with Fry. By then Anrep had already introduced into his home his cousin Maroussa Volkova, who had also left Russia after the revolution. Although the parting from Helen had not been

amicable, both he and Maroussa remained friendly with Bloomsbury; she was his "consort" until her death in 1956.

ANREP, Helen (1885–1965), wife of above: born Helen Maitland
in California, though of Scottish parentage. Her father, having
dissipated his money in Europe, failed to prosper as a wine-
producer in California and disappeared. She had no formal
education, her mother living successively in Stanford, New York,
Edinburgh and Florence, where Helen learnt singing and the
violin. After touring Italy with a small opera company, she and her
mother settled in Paris before the coming of the First World War.

Helen now began to take an interest in painting; she met the
artists Duncan Grant* and Henry Lamb;* with the latter she had a
brief affair. One of Lamb's friends was the Russian mosaicist Boris
Anrep (*supra*), who became Helen's lover. They had a daughter
Anastasia, but it was not until their son Igor was born in 1918 that
Boris and Helen were married; Boris's disapproval of illegitimate
sons was greater than his disapproval of marriage. After the war the
Anreps lived in Hampstead, London, together with Boris's cousin
Maroussa Volkova.

Helen Anrep accepted this situation until in the winter of 1924–5
she went to a party at Vanessa Bell's* Fitzroy Street studio and met
Roger Fry.* He was twenty years her senior, but they were
mutually attracted. Although the Anreps had a violent quarrel over
Fry immediately after the party, it took Helen a year to decide to
leave her husband, for fear of losing her children, but the break was
finally made in 1926. She and Fry took a house, 48 Bernard Street,
where they were to live until his death in 1934. Helen was not a
"Bloomsbury type" of intellectual, but she was a good listener and
talker. Fry himself testified to her influence over him; he could
relax in her company. She took great (sometimes critical) interest in
his work, and toured the art collections of Germany with him in
1928. In the same year she bought Rodwell House, near Ipswich in
Suffolk, as a home for her children in the school holidays.

Helen accompanied Fry on his last three trips to Italy (1929,
1931, 1934). During his final illness she had great difficulty visiting
him in hospital, as she was technically no relation. Bloomsbury,
however, treated her as his widow. She was a strong supporter of
Virginia Woolf* as Fry's biographer, and was happy to have the
story of her relationship with him included in the book. Helen
continued her interest in the arts, generously supporting the

Euston Road School for young artists, opened in 1937, although she had become much poorer after Fry's death. Indeed she nearly lost Virginia's friendship by borrowing £150 and failing to repay the loan; Virginia was upset, but Helen was happily oblivious of any coolness. Throughout her life she remained a part of the Bloomsbury circle, and was entertained at Charleston, Ham Spray and the Monk's House.

BAGENAL, Barbara (1891–1984), artist: born Barbara Hiles, daughter of a wealthy Liverpool cotton merchant who retired at fifty-eight and went to Paris to learn painting. Barbara also studied art, first in Paris, then at the Slade School (1913–14), where she met Brett* and Carrington,* and was one of the prettiest and liveliest of the "Cropheads" as Virginia Woolf* later called them. She took a studio in Pond Street, Hampstead, but it was through her work at the Omega Workshops and her visits to Lady Ottoline Morrell* that she came to know the Bloomsbury group, joining enthusiastically in all their activities.

During the summer of 1916 she was attached to David Garnett,* and stayed at Wissett Lodge where he and Duncan Grant* worked as conscientious objectors; she helped pull the plough, and took part in the packing-up to move to Charleston. By now she had met Nicholas Bagenal, ex-King's, Cambridge, and now in the Irish Guards. They spent a holiday at her parents' cottage in Wales, together with Carrington and Lytton Strachey.* In October Barbara fell foul of Virginia Woolf* by joining Garnett and Carrington in the "break-in" at Asheham (see CARRINGTON).

Camping in Charleston garden through the summer of 1917, Barbara made herself useful as always, helping Grant and Vanessa Bell* with the costumes for the New York production of *Pelléas et Mélisande*, amd painting floors and walls for Carrington and Strachey at Tidmarsh. She also became a regular member of the 1917 Club, now a haunt of "young Bloomsbury". In November 1917 the Woolfs took her on as apprentice at their Hogarth Press. They found her eager and willing, though careless at first; as she was given her meals, a night's lodging during an air raid, and a small share of the profits (2/6d on the first occasion) she was also cheap. She confided to Virginia her difficulty in choosing between

Nicholas Bagenal and Saxon Sydney-Turner,* who had belatedly
fallen in love with a life-long devotion; he wrote to her every day,
furthering her literary education with long quotations from the
poets. Despite the advice of both Virginia and Vanessa, she decided
to marry Bagenal, but to continue her relationship with
Sydney-Turner, perhaps because of her romantic attachment to the
idea of Bloomsbury; the wedding was in February 1918. On
8 November her first child, Judith, was born a month ahead of
Angelica Bell (Garnett*); two sons, Michael and Timothy, followed
later. Judith, a great friend of Angelica, often stayed at Charleston
or Cassis.

From 1918 Barbara Bagenal enjoyed a mainly domestic life with
her own children and those of friends. She saw much of the Bells
and Carrington, with whom she stayed after Strachey's death in
1932. By the Second World War she was separated from her
husband and, while still visiting her old admirer Sydney-Turner,
began to live with Clive Bell.* The two of them travelled
extensively in France and Italy, and Barbara saw Venice for the first
time. Although Vanessa Bell sometimes found her irritating, she
was grateful for her care of Clive, and she and Duncan Grant often
met the other couple on holiday. In 1960 Barbara and Clive stayed
at Menton while Vanessa and Duncan were at Roquebrune. Next
year it was Barbara who had to break to Clive the news that Vanessa
had died at Charleston, and she continued looking after him until
his own death in 1964. The rest of her life was spent in her house at
Rye, surrounded by Bloomsbury memories and visited by old
Bloomsbury friends. She took great interest in the restoration of
Charleston, and gave two of the most important pictures there,
Grant's *Lytton Strachey* and Vanessa Bell's *Saxon Sidney-Turner*.

BAKST, Léon (1866–1924), Russian painter, ballet designer: born
Lev Semuilovich Rosenberg in Grodno, later took his grandfather's
name. Bakst came from a prosperous Jewish family, but after his
father's death he was forced to work in support of his mother,
brother, two sisters and grandmother, while studying at the St
Petersburg Academy of Arts. A contemporary of Benois and
Nouvel, in 1890 he was accepted as a member of their circle, which
soon included Diaghilev.* After two years' study in Paris (1895–6)
he was one of the co-founders of Diaghilev's magazine *Mir iskusstva*
(World of Art) in 1899. Few of Bakst's paintings appeared in the
magazine, although many of the black-and-white illustrations were

his work. He painted a notable portrait of Diaghilev, but found his true vocation as a ballet designer when he designed *Die Puppenfee* at the Hermitage Theatre in St Petersburg (1903).

Bakst's most famous work, however, was done for the Diaghilev ballet in Western Europe. In 1906 he helped Diaghilev organise his exhibition of Russian art in Paris, and when the ballet company appeared there in 1909, it was Bakst's exotic décor for *Cléopatre* that seized the French imagination. Even more enthusiasm greeted *Schéhérazade* next year, and Bakst's bright colours and the oriental look became the newest fashion. Reactions to the first London season (1911) were similar; among those who took up the Russian dancers was Lady Ottoline Morrell*, and by 1912 Bakst was one of her frequent visitors in Bedford Square. His designs for *Jeux* (1913) may have been partly inspired by a summer's afternoon when, with Nijinsky,* he had tea with Lady Ottoline. At the sight of Duncan Grant* and Adrian Stephen* playing tennis against the background of trees and Georgian houses in the square, Bakst exclaimed *"Quel décor!"*

Although Bakst was capable of restrained design, as in *Spectre de la Rose*, his full-blown exoticism had more influence on Bloomsbury, as can be seen in the products of the Omega Workshop (see FRY, Roger). But Diaghilev, cut off from his Russian roots by the revolution and ever seeking novelty, forsook Bakst for Western artists in 1919. That year Bakst, who started his theatrical career with a ballet set in a toyshop, had expected to design *Boutique Fantasque*, but the French artist Derain* was chosen instead; Bakst was so hurt he did not speak to Diaghilev for two years. In 1921, however, he was the obvious choice for the great London revival of the full-length *Sleeping Princess;* he had, after all, seen the first dress-rehearsal in 1890. Diaghilev would have preferred Benois, but he would not come without guarantees. Bakst did much research for his ornate baroque setting and received the largest share of critical acclaim, though the ballet as a whole was a financial disaster. Wishing to keep up with post-war artistic trends, Bakst had asked for a Stravinsky opera, *Mavra*, to design in 1923; Diaghilev broke the contract for this, and was forced to pay Bakst 10,000 francs. This led to a violent quarrel; when Bakst died in December 1924, Diaghilev wept to think they could never now be reconciled.

BELL, Anne Olivier, *née* Popham, (1916–   ), born in London, daughter of Arthur Popham, Keeper of the Print Room in the

British Museum, and his wife Brynhild (see OLIVIER, Noel).
Popham had some contact with the original Bloomsbury circle and
their immediate successors at Cambridge when he was up at King's
College (Classical Tripos, 1911). Anne, usually called Olivier, was
educated at St Paul's Girls' School and the Courtauld Institute of
Art. During the Second World War she was in the Civil Service,
and afterwards on the Control Commission for Germany. She later
worked for the Arts Council, and it was over the Council's 1951 art
exhibition that she first met Vanessa Bell,★ although she had
contacts with artists on the Bloomsbury fringe before the war.
Vanessa invited her to Charleston as a model, and in 1952 she
married Quentin Bell;★ the couple have a son and two daughters.
When Quentin Bell left his post in Leeds in 1967, the family came
to live in Sussex, between Charleston and the Monk's House at
Rodmell. There Anne Olivier helped her husband in the research
for his biography of his aunt Virginia Woolf★ and herself began to
edit Virginia's diaries. She has played a great part in the restoration
of Charleston, as has her daughter Cressida, and is on the
committee of the Charleston Trust with her other daughter
Virginia.

BELL, (Arthur) Clive Heward (1881–1964), art critic: younger son
of William Bell, a rich coal-mine owner turned Wiltshire "squire",
who in 1897 refurbished his country home, Cleeve House, as a
pseudo-Gothic-*cum*-Jacobean mansion. Clive Bell was encouraged
to enjoy hunting and shooting, and went from Marlborough School
to Trinity College, Cambridge to read history in 1899; despite his
conventional upbringing he had already acquired not only a
mistress, but also a love of art. By a similar paradox the chubby,
ginger-haired figure in hunting-pink, first seen by Leonard Woolf★
crossing the Great Court of Trinity, won acceptance in the circle
that included Woolf, Lytton Strachey★ and Thoby Stephen,★ who
called him a cross between Shelley and a country squire. The
"Midnight Society", founded in 1900 to read plays, met in Bell's
rooms, and although his friends knew little of art they educated him
in philosophy and literature. At the 1900 May Ball he must have
met Thoby's beautiful sisters, Vanessa (Bell★) and Virginia
(Woolf★), but though Virginia later claimed to have talked to him at
length, there is no record of his first contact with Vanessa. To his
surprise Trinity rewarded his second-class degree with a research
studentship in 1902, and after spending part of July staying with

the Stephen family, he began his study of British foreign policy at
the Congress of Verona.

In January 1904 he went to Paris to look at the French archives,
but soon abandoned history for the Louvre. After meeting Gerald
Kelly* and other British art students, he moved to lodgings in
Montparnasse and joined the artists' gatherings at the "Chat Blanc"
in the Rue Odessa. Learning from his contemporaries again, he
transformed his natural eye for pictures into an educated one,
though he himself rarely tried to paint. In May he entertained the
Stephen girls as they passed through Paris, and on his return to
London attended their Thursday evenings in Gordon Square. By
1906 he was reviewing for the *Athenaeum*, and meditating a great
work, *The New Renaissance*, to deal with contemporary European
art, but Bloomsbury was more attracted by his conviviality and
lively conversation. He was soon in love with Vanessa, proposed
twice, and was accepted on 22 November 1906, two days after
Thoby Stephen died. They were married on 7 February 1907.

The Bells went to Paris in March, and on their return took over
46 Gordon Square, where they lived in comfort on the interest of
the £20,000 settlement from Mr Bell senior. They set the
Bloomsbury social tone, receiving friends informally while
ruthlessly chasing away bores, even family ones. In December 1907
they started a Play Reading Society, which met until the following
May. The birth of Julian (*infra*) in 1908 took most of Vanessa's
attention away from her husband, and he retaliated by a fierce
flirtation with his sister-in-law Virginia; their emotional relationship was always stormy, but he thought highly of her writing,
and she valued his criticism. From 1909 Bell was seldom without a
female companion, though he never wanted to end his marriage.
London society began to pall on the Bells, however, and they
thought seriously of removing to Paris permanently until their
meeting with Roger Fry* in 1910 changed the direction of their
lives.

Bell was soon engaged with Fry in arranging the first
Post-Impressionist exhibition of 1910, accompanying him to
France to choose the pictures, and their friendship endured even
after Fry became Vanessa's lover in 1911; the three of them went to
Italy together in 1912. However, Vanessa's renting of Asheham
House in Sussex disconcerted him, and Virginia's wedding in
August 1912 was even more of a blow, although he wrote an
affectionate letter to both Woolfs immediately afterwards. For
Fry's second Post-Impressionist exhibition (1912) Bell chose all the
English pictures, selecting mainly the works of his friends. He was

commissioned to write a book on Post-Impressionism, and in *Art* (published in 1914) he set out the theory of "significant form", rather than content, as being the essential quality that distinguishes an artistic work and appeals immediately to the senses. This theory was the hallmark of the "Clive-Fry" coalition that seemed to some to dominate the British art world between the wars. Clive Bell, now a recognised authority on modern painting, continued writing on art until after the Second World War; his books include *Since Cézanne* (1923), *Landmarks in Nineteenth Century Painting* (1927), *An Account of French Painting* (1931), and *Victor Pasmore* (Penguin, 1945).

Like the rest of Bloomsbury he disapproved of the First World War and flouted conventional opinion by producing a pamphlet *Peace At Once* (1915), which was publicly burned in London by order of the Lord Mayor. When conscription began in 1916, he "worked" on the Morrells'** Home Farm at Garsington, in reality spending more time at the house chatting to Lady Ottoline. Vanessa settled at Charleston from 1916 till 1919, with Grant and the two boys, Julian and Quentin (born 1910)*; Bell made her an allowance and stayed there often with his current mistress Mary Hutchinson.* In 1919 he returned to his beloved Paris, meeting the artists at the newly fashionable *Les Deux Magots*. London life for Clive Bell still centred on Gordon Square, but he had his book-lined room at Charleston and spent part of every summer there; he taught Julian to hunt and shoot, and treated Angelica (Garnett*) Vanessa's child by Grant, as his own daughter, almost forgetting that Grant was her father. After a break with Mary Hutchinson in 1927, he joined Vanessa at Cassis to begin writing his magnum opus, and eventually produced the slender *Civilization: an Essay* (1928). Virginia Woolf, to whom he dedicated it, said the start was brilliant and witty but in the end "Civilisation" turned out to be just a lunch party at 50 Gordon Square. In 1930 Bell was blinded in one eye by disease, but gradually recovered with the help of a specialist in Zurich. His vehement defence of Grant when his interior decorations for the *Queen Mary* were rejected in 1936 defeated its object by exaggerated ridicule of the Cunard company in *The Listener*.

The Second World War saw him serving on a British Council committee for sending art abroad, and in the Home Guard at Charleston. His close friendship with Barbara Bagenal,* his companion until his death, began in 1944. Bell did not care for the 1945 Labour government, and even contemplated emigration, but still continued to enjoy life, with holidays abroad and visits to friends. Although in 1959 he grumbled that it took him two hours to get up, next year he and Barbara were in Menton, livening up Vanessa's stay with Grant at nearby Roquebrune. In 1960, however, he broke his leg on the steps of a Menton church and was in the London Clinic when Barbara told him of Vanessa's death.

As well as books and essays on art, Clive wrote verse; a collection, *Poems* (1921), and a narrative poem, *The Legend of Monte Sibilla* (1923), were both published by the Hogarth Press, the latter book illustrated by Vanessa and Grant. In his 1956 collection of reminiscences, *Old Friends*, Clive Bell was at pains to deny the existence of "Bloomsbury". Yet it was his suggestion in 1917 that Roger Fry should paint a portrait of the group and, by his fierce defence of friends and contemptuous treatment of outsiders, he did as much as anyone to define its boundaries.

Clive Bell, *Old Friends* (London, 1956)
Leon Edel, *Bloomsbury, a House of Lions* (London, 1979)

BELL, Julian Heward (1908–37), writer, older son of Clive and Vanessa Bell:** born at 46 Gordon Square, the first Bloomsbury baby. A handsome, healthy, noisy child, who demanded all his mother's attention, Julian had a close relationship with her throughout his life. From 1916 to 1919 the family lived all year round at Charleston in Sussex, and later spent summers there. In this sanctuary of Bloomsbury pacifism, Julian and his brother Quentin *(infra)* played war games, went fishing and enjoyed country pursuits. They also produced a daily paper, the *Charleston Bulletin,* describing the day's events with jokes aimed at the adults. Education was provided partly by governesses, one of whom Julian is said to have pushed into a ditch. Vanessa read Homer, history, astrology and geology to the children, while from David Garnett* Julian learnt some science. His father guided his reading, as well as teaching him to hunt and shoot.

In 1919 Julian went to Owen's School, Islington as a day-boy; three years later he began to board at the progressive Quaker school, Leighton Park. No great scholar, he did well in subjects he liked, won a prize for speaking and enjoyed playing rugby. Although bullied at both schools, he learnt to fight back and was feared as well as popular. After a year in Paris, where his longing for the English countryside began to find expression in poetry, Julian went up to King's, Cambridge to read history (1927). Again he was not academically outstanding, but became an Apostle and wrote for literary magazines, especially *The Venture* edited by fellow Apostle and intimate, Anthony Blunt. Another particular friend was John Lehmann,* but Julian also had the first of many affairs with women, and described to his mother and often to his aunt, Virginia Woolf,* the progress of his love for either sex. He found time to go beagling once a fortnight and in his first year spoke often in the Union. His poetry became increasingly classical, and he began a research project on Pope and the eighteenth century; he was out of step with the writers of his own generation, like Auden and Spender, who were more acceptable in the literary establishment now dominated by Bloomsbury. His first book of poems, *Winter Movement* (1930) was well but not enthusiastically received, and he failed to obtain a fellowship at King's in either 1931 or 1934.

Politically Julian Bell was more in tune with his contemporaries. He worked for the Labour Party in the 1931 election and as a party organiser at Glynde, the village near Charleston. He also took part in the anti-war demonstration at Cambridge on 11 November 1933, driving his car reinforced with mattresses as a kind of tank. In this "good fight", as he called it, Guy Burgess was his navigator. Although he rejected the fashionable Cambridge Marxism of the 1930s, the rise of European Fascism gradually conquered his early pacifism. Yet he still revered the objectors of the First World War and edited their collected views in *We Did Not Fight* (published in 1935). Julian now had his own room in Taviton Street, Bloomsbury, where he produced a few more poems, articles and reviews. Virginia Woolf later blamed herself for not encouraging him more, and in fact Hogarth Press refused his last work, an essay on Roger Fry* (1936), though they published it in a posthumous collection (1938). He felt a need to make something of his life independently of Bloomsbury, and began to apply for posts abroad. In July 1935 he was appointed Professor of English at the National University of Wuhan, China.

Julian enjoyed Chinese food and amusements, including sailing and shooting, but found the teaching difficult until he came to the modern writers, who were for him Aunt Virginia and her friends. From the start of the Spanish Civil War, however, he wanted to return to Europe, and the disclosure of his affair with a colleague's wife provided the excuse. He meant to go straight to join the Republican army in Spain, but was persuaded to see his mother first. Julian was in England from March until June 1937, a time of great anguish for Vanessa Bell, who felt his intention to fight as a

blow to her principles as well as her feelings. To spare her he agreed
to become an ambulance driver rather than a soldier, and it was
while driving for Spanish Medical Aid that he was killed in the
battle of Brunete on 18 July 1937.

Peter Stansky and William Abrahams, *Journey to the Frontier.
Julian Bell and John Cornford: their lives and the 1930s* (London,
1966)

BELL, Quentin Claudian (1910–   ), writer, artist, art historian:
second son of Clive and Vanessa Bell.** Like his brother Julian
(*supra*), he was educated at Leighton Park School (1924), and spent
his holidays at Charleston in similar pursuits. With his aunt
Virginia Woolf* he wrote satires based on scenes from his parents'
life; she later called him sophisticated beyond his years. After
school Quentin studied painting in Paris, first spending some time
in Munich (1928). In 1929 he toured German galleries with his
mother and Duncan Grant,* and in 1931 they joined him in Rome,
where he had taken a studio.

Bell's career was interrupted in 1933 by an infection diagnosed as
tubercular and requiring convalescence in Switzerland. He began to
exhibit in 1935 and later added potting to his skills, setting up a kiln
at Charleston. During the Second World War Bell was not a pacifist
but was judged unfit for the services; he worked at first on Maynard
Keynes'* farm, then as an executive in Political Warfare. In 1952
he became Lecturer in Art Education at Newcastle University
(Senior Lecturer, 1956) and married Anne Popham (Bell*). With
their three children, Julian, Virginia and Cressida, they spent
summer vacations at Charleston. Bell then moved to Leeds
University, where he was Professor of Fine Art (1962–7). He held
posts at Oxford (Slade professorship 1964–5) and Hull (Ferens
professorship 1965–6). In 1967 he became Professor of the History
and Theory of Fine Art at Sussex University.

Professor Bell's first book, *On Human Finery* (1947) was a history
of fashion, and he has written much art criticism and theory. He is
also the author of *Bloomsbury* (1968), the prize-winning biography
Virginia Woolf (1972), and a novel *The Brandon Papers* (1985).
Since his retirement in 1975 he has lived in Sussex and, together
with his wife, played a great part in the restoration of Charleston by
the Charleston Trust, of which he was first Chairman.

BELL, Vanessa, *née* Stephen (1879–1961), painter: elder daughter of Leslie and Julia Stephen,★★ known as "Nessa", a grave and pretty little girl. She was devoted to her brother Thoby,★ teaching him his letters, sharing his lessons, and sometimes resenting the intrusions of the third child, Virginia (Woolf★). After Thoby left for school in 1894, however, the sisters became good companions, and it was agreed between them that Vanessa was to be an artist and Virginia a writer. 22 Hyde Park Gate was a gloomy house when Julia Stephen died in 1895, and Virginia had her first breakdown. Vanessa began to feel the strain of being responsible for a younger sister liable to mental illness, but she had already begun drawing lessons at home, and in 1896 was allowed to bicycle to classes at Arthur Cope's art school in South Kensington. The marriage and premature death of her half-sister Stella (Hills★) forced her to take over the housekeeping, and so confront her father's unreasonable rage over the weekly accounts. She developed the silent self-control in the face of others' emotions that made her appear formidably cold later in life, and also became an economical housewife. At the same time Vanessa was upset by her début in "society", under the wing of her very conventional half-brother, George Duckworth.★ Accustomed to her parents' intellectual friends, she hated the trivial, fashionable parties to which her father insisted she must go. She also suffered from George's kisses and caresses, though, unlike Virginia, she was not repelled by sex as a result. She fell slightly in love with her kindly widowed brother-in-law, Jack Hills,★ but George took the lead in destroying a relationship that could have no legal fulfilment in England.

Instead he helped widen Vanessa's horizon by taking her to Paris in April 1900, and in June that year she and Virginia visited Thoby at Trinity College, Cambridge, meeting some of his new friends at tea in his rooms and attending the May Ball. Next year Vanessa was one of twenty students admitted to the Royal Academy Painting School, where she had the advantage of technical instruction from a master technician, John Singer Sargent. The Stephens' social life was further enlivened by visits from Thoby's Cambridge set, including Clive Bell,★ and in 1903 Vanessa went to lectures on French Impressionism. However, Leslie Stephen's fatal illness in the period 1902–4 left his daughters little time for new relationships or ideas.

When their father died (February 1904) the family (Adrian★ now included) took a restorative trip to Venice and Florence, returning by way of Paris. Back in London, Vanessa accomplished the removal of the four Stephens to 46 Gordon Square in the then unfashionable district of Bloomsbury. She attended the Slade School of Art briefly in the autumn, but her chief concern was to decorate this first real home in a light, modern style, as unlike Hyde Park Gate as possible. In February 1905 Thoby began the Thursday evening "At Homes" whose regular attendants were the original Bloomsburyites. Apart from Clive Bell, they were more literary than artistic, so Vanessa organised the "Friday Club" for young artists to meet and exhibit their work. She was helped by Clive, but in August and again next summer refused his proposals of marriage. When both she and Thoby returned very ill from the family's Greek holiday in the autumn of 1906, she turned to Clive for comfort and on 22 November agreed to marry him; Thoby had died on the 20th.

After their wedding in February 1907, the Bells made 46 Gordon Square a centre for more intimate and exclusive Bloomsbury gatherings, with Vanessa enjoying a married woman's licence in speech and behaviour. She continued painting, mainly portraits of her friends and still lifes, even when on duty visits to Clive's parents' home in Wiltshire, a place she hated for its stuffy formality. Her children, Julian★ (born 1908) and Quentin (supra) (born 1910) were the main focus of her affection, but she could always leave them in their nurse's care in order to work or travel. After Julian's birth and Clive's subsequent flirtation with Virginia, the Bells' lives, though outwardly unchanged, were more detached from each other.

In 1909 Vanessa exhibited her still life Icelandic Poppies with the New English Art Club, but association with Roger Fry★ and his 1910 Post-Impressionist exhibition caused her to break with tradition and embrace a modern style. She and Fry painted happily together at the beginning of their Turkish trip with Clive and Harry Norton★ in April 1911, until a miscarriage made her seriously ill. Fry's nursing restored her health, and during her long convales-cence in England they became lovers. In the winter of 1911–12, together with her sister, she began renting Asheham House in Sussex. Fry was her first visitor and henceforward Vanessa adopted a casual country life for part of every year, though the Bells always kept rooms in Gordon Square and enjoyed the uproarious Bloomsbury parties. Some of Vanessa's paintings were included in the second Post-Impressionist exhibition in 1912, showing the influence of the new art on her use of colour. She had also begun to work with Duncan Grant,★ a younger artist whose pictures she admired, and with whom she gradually fell in love. To live with him she had to accustom herself to a triangular relationship, as

Grant was principally homosexual. They worked so well together and were temperamentally so compatible that Vanessa made lasting friends of most of his male lovers.

Virginia's marriage freed Vanessa from the main responsibility for her sister during her breakdowns, though she sat with Virginia all night after her suicide attempt (9 September 1913). Her own health improved, and from July 1913 she worked hard for Fry's Omega Workshops, of which she and Grant were co-directors. She continued using bold colour, but refined the representational element in her paintings, perhaps as a result of her involvement with design, until she began to produce purely abstract pictures. Yet her aesthetic pleasure in the external world prevented content from disappearing permanently. The outbreak of war in 1914 had little effect on Vanessa's life; she had let the Woolfs have Asheham and spent the summer of 1915 on the Sussex coast, mainly with Grant and his new friend David Garnett,* whose portrait both artists painted. When conscription was introduced in 1916, Garnett and Grant as conscientious objectors were allowed to do farm work. Vanessa accompanied them, first to Wissett Lodge in Suffolk, then by taking a lease of Charleston, four miles from Asheham. Here the three remained until 1919, visited by various members of Bloomsbury, while Clive and Maynard Keynes* had their own rooms in the house. Vanessa and Grant decorated Charleston themselves, and painted most of the furniture; the Charleston Trust has restored much of their work. Vanessa's own painting moved back from abstraction, and she began to illustrate and design covers for her sister's books. On Christmas Day 1918, she gave birth to Grant's child, Angelica (Garnett*), who developed into a beautiful girl with much of her mother's artistic talent.

Between the wars Charleston was only a summer home for Vanessa and her family; domestic help in the country proved difficult until in 1920 Grace Germany (Higgens*) came into their employment. In 1922, with Julian and Quentin away at school, Vanessa worked in Paris for two months and had her first one-artist show in London. She had joined the London Group of Artists in order to exhibit after the war, but attracted more critical attention through Keynes' London Artists' Association, who sponsored her 1930 exhibition. Her paintings, now more traditional but still full of strong colour, had great appeal, though she belittled them herself compared with Grant's work. The L.A.A. also publicised her collaboration with Grant in interior decorating and designs for fabrics and ceramics. During the late 1920s and early 1930s the two of them replaced the now defunct Omega, receiving commissions from Lady Dorothy Wellesley,* Kenneth (Lord) Clark, and Shell-Mex Ltd. They occupied adjoining studios at 8 Fitzroy Street, London, while in summer their working life centred on Charleston, and from 1927 also on La Bergère, the villa at Cassis Vanessa restored for her family.

Keynes and his wife, the ballerina Lydia Lopokova,* had settled near Charleston at Tilton, but the relationship between the two houses was sometimes strained, as Vanessa had resented Lydia's importation into the magic circle of Bloomsbury. In 1931 she and Grant annoyed Keynes by resigning from the London Artists, and began exhibiting jointly at Agnew's gallery, from whom they received a fixed salary offset against sales. Keynes' connection with the Camargo Society, however, gave Vanessa the chance to design two early Ashton ballets, *High Yellow* (1932) and *Pomona* (1933).

Quentin Bell's serious illness in 1933 caused his mother great anxiety, but a far worse shock was the fatal accident in 1934 to her old friend Roger Fry. Next year, however, Vanessa spent a pleasant spring and early summer in Rome with her children Quentin and Angelica. Yet she was still fondest of Julian, and her pride and joy in him was such that she saw him as fulfilling all the promise of her long-dead brother Thoby. In 1935 Julian took a university post in China. Vanessa lived for his letters, but saw him again only between March and early June 1937, for he left for the Spanish Civil War and was killed on 18 July.

His mother never really recovered from this blow. As always, she tried to keep her emotion suppressed except with Grant, whose companionship was more necessary to her than ever. With his example beside her she was gradually able to paint again, though only in the house and garden at Charleston. She took an interest in the newly-founded Euston Road School of Art, and began collecting Julian's papers for publication. By spring 1938 she faced the possible loss of Angelica, who began an affair with David Garnett, but when the couple came to live near Charleston, Vanessa accepted the situation. Once again she was settled in Sussex for the duration of a war, with Grant's mother as a temporary and Clive as a permanent guest. The studios in Fitzroy Street were gutted by an incendiary bomb in September 1940, and many of Vanessa's paintings destroyed. However, she had begun to paint freely again, and produced several portraits of friends, including Leonard Woolf,* Helen Anrep* and Desmond MacCarthy.* She and Grant had also been asked by Bishop Bell of Chichester to paint the murals in nearby Berwick Church. The task was finished in 1943, although Virginia Woolf's suicide in March 1941 had revived her sister's anguish at Julian's death.

Neither Grant nor Vanessa was invited to Angelica's wedding to Garnett in the spring of 1942, and Garnett did not go to Charleston with his wife until April 1943, when they were expecting their first child. Vanessa was delighted with this baby and subsequent grandchildren. Angelica's two oldest daughters often visited Charleston on their own, and later Quentin brought his family every summer; they restored some of the happiness the house had lost since 1937. In spite of a mastectomy in 1944, news of which she kept to herself as much as possible, Vanessa went on painting throughout the war and in 1946 she and Grant renewed their connection with the London Group. They also reverted to the habit of spending part of each year in France.

Although she welcomed Quentin's marriage to Anne Olivier Popham (Bell*) in 1952, Vanessa preferred on the whole not to meet too many new people, and could be very cool to those who wanted to satisfy their curiosity about Bloomsbury. Her life in the 1950s followed much the same course as ever; she painted now mainly to please herself, though her exhibition in February 1956 was successful. Official appointments to judge art competitions, including the Prix de Rome, occupied some of her time and from 1949 to 1959 she sat on the committee of the Edwin Austin Abbey Memorial fund to encourage mural painting. In 1959 she was very ill with pleurisy, and took her last trip abroad to Roquebrune with Grant in 1960. After visiting the Picasso exhibition at the Tate Gallery in the autumn, she did not leave Charleston again. On 4 April 1961 she had an attack of bronchitis, and died three days later.

Frances Spalding, *Vanessa Bell* (London, 1983)
Richard Shone, *Bloomsbury Portraits: Vanessa Bell, Duncan Grant, and their circle* (London, 1976)

BERENSON, Mary (1864–1945), born Mary (Pearsall) Smith in Philadelphia, daughter of Quakers Robert and Hannah Smith, and educated at Smith College (1880) and Harvard Annex, now Radcliffe (1884). While at college she became friendly with Walt Whitman, and met a young visiting Irish barrister from London, Frank Costelloe. In spite of her mother's horror at the involvement with a Roman Catholic foreigner, Mary married Frank in

September 1885. The ceremony was sweetened for her parents by the reception in Frank's old Oxford college, Balliol (the first to be held there) under the patronage of the Master, Dr Jowett.

Although the Costelloes had two daughters, Ray (Strachey★) and Karin (Stephen★), the marriage was unsuccessful. In 1888 Mary was asked to entertain a young Bostonian genius on a visit to England, Bernhard Berenson who had admired her from a distance at Harvard. He returned in 1890 and, in Mary's words, "When this beautiful and mysterious youth appeared . . . I felt like a dry sponge that was put in water". They toured the art galleries of England together, then moved on to Europe, at first accompanied by Frank Costelloe. By 1891 Berenson and Mary were living together openly, and eventually settled in Florence; the two Costelloe daughters were left in their father's custody until his death in 1899. Mary and Bernhard had collaborated in art history from the first and continued to work together after their marriage in 1900. Berenson's quarrel with Roger Fry★ over alleged plagiarism separated the Berensons from the English art world, and they divided their activities between Italy and the U.S.A., though Mary visited England regularly to see her daughters.

The marriages of Ray and Karin brought Mary Berenson into contact with the Bloomsbury group, but she remained cool towards what she described as "Gloomsbury" and was not "greatly exhilarated" at the fact that there was "generally a Strachey or two to lunch" just after Ray's marriage. She also quarrelled with Karin and Adrian over their pacifism in the First World War, most of which she spent in Italy.

Mary was increasingly ill between the wars; her illnesses were exasperated by loss of money in the slump of 1931, and an unnecessary operation. She still came to Britain every summer, however, and entertained her grandchildren in Florence, especially Ray's daughter Barbara. Indeed, from 1934 on, the visits of Barbara's son Roger were a joy to both Berensons. Mary was in England at the outbreak of war in 1939, but managed to get back to Florence. Berenson, as a non-Aryan, had to shelter in the Vatican between 1943 and the liberation in 1944. Mary died in March 1945, Berenson surviving her until 1959.

Barbara Strachey, *Remarkable Relations* (London, 1980)

BIRRELL, Francis Frederick Locker (1889–1935), journalist, drama critic and bookseller: was the son of Augustine Birrell (1850–1933), the literary critic, essayist, barrister, and Liberal politician. Augustine Birrell, himself the son of a Liverpool baptist minister, was an old friend of Leslie Stephen;* he entered the Cabinet as President of the Board of Education in December 1905 and was Chief Secretary for Ireland from January 1907 throughout the troubled period up to July 1916. Francis Birrell had none of his father's interest in politics. He was educated at Eton and King's College, Cambridge, where he met Lytton Strachey* for the first time in October 1909. By Christmas that year he was integrated in the Bloomsbury circle, visiting the Stephens in Fitzroy Square in the company of both Lytton and James Strachey,* as well as of Grant,* Keynes* and Norton.* He was also a friend of David Garnett,* whom he introduced to Lytton Strachey and with whom in 1914 he started a play-reading group, the Caroline Club; the name came from the club's first meeting-place, the home of their friends Hugh and Brynhild Popham (*née* Olivier), in Caroline Place.

Although Virginia Woolf* was occasionally bored with "Frankie" Birrell in her younger years, most of Bloomsbury liked him. They looked upon him as a happy, charming chatterer. To Keynes he was "a frivolous butterfly" but to others, as Gerald Brenan* later wrote, he seemed a modern Mr Pickwick. He was not, however, popular with D. H. Lawrence.* For in April 1915 Birrell's presence, with Garnett, as a guest of the Lawrences in Sussex, prompted the notorious outburst in which Lawrence likened the Cambridge-Bloomsbury set to a collection of maddening beetles. In June 1915 Birrell and Garnett joined the Friends War Victims Relief Mission. They crossed to France, and were stationed at Sommeilles, a war-ravaged village on the southern fringe of the Argonne Forest. Although Garnett returned to England in the following winter, Birrell remained with the Friends War Victims Mission until 1919, editing a magazine which kept American Quakers who were serving with relief teams in Europe in touch with each other.

From 1919 to 1924 Birrell and Garnett jointly ran a bookshop at 19 Taviton Street. It was furnished with Omega tables and patronised by post-war Bloomsbury, a connection which brought Birrell new friendships. Garnett sold his share of the bookshop to the bibliographer Graham Pollard in 1924 but Birrell retained his interest in it until 1927. He edited a series of books on "Representative Women" for the publishers, Gerald Howe; he also discussed with Leonard Woolf* the possibility of joining the

Hogarth Press, for whom he edited (in collaboration with F. L. Lucas) an anthology of "last words", *The Art of Dying*, published in November 1930. Although he visited the Garnetts occasionally at Hilton Hall, Huntingdon, Birrell was by now more closely attached to Raymond Mortimer.★ The two men spent the late spring of 1929 together at Charleston, writing a play; it was, however, never printed or produced. When in February 1931 the *Nation* was absorbed with the *New Statesman*, under the editorship of Kingsley Martin, Birrell became a regular critic, working closely with Mortimer. But he was also a friend of Dorothy Wellesley,★ the MacCarthys,★ Ethel Sands,★ Vita Sackville-West★ and Harold Nicolson.★ It was at Nicolson's request that in 1931 he contributed to *Action*, a periodical supporting Mosley's "New Party", not yet a Fascist movement.

In the following summer Birrell's health gave way; he underwent an operation for removal of a tumour on the brain. A second operation followed a year later, at a time when he was under great strain from the final illness of his father, who died in late November 1933. By then Francis Birrell himself was partially paralysed and was nursed for much of the following year by Raymond Mortimer. On 2 January 1935 he died, at Brighton.

BLANCHE, Jacques-Emile (1862–1942), French painter, art critic and author: born in Paris, where his father was a distinguished alienist who treated several French writers (including Guy de Maupassant) in his mental home at Passy. The young Blanche spent his summer holidays in Normandy and throughout his life was associated with the Dieppe artistic circle. He learnt much from Renoir and exhibited from 1877, when he was fifteen, until 1940. Probably his best known picture is the group painting of the Scandinavian impressionist, Frits Thaulow and his family in 1895 (*Musée d'Art Moderne*). Blanche is especially remembered for his portraits of French writers; but in Edwardian England he received several commissions from the aristocracy, particularly after he had painted Queen Alexandra in the year of the *Entente Cordiale*. Blanche first visited London in 1882 and was a friend of Whistler and Sickert;★ as one of the later Impressionists, he painted scenes in London and the English countryside. Back in Paris he was winning respect as an art critic and as a teacher; in 1906, largely on the recommendation of Simon Bussy,★ Duncan Grant★ was among Blanche's pupils at his Paris school, La Palette. Blanche maintained contact with Rothenstein* and the New English Art Club until 1940.

He wrote some twenty-five books, including the novel *Aymeris*. His early memoirs, *Les Cahiers d'un artiste* (1914–19), were followed by trenchant art criticism, *Propos de peintre* (1919–28), and *Mes Modèles* (1928)—prose portraits of six writers (Barrès, Gide, Proust, Moore, Hardy, James) whom he had painted. In January 1926 he met Virginia Woolf* in Chelsea. They became better acquainted in July 1927 when she was staying at Auppegard in Normandy, with Ethel Sands.* He wrote a perceptive study of Virginia Woolf for *Nouvelles Littéraires* (August 1927), introducing her *Kew Gardens* and *To the Lighthouse* to French readers in translation.

BOWEN, Elizabeth Dorothea Cole (1899–1973), novelist: born in Dublin, but spent her earliest childhood at Bowen's Court, Kildorrery, in County Cork, before crossing with her mother to Hythe in Kent at the age of seven. On leaving Downe House School in 1918 she travelled widely and began writing short stories; she married an education officer, Alan Cameron, in 1923. Her first novel, *The Hotel*, was published in 1927, when she already enjoyed a reputation for her two volumes of short stories. As she lived at that time in Old Headington, Oxford, she was soon taken under the wing of Lady Ottoline Morrell* at Garsington and later in Bloomsbury. She became friendly with Virginia Woolf* in 1932. After her husband began to work for the B.B.C., she would entertain literary London in their Regent's Park drawing-room, while he spent much of his time in a basement study, surrounded by portraits of favourite cats. Elizabeth Bowen was present at many Bloomsbury parties in the 1930s. By then, however, she had inherited Bowen's Court and was spending more and more time at Kildorrery, where the Woolfs were among her guests in the spring of 1934. She visited Rodmell some six weeks before Virginia Woolf's suicide.

Elizabeth Bowen published some twenty works of fiction as well as collected essays and reminiscences. Her much-praised Jamesian novel, *The Death of the Heart*, appeared in 1938, while the bombing of London in 1940–1 inspired some of her best short stories. She was created C.B.E. in 1948, four years before the death of her husband. In 1959 she sold their Irish estate and returned to Hythe for the last fourteen years of her life.

BOXALL, Nelly (?1889–?1963), cook; with her friend Lottie Hope worked for Roger Fry★ in Guildford, from where they both transferred to the employment of Leonard and Virginia Woolf★★ in February 1916. Lottie was a cheerful foundling, often in trouble and passed from one Bloomsbury household to another, but Nelly was a more complicated character. At first terrified of air raids in London, she became quickly bored with the country, especially when she and Lottie went to help Vanessa Bell★ at Charleston during the years 1917–18. She was an excellent cook and devoted to Virginia, but the emotional scenes involved every time she complained or gave notice were too much for her mistress's nerves. The enforced intimacy of a living-in servant irritated Virginia at the best of times. Unlike the previous generation of employers, she could not just give orders and ignore her, but was unable to make a friend of a totally uneducated woman. She acknowledged that Nelly's defects were the result of "the system", yet was shocked to find her servants voting Labour like herself in 1929; she did not relish being ruled by Nelly.

Expense was another problem as the Woolfs were not particularly affluent in the early 1920s, and it was not until 1927 that they managed to raise Nelly's wages by £5 a year. In August 1929 Virginia got up the courage to sack her, but weakly agreed to extend her notice until December, and then allowed her to stay after all. Nelly Boxall did not leave their service until April 1934, and then only after another series of scenes. Virginia made no further reference to her in her diaries or letters.

BRENAN, (Edward Fitz-) Gerald (1894–1987), Hispanophile author: born at Malta, the son of an army officer, spent his earliest years in India and South Africa before receiving formal schooling at Radley College, Abingdon, preparatory to passing the examination for the military academy at Sandhurst. Brenan, however, considered that he educated himself, acknowledging help from an older companion, John Hope-Johnstone (1882–1970), who lived near the Brenan home in the Cotswolds and interested his adolescent mind in art, poetry, necromancy and German philosophy. At the age of eighteen Brenan travelled with Hope-Johnstone across France and into Italy and Dalmatia, later visiting southern Germany. Brenan had run away from Sandhurst but joined the 5th Gloucesters in 1914, fought in the Ypres salient, on the Somme and in the second battle of the Marne. His courage won him, in 1918, the Military Cross and the Croix de Guerre.

Brenan's first Bloomsbury contacts came in 1919: through Hope-Johnstone, now editor of the *Burlington Magazine*, he knew Roger Fry;* and through Ralph Partridge,* a brother officer during the war, he met Carrington* and Lytton Strachey.* But on 25 September 1919 he set out for Spain and four months later settled at Yegen, on the southern slopes of the Sierra Nevada, between Granada and the coast at Almeria. This picturesque, remote and primitive village became his home until December 1934. As early as April 1920 he was visited there by Partridge, Carrington and Strachey (who found mule travel in the mountains exhausting and alarming). Carrington fell in love with Brenan and, after her marriage to Partridge, continued a secret correspondence with him. Brenan visited England in the summer of 1921 and again in May–June 1922, when he met the Woolfs** for the first time, and much impressed them by his conversation. Partridge's discovery in that summer of Brenan's relationship with Carrington led to a rift, but reconciliation followed twelve months later; and a, sometimes stormy, friendship between the two men continued for another thirty-seven years. The Woolfs were Brenan's guests at Yegen in April 1923, and so later was Roger Fry. Often he was in England, sometimes as a private tutor, the children of Boris Anrep* being his pupils briefly. A great-aunt's allowance of £50 a year and some small legacies staved off the threat of penury. He wrote some poetry and began several novels; the most successful, *A Holiday by the Sea*, was published in 1961. In 1930 he married the American poet, Gamel Woolsey (1899–1968), and was in England the following winter when Strachey and Carrington died.

In 1934 the Brenans (with an adopted daughter, Miranda) moved from Yegen to Churriana, near Malaga. They left for Gibraltar and England seven weeks after the Civil War began and did not settle in Spain again until 1953. Enforced exile at Aldbourne, on the Berkshire–Wiltshire border, inspired Brenan to put on paper his sympathetic understanding of Spanish life and literature and he completed three major works: *The Spanish Labyrinth* (1943); *The Face of Spain* (1950); and *The Literature of the Spanish People* (1953). On his return to Churriana he wrote *South from Granada* (1957), recalling his early years in Spain. The book includes perceptive character sketches of Lytton Strachey and Virginia Woolf, each of whose visits to Yegen merits a separate chapter. *A Life of One's Own* (1966) described his childhood and his wartime experiences while *Personal Record* (1974) was an autobiographical account of half a century. His most scholarly work was *St John of the Cross, his life and letters* (1971). In 1969 he moved to the mountain village of Alhaurin el Grande. Britain honoured him belatedly with a C.B.E. in 1982. After a brief experience of an old people's home in Pinner in 1984, he was brought back to Alhaurin where the municipality cared for him, respected as a "living monument" of Spain, until his death on 19 January 1987. He left his body for dissection by the medical faculty of Malaga University.

BRETT, Dorothy Eugenie (1883–1977), painter: born in London, daughter of second Viscount Esher and his Belgian wife Eleanor. Lord Esher, a Secretary of the Office of Works, was a power behind the throne and advised Queen Victoria, King Edward VII and King George V. His family were brought up so close to Windsor Castle that royalty visited them through a private gate, and his daughters, Sylvia and Dorothy, went to dancing-classes with the Queen's grandchildren.

Dorothy's début in 1902 was delayed by appendicitis and after an operation by the King's doctor, by complications that may have caused her later deafness. Edward VII had a more successful operation for the same illness and Dorothy was able to attend his postponed Coronation and be presented at Court. She was not a success in the marriage market, however, always preferring to paint and draw by herself rather than go to débutante dances. The main influence on her at this time was Margaret Brooke, wife of Rajah Brooke of Sarawak, the first object of the violent "crushes" that formed the pattern of Dorothy's life. Sylvia Brett later married Margaret's son and became the last white Ranee of Sarawak.

In 1910 Dorothy's father was persuaded with difficulty to let her enter the Slade School of Art. Although she was much older than the other students, she had found her proper setting; she cut her hair, wore breeches, and was called just "Brett", in the Slade fashion. Carrington,* ten years her junior, became her closest friend. Brett moved to a studio of her own where she could entertain her friends, who now included fellow-student Mark Gertler.* Through him she met other artists and Lady Ottoline Morrell,* to whom she soon developed a passionate attachment. From 1915 to 1919 she was almost a fixture at Garsington. Here she painted and battled against increasing deafness to join in the conversation of such guests as Lytton Strachey* and the Woolfs.** During this, her most "Bloomsbury" period, Brett also met the two next great loves of her life, Middleton Murry* and D. H. Lawrence.*

In 1916 she rented Maynard Keynes'* house, 3 Gower Street, which she called the "Ark"; she shared it with Murry and Katherine Mansfield,* while Carrington lived in the attic. The lease ended in 1917, with an acrimonious exchange of letters between Brett and Keynes about rent arrears and damage to furnishings. She then moved to Hampstead, giving lodgings at different times to Gertler and the Murrys and holding Thursday evening parties in imitation of Lady Ottoline and Bloomsbury. After Katherine Mansfield's death in 1923, Brett told Virginia Woolf that she was in "contact" with the dead woman. The widower Murry may have become her lover for a short time.

Next year Brett broke with her old life entirely to join D. H. Lawrence and his wife in their "ideal community" in Taos, New Mexico. Apart from a visit to Europe with the Lawrences in 1925–6, she spent the rest of her life there, caring for Lawrence's ranch in his absence, riding with him when he was there, and quarrelling with Frieda Lawrence and his local friend Mabel Luhan. She wrote a memoir of Lawrence after his death (1930) and painted huge canvases of Indian ceremonies. Brett died in New Mexico just before her ninety-fourth birthday.

Sean Hignett, *Brett: From Bloomsbury to New Mexico* (London, 1984)

BROOKE, Rupert Chawner (1887–1915), poet: born and educated at Rugby School, where his father was a housemaster. On holiday at St Ives, Cornwall in 1893, he played cricket on the beach with the Stephen family, including Virginia (Woolf*). At Hillbrow Preparatory School he was a friend of James Strachey* and at Rugby of Geoffrey Keynes.* He went up to King's College, Cambridge, in 1906 as a Classics scholar and was elected to the Apostles in his first year. An interest in acting led to his famous performance as Mephistopheles in Marlowe's *Dr Faustus* in November 1907 and to the foundation of the Marlowe Society a year later, with Brooke as first President. But he was also interested, and active, in Fabian Society politics.

In the first part of the Classical Tripos he gained second-class honours, May 1909; thereafter he decided to concentrate on English, hoping for a Fellowship. He took lodgings in the village of Grantchester later that summer and began to write poetry for several journals; his *Poems 1911* was eventually published by Sidgwick and Jackson on 3 December 1911. By then he had moved into the Old Vicarage, Grantchester, after spending three months of that year on the first of several courses in Munich. Among the friends entertained at Grantchester in August 1911 was Virginia Stephen, who was rather proud of having joined a naked bathing-party in the Granta, and she was later persuaded to accompany him on a camping trip in Devon.

The "Neo-Pagans"—the Brooke circle—were never quite identified with the Bloomsbury group and a definite break occurred after a curious incident at West Lulworth in Dorset, where Brooke joined a reading party on 27 December 1911. For some years he had been conducting an on-off affair with Katharine Cox,* whom he first met at Newnham College in 1908. At West Lulworth on New Year's Day Brooke feared she had fallen in love with the painter Henry Lamb,* an episode he blamed on their fellow guest, Lytton Strachey.* Brooke, who was at that time seeking to complete a dissertation for a Cambridge fellowship, overdramatised the incident and suffered a nervous breakdown. Although he never forgave Lytton or Lamb he did not break with Ka Cox (who was with him in Germany in February 1912) and later that year he stayed with James Strachey in Rye and visited the Woolfs in Sussex.

Brooke failed to gain a Fellowship at King's College in 1912 but was successful in March 1913. New interests took him away from his Bloomsbury contacts: he was closely associated with the family of the Prime Minister, Asquith, and he began a platonic affair with the actress, Cathleen Nesbitt. His emotions were, however, so confused that he resolved to take a long holiday in America, Canada and the Pacific, seeking peace of mind, and writing a series of articles about his travels for the *Westminster Gazette*. He arrived back in England early in June 1914. Soon afterwards he was caught up in the patriotic fervour which produced his famous five "War Sonnets". Lieutenant R. C. Brooke, R.N.V.R., joined the naval division sent to Antwerp in November, sailing for the Dardanelles on 1 March 1915. He contracted blood poisoning and died aboard a French hospital ship on St George's Day; his body was buried on Skyros. The First Lord of the Admiralty, Winston Churchill, wrote an obituary published in *The Times* three days later. There had indeed been a break with Bloomsbury in his last year of life.

John Lehmann, *Rupert Brooke* (London, 1980)
C. Hassall, *Rupert Brooke* (London, 1964)
G. Keynes, *The Letters of Rupert Brooke* (London, 1968)

BUSSY, Dorothy (1865–1960), born Dorothy Strachey, elder sister of Lytton Strachey,* third surviving child of Sir Richard and Lady Strachey.** She accompanied her mother back to India in 1868 and was bridesmaid to the Viceroy's daughter at the age of three. Dorothy was educated at "Les Ruches", the Fontainebleau school of Mlle Souvestre,* for whom she conceived a schoolgirl passion, and whom she later portrayed as "Mlle Julie" in her novel *Olivia*, published anonymously in 1948.

Once her school days were over, Dorothy stayed at home as housekeeper, apart from teaching at Mlle Souvestre's new school in Wimbledon. She coached her younger sister Pernel* for Cambridge entrance, and made a favourite of Lytton among the smaller children. With her next sister Philippa,* she gave parties at their Lancaster Gate house, and entertained many young men, but had no serious love affair until in 1900 she met the painter Simon Bussy.* He was poor and of obscure origin, and the Stracheys at first opposed the match, but in 1903 the couple were allowed to marry. Sir Richard bought them a house, La Souco, at Roquebrune in the south of France, and one daughter, Jane (*infra*) was born in 1906. The marriage lasted, in a detached way, in spite of Dorothy's habit of never speaking her excellent French; a common Strachey idiosyncracy.

A visit to Cambridge in 1918 altered Dorothy's placid life. She met the writer André Gide, and began an intense, romantic friendship with him that lasted until his death in 1951, although the word "love" did not enter their correspondence until 1948, when both were over eighty. Dorothy translated most of Gide's works into English. Gide was a frequent visitor to Roquebrune, and the Bussys, or sometimes Dorothy alone, stayed in his Paris flat in September on their return from their annual London visit; they occupied the top two floors of 51 Gordon Square every summer from 1932 onwards. Dorothy survived Gide and her husband, but senility mercifully prevented the knowledge that she had outlived her daughter also, by two weeks. Her portrait by her husband is in the Ashmolean Museum, Oxford.

BUSSY, Jane Simone (1906–60), painter, only child of Simon and Dorothy Bussy:* born at Roquebrune early in March 1906 at a time when her uncle, Lytton Strachey,* was convalescing three miles away, at Menton. Although technically a Frenchwoman, Jane Bussy spent several months of each year for most of her life in

England, much of it in Bloomsbury, and she became particularly attached to the Charleston circle, her mother's cousin, Duncan Grant,★ and Vanessa Bell★ and her family. These feelings were reciprocated; she was a welcome guest at Charleston, where she often participated in the summertime domestic theatricals; and in 1947 Professor Quentin Bell's★ first book, *On Human Finery*, was dedicated to her. She was also a friend of Rachel MacCarthy★ and Frances Partridge★ and was one of the younger guests at the Memoir Club on 9 September 1938 when Keynes★ defended "Old Bloomsbury's" aestheticism, then under attack from Leavis and others.

Jane Bussy first exhibited in London in the spring of 1935 at the Lefevre Gallery, her painting skills concentrating on still life, especially fruit and flowers. She possessed a natural artistic perception, which was sharpened by the family's friendship with Matisse;★ and she had, too, a feeling for French literature, stimulated by conversations with Gide and Paul Valéry. This cultural sensitivity, hardened by left-wing political convictions, endeared her to Virginia Woolf,★ to whom in the summer of 1934 she gave lessons in conversational French. It was generally considered by her Bloomsbury friends that "Janie's" talents suffered from the social burden of an over-dominant mother.

France's military defeat in 1940 left the Bussy family cut off from England for most of the war. They were forced to move from Roquebrune into the Rue Verdi in Nice, fifteen miles away, where they gave hospitality to Matisse. Jane Bussy's politics made her naturally hostile to the Vichy collaborationists and sympathetic to the Resistance. As early as June 1945 mother and daughter were able once more to stay in Gordon Square and at Charleston; the Bells and Duncan Grant soon returned these visits, with Jane Bussy by now effective hostess at Roquebrune. After her father's death in May 1954 she spent more time in London, caring for her increasingly senile mother and her two aged aunts, Marjorie★ and Philippa Strachey,★ at their home in 51 Gordon Square. It was there that fumes from a faulty gas water-heater in the bathroom caused her death in a tragic accident a month after her fifty-fourth birthday.

BUSSY, Simon Albert (1869–1954), French painter: born into a peasant family at Dôle, on the edge of the Jura. He studied painting at the École des Beaux-Arts in Paris under Gustave Moreau, was complimented by Degas for his pastels of trees, and received an "honourable mention" in the Salon of 1894. Matisse* was a fellow-pupil in Moreau's class and became a life-long friend. In the winter of 1901–2 Bussy came to London and took a studio in Kensington. He painted portraits of several members of the Strachey family and in February 1903 became engaged to Dorothy Strachey (BUSSY, Dorothy). They were married later in the year and settled at La Souco, their Roquebrune home for half a century. His illustrations for Francis de Miomandre's *Bestiaire* were much praised. A notable exhibition at Leighton House in 1907 emphasised the thoughtful restraint with which he employed colour. His standards remained high, for himself, for his daughter Janie (*supra*), and for others. He advised his wife's cousin, Duncan Grant,* early in his career, to strengthen his self-discipline by working regular hours and to learn technique by copying the great Florentine masters. Bussy, the ablest portrait pastellist of his generation, also had a good eye for landscape, notably in London, Venice and North Africa. He suffered a stroke in May 1954, dying in London at the end of the month.

C

CANNAN, Gilbert (1884–1955), novelist: born in Manchester, educated at Manchester Grammar School, he read law at Manchester University and Cambridge, and was called to the Bar in 1908. He became first an actor, then a drama critic, and finally a novelist; his first novel, *Peter Homunculus*, appeared in 1909. By then he had married J. M. Barrie's ex-wife Mary, who left her husband for Cannan in 1904, bringing with her Barrie's huge Newfoundland dog Luath, the original "Nana" in *Peter Pan*. All three lived in the Mill House, Cholesbury, Buckinghamshire. The Cannans were part of Lady Ottoline Morrell's★ circle, and friendly with D. H. Lawrence★ and Middleton Murry.★ They lent the Mill House to several Bloomsbury friends, notably to Mark Gertler★ during his affair with Carrington (*infra*). In 1916, however, Cannan published a novel, *Mendel*, based on Gertler's life, and the revelations in it destroyed their relationship; it was poorly written as well, according to Bloomsbury critics. In 1917 Cannan had the first of many breakdowns, but recovered enough to leave his wife and write more novels during sane periods. One of these, *Pugs and Peacocks* (1921) offended Lady Ottoline. In 1924 Cannan was committed to a mental hospital for the rest of his life.

CARRINGTON, Dora de Houghton (1893–1932), painter: born in Hereford, daughter of Samuel Carrington, a railway engineer with the East India Company, who in retirement at the age of fifty-six married a governess, Charlotte Houghton. Dora was the fourth of five children, and was particularly fond of her brother Edmund (Teddy), a year older than herself. All the children had a happy relationship with their father, who led the outdoor games

and expeditions they enjoyed in the summer, but found their
mother dominating and obsessed with "what people would think".
As a Sabbatarian she made Sunday a day of misery for the family;
Dora in particular became used to deceiving her parents about her
activities.

The Carringtons moved to Bedford in 1902, where Dora went to
the high school for girls. The only subjects to interest her were
drawing and natural history, and in 1910 she entered the Slade
School of Art. As she hated her first name, she adopted the current
Slade habit and was known simply as "Carrington"; she also
cropped her hair, pretending at home that it was done for a
fancy-dress party. Carrington was now an attractive girl, blue-eyed
and fair-haired, with a shy and breathless manner of speech.
Among her particular friends at the Slade were Dorothy Brett* and
Barbara Hiles (Bagenal*), while Mark Gertler* was seriously in love
with her. However, she shunned any sexual relationship, resenting
her own female physical nature.

Visits to Lady Ottoline Morrell* at Garsington introduced her to
a wider literary and artistic circle, including some members of the
Bloomsbury group, She started filling in the gaps in her education
by reading history and literature, and sharing the studies of her
younger brother Noel, though her spelling remained erratic. In
December 1915, while staying at Asheham house in Sussex,
Carrington met Lytton Strachey.* Although homosexual, Strachey
got on well with women, but he seems also to have been physically
attracted by Carrington's boyish charm. The story goes that she
tried to avenge his attempt to kiss her by cutting off his beard as he
slept, but when Strachey opened his eyes and looked at her she fell
in love with him. Their friendship progressed by way of a holiday in
Wales with Barbara Hiles and her fiancé Nicholas Bagenal, and a
walking tour on their own, until by autumn 1916 Carrington was
looking for a house that they could share. Meanwhile she lived first
in a communal house rented from Maynard Keynes* and then with
Alix Sargant-Florence who later married James Strachey.** In
October 1916 her brother Teddy was reported missing on the
Somme, a loss from which she never quite recovered.

It was a repeated pattern in Carrington's life that in spite of her
devotion to Strachey she attracted and was attracted by other men.
If he was her father-figure (she addressed him in early days
sometimes as "grandpère"), the younger men may have been
substitutes for her brother. Mark Gertler was finally allowed to
become her lover in December 1916, but his jealousy of Strachey
and his violent nature finished the affair in 1917. Next year she met

Ralph Partridge,* an Oxford friend of her brother Noel. He fell in love with her and eventually persuaded her to marry him in May 1921, aided by the fact that he was no threat to her relationship with Strachey. Even before the marriage Carrington began a much more passionate affair with Partridge's friend Gerald Brenan,* which aroused Partridge's fury when he discovered it in 1922. Carrington's last liaison resulted in pregnancy and an abortion in 1929. She also had emotional attachments to some of her women friends, notably the American Henrietta Bingham, whom she met in 1923, and Julia Strachey,* Lytton's niece.

By the end of 1917 Strachey had taken the Mill House, Tidmarsh, and Carrington moved in with him, "looting" as much furniture as she could from her parents' home. The success of *Eminent Victorians* in 1918 began to make Strachey's fortune, and Carrington's father died, leaving her a small income. Ralph Partridge fitted comfortably into the *ménage* as Carrington's husband and in 1924 he and Strachey bought the lease of Ham Spray House, near Hungerford; here the three lived out their lives. In 1926 a break-up threatened because of Partridge's love for Frances Marshall (Partridge*), but she and Carrington worked out a settlement that allowed Partridge to continue his rôle of essential prop to the Ham Spray household.

Carrington was not at first whole-heartedly accepted by the Bloomsbury group; all the young "Cropheads", as Virginia Woolf called them, were often subjects of criticism by their elders. She was particularly unfortunate in taking a good deal of blame for the "burglary" of Asheham house in October 1916. With David Garnett* and Barbara Hiles, she broke in for a night's shelter, and had to dine alone with the Woolfs to make their excuses. Eventually it became apparent to Strachey's friends that Carrington had made him a comfortable and beautiful home. As long as he was with her, she was happier in Wiltshire than in Bloomsbury, riding, making wine and sloe gin, pickling and preserving, and entertaining guests. Strachey furthered her literary education, but she had less time for her own painting, and not so much encouragement; none of her lovers after Gertler were artists. Best known of her portraits are those of Lytton Strachey and his mother, the latter looking like "the Queen of China" as Carrington said in a letter. Other subjects were her father, E. M. Forster,* David Garnett, and Gerald Brenan, as well as landscapes in England and abroad. Her letters are illustrated with lively cartoons. She also produced woodcuts for the Hogarth Press, and painted inn signs, murals and tiles. Most of the portraits are privately owned, but Lady Strachey's is in the

Scottish National Portrait Gallery, and Forster's in the National Portrait Gallery.

Carrington spent much time on her own at Ham Spray, when Strachey was abroad or in London. She visited France with the Johns, and stayed with Gerald Brenan in Spain. New friends came into her life, like Bryan and Diana Guinness (*née* Mitford) at whose nearby house she painted a mural. But whatever might be her surface preoccupations, Lytton Strachey was the centre of her existence. His fatal illness began in November 1931; on 20 January 1932 he became suddenly worse, and that night Carrington attempted suicide through breathing exhaust fumes in the garage. She was saved by Ralph Partridge, and recovered in time to see Strachey die on the afternoon of 21 January. Although her friends, the Partridges and Stephen Tomlin★ in particular, tried to watch her from that time onwards, she managed to borrow a gun from the Guinnesses, ostensibly to shoot rabbits, and shot herself on 11 March. Ralph Partridge, David Garnett and Frances Marshall arrived at Ham Spray while she was still alive, but she died later that day. Two days before Strachey's death he said "I always wanted to marry Carrington and I never did".

Carrington, *Letters and Extracts from her Diaries*, ed. David Garnett (London, 1970)
D. Gadd, *The Loving Friends* (London, 1974)

CASE, Janet Elizabeth (1862–1937), teacher: youngest of six daughters of William Case and his wife Sarah who kept a co-educational school, Heath Brow, in Hampstead. Janet was educated there, then followed her sister Esther to read Classics at Newnham College, Cambridge (1881–5, Class II and I). She was the first woman to act in the university's Greek play, appearing as Athena in Aeschylus' *Eumenides* (1885). Janet Case lived in Hampstead with her sister Euphemia ("Emphie"), and taught Greek in schools and to private pupils, among them Virginia Stephen (Woolf★). In 1905 she published an edition of Aeschylus' *Prometheus Unbound*. She supported Home Rule for Ireland and divorce law reform, and belonged to the Women's Co-operative Guild, the Labour Party and the Peace Pledge Union, until ill-health forced her to give up these activities. In 1920 she retired to Lyndhurst in the New Forest with her sister and from there wrote the "Country Diary" in the *Manchester Guardian* from 1925 until her death. Virginia Woolf, in her *Times* obituary of Janet Case, said that she could teach grammar to the classicist and "reading" Greek to the non-specialist with equal inspiration, but preferred the society of the latter. Virginia herself often went to Hampstead for tea and gossip.

CECIL, (Lord Edward Christian) David (1902–86), literary critic and biographer: the younger son of the fourth Marquess of Salisbury and thus a grandson of Queen Victoria's last Prime Minister. He was educated at Eton and Christ Church, Oxford, where he was also a Fellow of Wadham College from 1924 to 1930, becoming a Fellow of New College in 1939 and holding the Goldsmith Chair of English Literature from 1948 until his retirement in 1969. His first book, *The Stricken Deer* (1929), was a study of Cowper; it was followed by brief biographies of Walter Scott (1933) and Jane Austen (1935), printed lectures on the *Early Victorian Novelists* (1934), a two-volume biography of Queen Victoria's first Prime Minister (*The Young Melbourne* in 1939 and *Lord M.* in 1954), a study of *Hardy the Novelist* (1943), a biography of Beerbohm (*Max*, 1964), *The Cecils of Hatfield House* (1973), and other scholarly works, all elegantly written with imaginative sympathy for his subject.

Lord David became a member of Ottoline Morrell's★ admiring circle of undergraduates at Garsington where, in June 1923, he met Virginia Woolf★ for the first time. It was not, however, until a party given by Ethel Sands★ in Chelsea at Christmas 1927 that he made a deep impression on her, and on Vanessa Bell.★ He was an observant guest at many Bloomsbury parties, fascinated by the group's "mannerisms of voice and phrasing . . . rather breathless way of talking and . . . very solemn face": "When they shook hands they didn't smile, they just handed the hand", he once recalled in a television interview. In October 1932 he married Rachel MacCarthy;★ their first son (the actor Jonathan Cecil) was born in February 1939. They remained on the fringe of Bloomsbury, Lord David later contributing the life of Lytton Strachey★ to the *Dictionary of National Biography*. After retiring from Oxford they lived mainly in Dorset, at Red Lion House, Cranborne, where Lord David died on New Year's Day 1986.

CECIL, Lady Robert, *née* Eleanor Lambton (1868–1959), a granddaughter of "Radical Jack" Lambton who, as Lord Durham, drafted the famous Report (1839) on responsible government for Britain's colonies. In 1889 "Nelly" Lambton married Robert Cecil, third son of the then Prime Minister, Lord Salisbury; this happy, though childless, marriage lasted to within nine weeks of seventy years. She was a woman of sturdily independent mind who, despite the Cecils' High Tory traditions, voted Labour in the 1945 General Election. Her husband—Nobel Peace Prize laureate in 1937—was largely responsible for the form and structure of the League of Nations. As Viscount Cecil of Chelwood, he sat in Baldwin's Cabinet, 1924–7.

Virginia Stephen (Woolf★) first met Nelly Cecil in June 1903, as a friend of Violet Dickinson;★ she corresponded with her from 1904 until 21 March 1941. Conversation with Lady Robert was difficult as she was almost totally deaf by the age of thirty, but she had a fine sense of humour, shrewd political judgement and good literary taste, acting for many years as an (anonymous) publisher's reader. She wrote an unpublished novel and in 1907–8 shared book reviewing in *The Cornhill* with Virginia Stephen. Letters to her friend Gwendolen Osborne show that Lady Robert recognised Virginia's gifts as early as March 1906, nine years before her first book was published. In 1905 she commissioned Vanessa Bell★ to paint her portrait, but she became critical of Gordon Square society, particularly of the influence of Clive Bell,★ whom she considered silly and decadent; and it is probable that her article in the *National Review* for November 1907 mocking the fear of conventional respectability held by "the artistic person" was a gently ironical reproach to young Bloomsbury. Nevertheless the friendship with Virginia Woolf remained unimpaired; and at Virginia's request in 1917 Lady Robert wrote to her brother-in-law, Lord Salisbury, Chairman of the Conscientious Objectors' Board, on behalf of Duncan Grant.★

Viscountess Cecil of Chelwood died on 24 April 1959, five months after her husband.

Kenneth Rose, *The Later Cecils* (London and New York, 1975)

COLE, (William) Horace de Vere (1881–1936), hoaxer and art connoisseur: the son of Major W. V. Cole of the Third Dragoon Guards, who died from cholera in India when his son was ten. The

Coles, by origin stolid Norfolk farmers, were suddenly made wealthy through the business acumen of Major Cole's father, who became a city merchant in London. Horace Cole was brought up by these grandparents at West Woodley, near Newbury, the house he eventually inherited. On leaving Eton in 1899 he sought a commission in his father's old regiment and was wounded in the later stages of the Boer War. In 1902 he went up to Trinity College, Cambridge, where he was a friend of Adrian Stephen.★ From his mother's family, the Anglo-Irish de Veres, "Molar" Cole—as Horace was nicknamed—inherited an impish sense of the ridiculous. He delighted in staging elaborately prepared hoaxes: on 5 March 1905 Cole and Stephen fooled the Mayor of Cambridge and other civic dignitaries into receiving the suite of "the Sultan of Zanzibar's uncle". In 1908–9 Cole brought a touch of light-hearted idiocy to Bloomsbury as a frequent visitor to 29 Fitzroy Square when Adrian Stephen was living there with his sister, Virginia: both Adrian and Virginia took part in the notorious *Dreadnought* hoax of 1910, the details of which Cole leaked to the press; this apparent desire for newspaper publicity cut his links with Bloomsbury. A year later Cole's sister Ann married the rising Birmingham politician, Neville Chamberlain (Prime Minister 1937–40). Cole was a patron of Augustus John, wrote some verse and collected pictures. He married Denise Daley, from Galway, and died at Honfleur in late February 1936.

COLEFAX, Lady Sibyl, *née* Halsey (c.1875–1950), society hostess: born into a family with traditions of service in India, although her grandfather, James Wilson, had been first Editor of *The Economist*. In 1901 she married the barrister, Arthur Colefax (1866–1936, an M.P. for ten months in 1910, knighted in 1920). At Onslow Square and, in particular, at Argyll House she established a salon—political, literary, musical and artistic—which, during the inter-war years, won her eminence in a wider circle than was enjoyed by her rival hostesses, Lady Oxford and Asquith, Lady Cunard and Lady Ottoline Morrell.★ After her husband's death she continued her parties, on a smaller scale, at her home in Lord North Street, Westminster.

Lady Colefax cultivated the "Bloomsberries" from 1922 onwards although her social values were the antithesis of theirs. Most Bloomsbury intellectuals treated her disdainfully, "an unabashed hunter of lions", was Leonard Woolf's★ description of her. But

Lytton Strachey* and Virginia Woolf* frequently went to Argyll House, and Lady Colefax visited the Woolfs at Rodmell on several occasions. Although she may well have been invited, Virginia Woolf did not go to the last "brilliant party" in Argyll House on 11 June 1936, lovingly described by Harold Nicolson* in the first volume of his *Diaries and Letters,* which was attended by King Edward VIII and Mrs Simpson; but she was Lady Colefax's guest three months later, shortly before she moved out. On one evening between October and February of that winter Virginia Woolf gave a paper to the Memoir Club, "Am I a Snob?", which mocked Lady Colefax's social pretensions. But the two women remained friends.

J. Schulkind (ed.), *Moments of Being* (London, 1976)

COX, Katherine Laird ("Ka") (1887–1938), born in London, daughter of Henry Cox, a stockbroker, and educated at St Felix's School, Southwold. Her mother died when Ka was young and her father in 1905, just before she entered Newnham College, Cambridge, so that she developed a responsible and maternal attitude to her family and friends. She read history at Newnham from 1906 to 1910, gaining a Class II in both parts of the Tripos. At Cambridge Ka was a member of the set that revolved around Rupert Brooke,* sometimes known as "Neo-Pagans", and after a brief love-affair with Jacques Raverat,* she became one of Brooke's most constant companions. The Neo-Pagans had many connections with Bloomsbury, and in 1911 Ka first met Virginia Stephen (Woolf*); Virginia gave her the nickname of "Bruin" or "the Bear", probably because of her sturdy yet cuddly appearance and shiny brown hair.

Over Christmas and New Year of 1911–12, Ka's affair with Rupert Brooke took a more serious turn. She had become acquainted with the painter Henry Lamb,* who made several drawings of her. Brooke developed a violent jealousy of Lamb while all three were staying near Lulworth in Dorset and the intensity of his feelings convinced him that he loved Ka. During 1912 he persuaded her to join him in Verona and Munich in February, and in Berlin in May. She was still seeing Lamb, and in March nursed him and dressed his wrist after a riding accident, but he did not care for her Bloomsbury friends and soon tired of the affair. However Brooke could never bring himself to the point of marriage, and in June 1913 wrote Ka a farewell letter from New York. Meanwhile she had become more intimate with Virginia Woolf, and helped nurse her in her mental illnesses of 1913. Indeed it was Ka who discovered the unconscious Virginia after her suicide attempt on 8 September of that year, and she was of great help to Leonard Woolf* during his wife's convalescence, often persuading the sick woman to eat when no one else could. She saw Rupert Brooke once more in 1914, and on 10 March 1915 in his final letter to her, he claimed to regard her as almost his widow and the best thing he had found in life; she was to have all his papers after his mother's death.

Ka Cox spent the rest of the war organising Serbian refugee camps in Corsica, and then as a temporary civil servant. In September 1918 she married William Arnold-Forster, a painter serving in the R.N.V.R. The couple lived in Lancaster Place and later in Aldbourne, Wiltshire, but after the birth of their son Mark in 1920 they took the Eagle's Nest, a house high on the moors above Zennor in Cornwall. Virginia Woolf greatly envied their Cornish home, though not Ka's activities when she became a J.P. (1928) and a member of Cornwall's Education Committee (1931). She still visited London frequently and the Woolfs stayed in Zennor several times, but Virginia had no great opinion of Arnold-Forster. She thought Ka's defence of her marriage was a complacent façade hiding dissatisfaction; that her life had ended with Rupert Brooke's death and she had played a part ever since. Virginia also felt that her own relationship with Ka was strained because "she had seen me mad". Their friendship and Ka herself are described in Virginia Woolf's diary entry of 25 May 1938; she had just heard of her friend's sudden death from heart failure three days before.

D

DAVIDSON, Angus Henry Gordon (1898–1980), art critic:
educated at Magdalene College, Cambridge. He became associated
with post-war Bloomsbury in the summer of 1924 as a friend of
Duncan Grant,★ but his brother—the painter Douglas Davidson—
was already a friend of Lytton Strachey★ (who, by the following
spring, was much attracted by Angus Davidson, too). Leonard
Woolf★ employed him at the Hogarth Press from December 1924 to
December 1927 but Davidson was too charmingly ineffectual to
satisfy Woolf's standards. He contributed art criticism to several
London periodicals and became Secretary of the London Artists'
Association before retiring to Cornwall to write *Edward Lear,
Landscape Painter and Nonsense Poet*, which was published in 1938.
In later years he translated several novels by Alberto Moravia.

DAVIES, Margaret Caroline Llewelyn (1861–1944), General
Secretary of the Women's Co-operative Guild: born in Marylebone,
the only daughter of the Reverend John Llewelyn Davies
(1826–1916), a pioneer Christian Socialist, who had coached Leslie
Stephen★ before he went up to Cambridge. Margaret Llewelyn
Davies was educated at Girton College, Cambridge (1881–3), taking
up her post with the Co-operative Guild in 1889 and holding it until
she was sixty. Leonard Woolf★ knew two of her brothers as senior
Apostles at Cambridge. She became a friend of the Woolfs in 1912,
introducing Leonard to co-operative socialism, and helping
Virginia (Woolf★) in her bouts of mental depression. Although
interested in "Bloomsbury" she remained an outsider, living in
Hampstead; but she would argue amicably with Virginia over art
and questions of morality. She outlived six brothers, one of whom

(Arthur) was the father of the five sons who were befriended by Sir James Barrie and became the first recipients of his *Peter Pan* stories.

DERAIN, André (1880–1954), French artist: born at Chatou, ten miles west of Paris. In the early 1900s he became fascinated by colour as an expressive rather than a descriptive form and—with Matisse,* Braque and others—was one of the *fauves* ("wild beasts"), whose experiments with yellows, blues, greens, reds and purples amazed the critics at the Salon d'Automne in 1905. In 1906 and 1907 he visited London, adding scenes beside the Thames and the Serpentine to the more familiar paintings of his native countryside around the Seine. Both Clive Bell* and Roger Fry* soon perceived Derain's significance and his esteem rose among the Bloomsbury artists after some of his works were hung in the "Modern French Artists" exhibition at Brighton in June 1910, five months before Fry selected more of his paintings for the first Post-Impressionist exhibition. A wider range of Derain's work— the later canvases more restrained in colour and influenced by cubism—was shown at the second Post-Impressionist exhibition.

Like Picasso,* Derain was attracted by the artistic possibilities of the Russian ballet and designed the décor for Massine's* *La Boutique Fantasque,* in which Lopokova* attracted much attention at the London première in June 1919; the critics noted, with some surprise, that Derain "employed the most restful of hues". Vanessa Bell* lent Derain a flat at 36 Regent Square; he lived simply, scorning evening dress and using a small studio in the seedy Seven Dials district. In Paris he presided with natural authority over the artists who gathered in *Les Deux Magots,* a group to whom he introduced the Bells and Duncan Grant.* He became increasingly traditionalist, with browns and olive green replacing the rich colours of earlier years, but some later ballet designs were strikingly effective, notably his re-creation of Directoire Paris in Massine's *Mam'zelle Angot* (1947). He died on 11 September 1954 in Paris after being knocked down by a car near his home at Chambourcy.

DIAGHILEV, Serge Pavlovich (1872–1929), Russian impresario: born, the son of a Guards officer, in army barracks at Gruzino, 150 miles south-east of St Petersburg. He settled in the capital as a law student in 1890 and established his primacy within a group of young and progressive writers, musicians and painters (who included Bakst★ and Alexander Benois). From 1899 to 1904 he managed and edited the magazine *Mir iskusstva* ("The World of Art"), thereafter concentrating on organising art exhibitions in St Petersburg and Paris. He brought Russian opera to Paris in 1908 and scored sensational triumphs with the ballets he mounted for Paris seasons in the early summer of 1909 and 1910. When Nijinsky★ resigned from the Maryinsky Theatre in St Petersburg in 1911, Diaghilev established his Ballets Russes as an independent touring company to which he gave his own name. Although suffering from diabetes, and often buffeted by fortune and creditors, he continued to direct the Ballets Russes until his death at Venice on 19 August 1929. The company never performed in Russia but had its headquarters in Monte Carlo.

"The Ballets Russes de Serge Diaghilev" opened at Covent Garden on 21 June 1911, their first London visit coinciding with George V's coronation. The revolutionary integration of modern music, bright design and daringly original choreography captivated London society. They returned to London for a second season in October 1911 and a third in June 1912. Among hostesses eager to entertain Diaghilev, Nijinsky and Bakst was Lady Ottoline Morrell★ and it was during this third season that the "Russian dancers" were particularly taken up by Bloomsbury. Diaghilev was back in London with his company in 1913 (twice) and 1914, finishing a season at Drury Lane eleven days before Britain went to war with Germany.

On 5 September 1918 Diaghilev saw his company open at the London Coliseum; the Bloomsbury circle renewed old friendships and made new ones, notably the attachment of Keynes★ to Lopokova;★ and Diaghilev also brought Derain (*supra*) and Picasso★ to London. So successful was the season that Diaghilev remained in London until March 1919 and, after a short visit to Manchester, transferred from the Coliseum to the Alhambra Theatre in April and to the Empire Theatre from October to December. On armistice night (11 November 1918) Diaghilev and Massine★ accompanied Osbert Sitwell★ to the party given by the barrister, Montague Shearman,★ in his Adelphi flat at which most of the Bloomsbury group were present. All joined in the dancing except Diaghilev who, even on so festive an occasion, was too conscious of his dignity—and, unlike Lytton Strachey,★ too protective of his homosexuality—to be seen jigging around the floor with the Bloomsbury "cropheads".

Diaghilev returned with his company to London in each of the following nine years, apart from 1923. Except when Lopokova was dancing, his visits aroused less interest among the Bloomsbury intelligentsia than in 1912–13 and 1918–19. The most ambitious production was *The Sleeping Princess*, mounted with Bakst designs at the Alhambra and opening on 3 November 1921. It was too old-fashioned for Bloomsbury, making Lytton Strachey "feel sick", mainly because of Tchaikovsky's "degrading" music. Diaghilev, however, remained in favour with the wealthier patrons and began to recruit English-born dancers to his company. It was at Covent Garden on 24 July 1929 that Diaghilev saw his Ballets Russes dance for the last time, presenting a royal gala in honour of King Fuad of Egypt.

R. Buckle, *Diaghilev* (London, 1979)
S. L. Grigoriev, *The Diaghilev Ballet 1909–1929* (London, 1953)
O. Sitwell, *Laughter in the Next Room* (London, 1949)

DICKINSON, Goldsworthy Lowes (1862–1932), Cambridge don and political philosopher: born in London, the grandson of W. S. Williams, who "discovered" Charlotte Brontë for the publishers Smith, Elder. "Goldie" Dickinson was a classicist educated at Charterhouse and King's, Cambridge, of which college he became a Fellow in 1887 after a half-hearted attempt to study medicine. From that academic year a deep, lasting friendship developed between Dickinson and the newly elected Apostle, Roger Fry* (whose 1893 pastel of Dickinson is in the National Portrait Gallery). Subsequently Dickinson's sceptical Platonism influenced younger Apostles but, although he became a close friend of Leonard Woolf* and Lytton Strachey,* his strongest Bloomsbury link remained his intimacy with Fry. Apart from a natural misogynism, he was tolerant and liberal-minded, his political opinions softening with the passage of time into an anaemic radicalism. His *The Greek View of Life* was published in 1896, the year in which he became a lecturer in political science at Cambridge.

As early as August 1914 Lowes Dickinson invented the phrase "a League of Nations" and he continued to promote causes devoted to international peace and reconciliation for the remainder of his life. His suspicion of secret diplomacy made him an active member of the Union of Democratic Control from its inception in September 1914 and he was a founder of the League of Nations Union. His best-known book *The International Anarchy, 1904–14* (1926), persuasively argued in graceful prose that Germany was less responsible for the First World War than any other Power. But, despite his concern for world affairs, he remained an agreeably cloistered eccentric, wearing in his Cambridge rooms a mandarin hat he had brought back in 1912 from an extended visit to China. Death in August 1932 from a bungled prostate operation spared him the disillusionment of seeing the League he championed spurned by politicians he had sought to enlighten.

E. M. Forster, *Goldsworthy Lowes Dickinson* (London, 1934)
D. Proctor, *Autobiography of Goldsworthy Lowes Dickinson* (London, 1973)

DICKINSON, Violet (1865–1948), friend of the Stephen family: born at Chapmanslade, near Frome. As a girl in Somerset, she was a close friend of Stella Duckworth (Hills*) and thus became a frequent visitor to Hyde Park Gate throughout the childhood of Vanessa (Bell*) and Virginia (Woolf*). She was over six feet tall, an impressive woman but hardly a beauty; although she was liked in conventional London society, she never married but lived for most of her life with her brother Oswald Dickinson (1867–1954), a barrister, who in 1912 became Secretary to the Commissioners in Lunacy. Their town house was off Manchester Square, Marylebone, but they preferred Burnham Wood, Welwyn. In 1919 Violet Dickinson edited and published the letters of her maternal great-aunt, Emily Eden, the early Victorian novelist and traveller in India.

Despite the seventeen years between the two women she was from 1902–11 Virginia Stephen's closest friend and confidante. She introduced Virginia to Lady Robert Cecil*—with whom Violet went on a world cruise in 1905—and to the daughters of the Marquess of Bath, Lady Beatrice Thynne and the Countess of Cromer. After Virginia had shown severe mental disorder while convalescent at Burnham Wood in 1904, Violet showed remarkable patience and sympathy, arranging for Virginia to contribute articles to the Protestant journal, *The Guardian*, in December 1904, her first literary undertaking. Virginia treated her strangely in November 1906 when Thoby Stephen* died, concealing the news from her for four weeks, even inventing details of meals he had allegedly eaten and discussing in her letters how he would spend Christmas. If this macabre deception was intended to spare her friend pain when she was herself ill, it failed. Predictably, Violet

Dickinson read of Thoby's death before hearing of it from his sister.

She continued, however, to treat Virginia Stephen with charitable sympathy. At first both Violet and her brother were frequent visitors to 29 Fitzroy Square, although not to the Thursday evening "At Homes". Gradually the ardour of Virginia's passion waned, for her Bloomsbury interests were at variance with Violet Dickinson's Quaker sympathies. Although Virginia Woolf herself attributed the cooling of their friendship to the occasion in 1911 when Violet Dickinson reproached her for sharing a house in Brunswick Square with young men, it is clear from the printed letters that there had been passing "estrangements" for several years. There was never a definite breach or a quarrel but merely a divergence of interest. In December 1936 Violet Dickinson returned typed and bound copies of more than three hundred letters she had received from Virginia Woolf, but their correspondence continued until the autumn of 1940.

DUCKWORTH, George Herbert (1868–1934), public servant: the elder son of the barrister, Herbert Duckworth (1833–70) whose widow became Julia Stephen.★ George was therefore the half-brother of the Stephens' children, Vanessa (Bell★), Thoby,★ Virginia (Woolf★) and Adrian; after Sir Leslie's★ death in 1904 he was titular head of the family.

George was educated at Eton, where he was a good cricketer, keeping wicket against Harrow in the 1886 match. After coming down from Trinity College, Cambridge, he was for ten years unpaid Private Secretary to Charles Booth, whom he assisted to prepare his great *Life and Labour of the People in London*. When Austen Chamberlain entered the Cabinet in 1902 George acted as his Secretary but he never became a politician. In 1908 Duckworth was appointed Secretary of the newly established Royal Commission on Historical Monuments in England, with responsibility for publishing surveys of some 3,000 historically significant buildings, earthworks and stone constructions from earliest times until the coming of the House of Hanover. This great project absorbed his working life, although during the First World War he also served the Ministry of Munitions and subsequently presided over the government's "Land Trust" to settle ex-servicemen in Ireland, as well as co-ordinating plans for the Eton College War Memorial. In September 1904 he married Lady Margaret Herbert, daughter of the Earl of Carnarvon; they settled in Sussex, at Dalingridge Place, near East Grinstead, and had four sons. He was made a Companion of the Bath in 1919 and knighted in 1927.

Duckworth was Vanessa's chaperon in Paris (1900) and in Rome and Florence (1902) and he treated Virginia with patience in her earliest nervous breakdowns, allowing her to rest for two months at Dalingridge Place in 1913 after her attempted suicide. In 1920, or early 1921, she told her friends in the Memoir Club that both her half-brothers—particularly George—had occasionally sexually interfered with her as a child, a point she also made in her letters. This tale possibly over-dramatised George's behaviour, although excessive affection may have left an innocent mind disturbed by sexual responses. Both his half-sisters resented his attempts to launch them into London society before their marriages, regulating what they should say, do, and wear; they mocked his strictures on the early days of Old Bloomsbury and his social snobbery. Some of George's foibles may have helped his half-sister create Hugh Whitbread in *Mrs Dalloway;* but, at Dalingridge Place, he was more of a P. G. Wodehouse character. Some ten years after the Memoir Club reminiscences Virginia Woolf could write of "poor George", not with revulsion, but in puzzled endearment; in July 1931 he sent her three copies of a letter he wrote to *The Times* on pigs. He died on 27 April 1934 while on a visit to Freshwater, in the Isle of Wight. When his first cousin, H. A. L. Fisher,* paid tribute to him in *The Times* three days later he praised, in particular, Duckworth's "genius for happiness" and love for his garden and his pigs. "It delighted him", Fisher wrote, "to be an arbiter of wines and dishes, to legislate on the breaking of an egg, to prescribe the one artistic method of preparing a rabbit, and to launch a crusade for the improvement of Sussex cooking".

DUCKWORTH, Gerald (1870–1937), publisher: younger brother of George Duckworth (*supra*), educated at Eton and Clare College, Cambridge. In January 1898 he founded the publishing house, Duckworth and Co., which brought out Virginia Woolf's* *The Voyage Out* in 1915 and *Night and Day* in 1919. He escorted his half-sisters and half-brothers to Venice in 1904, but was not popular with them. At the age of fifty he married Cecil Scott-Chad from Norfolk. He died in Milan in September 1937.

DUCKWORTH, Stella (1869–97) see HILLS, Stella.

E

ELIOT, Thomas Stearns (1888–1965), poet, critic, dramatist: born in St Louis, Missouri, the youngest child of Henry Eliot, a prosperous business man, and a member of a Unitarian family deriving originally from East Coker, Somerset. Eliot attended private schools, and then read French literature at Harvard. After graduation in 1910 he spent a year in Paris, returned to Harvard for doctoral studies in philosophy (1911–14), and went to the seminars of the visiting lecturer Bertrand Russell,* who became a friend. With a travelling fellowship to Europe Eliot arrived in London in 1914 and lodged in Bloomsbury, at 28 Bedford Place; however, his first literary contacts were other expatriate Americans, notably Ezra Pound. In the autumn he went up to Merton College to continue his philosophical studies, but found wartime Oxford boring.

Eliot had already given poetry the preference over philosophy and in 1915 "The Love Song of J. Alfred Prufrock" was published in the Chicago magazine *Poetry*. In the same year he met and married Vivienne Haigh-Wood; they made their first home in Russell's Bury Street flat. Soon Vivienne's mental and physical illnesses made a steady income imperative, so Eliot became a teacher, then a clerk in Lloyds Bank. Meanwhile he had met Lady Ottoline Morrell* and visited her house at Garsington, where he was introduced to many of the Bloomsbury group.

It was not until 1918 that he first met Virginia Woolf,* when he took his poems to Hogarth House. The Hogarth Press was to produce *Poems* (1919) and the English edition of *The Waste Land* (1923). Virginia took a great, sometimes exasperated, interest in Eliot's work and circumstances; she felt that he needed more "spunk". In 1922 she was on the committee of Lady Ottoline's "Eliot Fellowship Fund", and was writing round for donations of £10 a year to rescue him from the bank. The attempt failed, partly through the embarrassing publicity of another fund started at the same time by Ezra Pound, but mostly because the Eliots thought it too risky to give up a secure job; £50 was finally handed over to them. With Lady Rothermere's support Eliot was able to start his own literary magazine, *The Criterion*, published from 1922 until 1939, but Virginia Woolf could not persuade him to try for the post of literary editor of the *Nation*.

A coolness came over Eliot's relationship with the Hogarth Press when he joined the publishing firm of Faber in 1925. The ideas behind his work became less acceptable to Bloomsbury after his conversion to Anglo-Catholicism and reception in the Church of England in 1927, the year he also became a British subject. Virginia Woolf in particular attacked his religious pageant *The Rock* (1934), nor was she greatly impressed by *Murder in the Cathedral* (1935) or *The Family Reunion* (1939). Yet they remained friends, and he gave her advance copies of his later works. After his separation from his wife in 1933, Virginia tried to find him rooms, but he finally lodged at the vicarage of St Stephen's, Gloucester Road, where he was churchwarden from 1934. Eliot attended Bloomsbury parties throughout the 1930s and stayed at Rodmell for several weekends, going to early service at the nearby church. Virginia had in fact invited him for 5 April 1941, a week after the day on which she drowned herself.

During and after the Second World War Eliot's stature as dramatist, critic and the foremost living English poet greatly increased. In 1938 Cambridge had awarded him an honorary degree, and in 1948 he received the Nobel Prize for Literature and the Order of Merit. He married Valerie Fletcher in 1957.

Peter Ackroyd, *T. S. Eliot* (London, 1984)

ETCHELLS, Frederick (1886–1973), artist and architect: was educated at the Royal College of Art, subsequently developing his technique as a painter in Paris, where he had a studio and met Braque, Modigliani and Picasso.* He was a friend of Wyndham Lewis* and Roger Fry* and collaborated with Duncan Grant* in painting murals for the Borough Polytechnic in South London in the summer of 1911, and for Keynes* in Brunswick Square. For over a year he was closely associated with the Bloomsbury artists and became a particular friend of Adrian Stephen.* Both Frederick and his sister Jessie Etchells were members of Vanessa Bell's*

Friday Club. Frederick was among the guests at the Woolfs' wedding in August 1912, but from comments made by Virginia Woolf* in a letter to Janet Case he appears to have been unknown to her. Fry included some of Etchells' paintings at the second Post-Impressionist exhibition and both Frederick and Jessie were among the English artists exhibited at the Galeries Barbazanges in Paris in July 1912. Later that summer Frederick and Jessie Etchells followed Roger Fry as Vanessa Bell's first guests at Asheham. Vanessa found Etchells an irritating companion, and when she painted a scene which depicted brother and sister painting, she omitted all details of expression; the work was later purchased by the Tate Gallery.

Frederick Etchells was a founder member of the Omega Workshops but he seceded with Wyndham Lewis in 1913 and was, for a time, associated with Vorticism. But even before the First World War Etchells was practising as an architect and this became his chosen profession. He was elected a Fellow of the Royal Institute of British Architects and translated two of Le Corbusier's studies, *Vers Une Architecture* and *Urbanisme*. He specialised, however, in church buildings and in 1941–2 was once again associated with Vanessa Bell and Duncan Grant as advisory architect for the interior decoration of Berwick parish church, on the Downs near Charleston. Etchells—who lived with his wife and daughter, not in Sussex, but near Wantage in Berkshire—was also co-author with Canon Addleshaw of *The Architectural Setting of Anglican Worship* (1948). He died in August 1973.

EVEREST, Mrs Louie (1912–), cook-general: the daughter of a labourer on Rudyard Kipling's estate at Burwash. While living at Southease with her two boys in the summer of 1934 she applied for the post of cook at Monk's House, attracted by an advertisement which promised rent-free accommodation in a cottage at Rodmell. To her surprise Leonard and Virginia Woolf** drove over to Southease to interview her, later writing to offer her the job at 7/6d a week. She worked at Monk's House until Leonard Woolf's death in 1969 and was an active member of the local Labour Party, speaking out at meetings attended by her employers and by Vanessa Bell.* In 1962 she married for a second time, her husband being Konrad Mayer. Two years after Leonard Woolf's death she contributed some 4,000 words of reminiscences to Joan Russell Noble's *Recollections of Virginia Woolf*. As well as recalling Virginia

Woolf's elation at completing *The Waves* and the tragedy of her last days, Mrs Mayer noted down her impressions of some "Bloomsbury" guests. These included the weekend visits of T. S. Eliot,* whose room she would find empty when she brought the Sunday breakfast for, while "Mr and Mrs Woolf never went to church, . . . he went every Sunday".

F

FISHER, Herbert Albert Laurens (1865–1940), historian and Cabinet minister: born in London, his father, H. W. Fisher, being Private Secretary to the Prince of Wales. His mother (*née* Mary Jackson) was a sister of Julia Stephen.* Early education at Winchester and New College, Oxford, was followed by post-graduate study at Gottingen and Paris. He returned to Oxford as a Fellow of New College in 1888 with a great admiration for French historical teaching and became a specialist on Napoleonic statesmanship; his *Napoleon*, the first compact life of the Emperor, was published in 1912 for the Home University Library (of which he was a founder editor). He had been Vice-Chancellor of Sheffield University for two years when, in 1916, Lloyd George appointed him President of the Board of Education (i.e. education minister), and he entered the Commons for a Sheffield constituency after an unopposed by-election. Fisher was responsible for an education act which, in 1918, raised the school-leaving age to fourteen and for establishing the Burnham Scale as a basis for teachers' salaries. He left office in 1922 but remained an M.P. until 1926 when he was elected Warden of New College. His best-known work, the three volume *History of Europe* was published in 1936, a year before he received the Order of Merit.

His first cousin, Virginia Woolf,* complained of Fisher's donnishness but took a grudging pride in his political achievements and was flattered by a surprise visit which he made to her at Richmond on 13 October 1918 to tell her "we won the war today". Leonard Woolf*—who was defeated by Fisher in the General Election of 1922—described in *Downhill All the Way* how Fisher would "discourse lyrically" about "L.G. . . . in Downing Street". Of Fisher, Woolf wrote, "His face and his mind had the gentle, pale, ivory glow, the patina which Oxford culture and innumerable meals at College high-tables give to Oxford dons". Fisher died on 18 April 1940, a week after being knocked down by a lorry on the Embankment while on his way to chair an appeal tribunal for conscientious objectors; his mother had been fatally injured by a car outside Chelsea town hall in August 1916.

D. Ogg, *Herbert Fisher, 1865–1940, A Short Biography* (London, 1947)

FISHER, William Wordsworth (1875–1937), naval officer, brother of the above. Born in Seaford, the eighth child of H. W. Fisher and his wife Mary (a sister of Julia Stephen★). Entered the Royal Navy at the age of thirteen becoming, by 1906, an outstanding gunnery officer. In May 1909 he was appointed Flag Commander of H.M.S. *Dreadnought*, the earliest all-big-gun battleship. As one of the officers deceived by the *Dreadnought* hoax he unknowingly helped entertain his cousins Virginia (Woolf★) and Adrian Stephen★ aboard the battleship in 1910. Since he regarded the hoax as an insult to the senior service, Fisher thereafter ostracised his cousins. He commanded H.M.S. *St Vincent* at Jutland and was Commander-in-chief of the Mediterranean Fleet from October 1932 to March 1936. Admiral Sir William Fisher collapsed and died while taking the salute at a parade in Portsmouth on 24 June 1937, after overtaxing himself in organising the Coronation naval review at Spithead.

FORSTER, Edward Morgan (1879–1970), writer: born in London, son of Edward Morgan Forster, architect, a dreamy and ineffectual man, who died from tuberculosis in 1880. Forster was brought up without male influence and treated tenderly as a potential consumptive. His maternal grandmother, his great-aunt, six aunts or cousins, their female friends, maids and nurses dominated his early years. He was devoted to his mother, who survived until 1947, when she was ninety, and thoroughly enjoyed his life with her at Rooksnest, the country house at Stevenage as beloved as the house in *Howards End*.

At eleven he was sent to board at a preparatory school at Eastbourne, and at fourteen to Tonbridge School. Forster was regarded as a cissy at both schools and suffered a certain amount of bullying, developing a hatred of the English public school system that lasted all his life. King's College, Cambridge, which he entered in 1897 to read Classics, brought release. His tutor, Nathaniel Wedd, introduced him to socialism, atheism and Ibsen, and after gaining a second class, Forster took a fourth year to study history. Although he now had as tutor the flamboyant homosexual Oscar Browning, a greater influence was Lowes Dickinson.* In 1901 Forster was elected to the Apostles society, whose intellectual, all-male exclusiveness suited him well.

After Cambridge Forster had no immediate need to earn a living, thanks to his great-aunt's legacy, and with his mother he spent a year travelling in Austria and Italy. He had already written articles for university magazines, but Italy inspired his first short story, *The Story of a Panic*, and the plan for a novel about "Lucy and her cousin" staying in a *pensione* (later *A Room with a View*). On his return home Forster took a weekly Latin class at the Working Men's College in London, where he taught for twenty years. In 1903 he also began to write for the *Independent Review*, a magazine started by his Cambridge friends led by G. M. Trevelyan; the first cover was designed by Roger Fry.* Forster was gradually drawn into the Bloomsbury circle, which had not yet acquired its distinctive identity. A fringe member, Sydney Waterlow,* introduced him to his aunt, the German writer Elizabeth von Arnim, as tutor for her children. Forster spent the early summer of 1905 in Germany, and in October his first novel, *Where Angels Fear to Tread* was published and enthusiastically reviewed. Yet he was still unsettled in both his personal and professional life. He felt an unrequited romantic affection for an old Cambridge friend, and also for a Moslem Indian pupil, Syed Ross Masood.

Next year his autobiographical novel *The Longest Journey* came out and was generally disliked, especially by Bloomsbury; Lytton Strachey called it a "dreary fandango". *A Room with a View* (1908) was a success, however, and *Howards End* (1910) an even greater one. Forster was now an accepted Bloomsbury literary figure, reading a much-praised paper at Vanessa Bell's* Friday Club and having his portrait painted by Fry. Meanwhile he had become emotionally estranged from his mother and, to further his friendship with Masood, decided to go to India. As part of his preparation, Leonard Woolf,* who had just returned to England, taught him to ride on Putney Common.

In October 1912 Forster sailed for India, accompanied by Lowes Dickinson and Robert Trevelyan;* they were entertained together by the Maharajah of Chhatarpur, but Forster also travelled

about on his own or with Masood. He met for the first time the
Maharajah of Dewas Senior, later his employer, and visited the
Barabar Hills (model for the "Marabar Caves" in *A Passage to
India*). When he returned to England he still felt ineffective and
unfulfilled, and decided to sublimate his unsatisfied emotions by
writing a novel of homosexual love. *Maurice* could not be published
till after his death, but he used it as a touchstone, showing it to
those whose opinion he valued. Lytton Strachey★ admired it
unenthusiastically. Forster's literary relationship with Virginia
Woolf,★ who respected him greatly as a critic of her own work, was
impaired by the fact that he dared not let her see *Maurice*. By 1914
he had become friendly with Lady Ottoline Morrell★ and, in a
quarrelsome way, with D. H. Lawrence★ as well as the Bloomsbury
set.

The coming of the First World War further depressed Forster's
spirits and inhibited his writing. Unlike some of his pacifist friends,
he agonised over the effects of war from the start. He managed to be
sent to Alexandria as a "searcher" for the Red Cross in 1915,
interviewing wounded soldiers to try to trace others who were
missing. In Egypt he had his first real love affair, with a
tram-conductor, Mohammed el Adl, and on his return to
England in January 1919 he continued to help Mohammed and his
family; he took up the cause of the *fellahin* against the British
occupation.

Although Forster enjoyed literary life in London and joined in
founding the Bloomsbury Memoir Club, he was writing nothing of
importance himself. When in 1921 the Maharajah of Dewas invited
him to become his Secretary, indignation at the injustices of the
British Empire inclined him to accept. Forster's second visit to
India confirmed his previous view of the British. He regarded their
new conciliatory attitude to Indians as hypocritical, and wrote an
article attacking the Prince of Wales' visit as an impertinence.

He began a novel in India and continued it after his return to
England in 1922, while helping other authors, among them David
Garnett★ and a new friend, J. R. Ackerley, for whom he found a
post as Secretary to the Maharajah of Chhatarpur. Other additions
to his circle were Sebastian Sprott,★ and T. E. Lawrence; Forster
gave Sprott and Ackerley generous gifts of money. Encouraged by
Leonard Woolf, and inspired by Ackerley's letters from India and
Lawrence's *Seven Pillars of Wisdom*, Forster at last completed *A
Passage to India* (1924). It was an immediate success with all except
some indignant Anglo-Indians, yet it was his last novel.

Forster was active professionally through the 1920s and 1930s, however. In 1927 he gave the Clark lectures in Cambridge, on the novel. He received help in advance from Virginia Woolf, and had already praised her *Mrs Dalloway*, but at Cambridge he attacked her artistic method. When the lectures were published as *Aspects of the Novel* she responded with an unfavourable review which caused a temporary rift between the writers. As well as writing criticism and essays, Forster was becoming more involved with public issues. He began to broadcast from 1932 onwards, took a strong stand against Fascism and Nazism, and in 1934 was made President of the new National Council for Civil Liberties. The London social round appealed to him less, especially as he had attained a stable relationship with a policeman, Bob Buckingham, to whom Ackerley introduced him. Buckingham and his wife and son were his substitute for a family as he grew older.

At Abinger in Surrey, where he and his mother now lived, Forster took a squire's part in village activities, writing the book of the 1934 pageant in aid of the church restoration fund, with Vaughan Williams' music. A prostate operation in 1935 caused him to withdraw further from outside activities, and the years of the Second World War were mainly spent at Abinger. However, he continued to broadcast for the B.B.C., giving regular talks to India until after the war. He used his position to defend broadcasters against attempted government censorship, and was President of the N.C.C.L. again in 1942.

In 1944 Forster was with his mother when she died, and was then given notice to quit the Abinger house by its owners. King's, Cambridge came to his rescue with an Honorary Fellowship, a room in college, and lodgings in the town. Forster divided his residence between his London flat (now in Chiswick) and Cambridge; he taught a little in college and met the revived Apostles society. New experiences included a visit to the U.S.A. in 1947, and writing the libretto of an opera, *Billy Budd* (1951), for his old acquaintance, Benjamin Britten. Forster was made a Companion of Honour in 1953 and received the Order of Merit in 1969. After several illnesses and minor strokes, he died at the Buckinghams' Coventry home on 7 June 1970.

Although he shared so many of the Bloomsbury group's views, Forster was always rather detached from the rest. They were inclined to regard him with amused indulgence, as a "mouse" (Virginia Woolf) or "taupe" (mole—Lytton Strachey); the sharp, brilliant Bloomsbury manner did not come naturally to him. He enjoyed a quiet malicious gossip, but quarrelling or ridicule directed against himself reminded him that he had a train to catch to Weybridge or Abinger, and he would disappear, in his shabby raincoat and old cap (though generous to others, he never spent much on himself). He gave the impression of a very private man.

P. N. Furbank, *E. M. Forster: A Life* (2 vols, London, 1978)

FRY, Isabel (1868–1957), teacher: daughter of Sir Edward and Lady Fry, younger sister of Roger Fry.* She wanted to go up to Cambridge, but her mother feared she might marry one of Roger's friends like Lowes Dickinson,* an unlikely fate. In any case there could be no better education for a Fry girl than listening to the conversation at her father's dinner table. However, Isabel got away to teach at Roedean School in 1891, then started her own "Farmhouse School" in Buckinghamshire. Here the children of Bloomsbury were sent in the 1920s. They learnt practical country skills, economics, morality (not religion) and English grammar on Isabel's own system. They remembered their headmistress as a formidable lady in tweed drawers, who painted, sang comic songs and wrote the school plays. She had decided opinions, despising Bertrand Russell* for instance as an "odd little man", but thought highly of her own brother's work. When the miners' strike of 1926 ended in defeat Isabel's egalitarian principles were outraged at the idea of educating privileged children any longer, and in 1927 she closed her school to become a teacher in the Rhondda Valley in Wales.

FRY, Joan Mary (1862–1955), daughter of Sir Edward and Lady Fry, second of Roger Fry's* older sisters. In 1908 Roger's wife Helen became permanently insane, and Joan looked after her brother's children, Julian and Pamela, at first on a farm near their grandparents' country home, Failand House by Bristol. She remained the family housekeeper until 1916, moving with them in 1909 to Durbins, the Guildford house Roger designed for himself. She disliked his involvement with Clive and Vanessa Bell** and found his Bloomsbury friends difficult to entertain, especially as they usually neglected to talk to her. In 1916 she moved into her own Guildford house.

Joan Fry remained a life-long member of the Society of Friends. She was one of the first Quakers to visit Germany in 1919, and continued to work there every year until 1933, playing a great part in re-establishing the old Friends Meeting House at Bad Pyrmont, first used after the Napoleonic Wars. Later she was Chairman of the Friends Allotment Committee, founded in 1930 to provide allotments for British unemployed, and in 1939 set out with a party of Friends who tried unsuccessfully to visit Germany and prevent the coming war. In 1947 she flew to spend her eighty-fifth birthday with the German Quakers at Bad Pyrmont.

FRY, (Sara) Margery (1872–1957), university don, penal reformer: daughter of Judge Sir Edward Fry and his wife Mariabella, younger sister of Roger Fry (*infra*), known in the family as "Ha". Margery was educated at Miss Lawrence's School, Brighton (later Roedean) and read Mathematics at Somerville College, Oxford, where she became librarian in 1898. From 1904 till 1914 she was warden of a students' hostel (eventually University House) at Birmingham University. She followed the family's Quaker tradition, serving in the Friends' War Victims Relief Mission in France (1915–17), and from 1919 as Honorary Secretary of the Howard League for Penal Reform.

From then until 1926 Margery shared a house in Camden Town with her brother Roger; she used a room on the ground floor, with an appropriate view of Holloway Prison, as a combination of sitting-room and office for the Howard League. Her efforts helped to put penal reform on the agenda of the League of Nations. From 1926 to 1931 she was Principal of Somerville, then resumed her voluntary activities with a mission to China for the Boxer Indemnity Fund, helping to restore Chinese universities damaged in the Boxer Rising. She was a Governor of the B.B.C. and on the Treasury and University Grants Committees. Margery published pamphlets on penal reform and one book, *Arms of the Law* (1951).

Margery's connection with the Bloomsbury group was solely through Roger, and she often found them difficult guests while she was living with her brother. In the spring of 1932 the Frys went with Leonard and Virginia Woolf** to Greece; Margery began to admire Virginia and told her the story of her life. As her brother's literary executor after his death in 1934, she did not at first want Virginia Woolf to write his biography, preferring the idea of essays by different people, including herself; Virginia's diaries show how often she was irritated by Margery's suggestions after the work was started. When the *Life* was published in 1940, however, Margery Fry greeted it with "unbounded admiration".

FRY, Roger Eliot (1866–1934), painter, critic: born into a strict and distinguished Quaker family in Highgate, London, son of Judge Sir Edward Fry. Roger was educated at St George's School, Ascot, and Clifton College, where his great friend was John McTaggart, the future philosopher. At King's College, Cambridge (1885–9), Fry gained a Double First in Natural Sciences, shook off his shyness and was elected to the Apostles (1887). Under the influence of McTaggart and Lowes Dickinson,* he abandoned formal religion, though he never lost a belief in the spiritual element of man's nature.

Fry wished to become a painter but, to appease his father, twice tried for a Fellowship before leaving Cambridge for Francis Bate's Hammersmith art school in 1889. In 1891 he visited Italy and a year later spent two months at the Académie Julian in Paris. Back in England he shared a studio with Robert Trevelyan,* whose poems he illustrated, painted with the New English Art Group, and attended Sickert's* classes while intensifying his studies of Italian art. In 1897 he married a fellow artist, the beautiful but unstable Helen Coombe. He wrote articles for the *Athenaeum* and the *Burlington Magazine* and in 1899 produced his first book, *Giovanni Bellini*. Helen Fry's recurring mental illness forced him to seek a regular income, but hampered his career; he accepted the curatorship of New York's Metropolitan Museum in 1906, but was unable to remain in America. He was the museum's European adviser until his dismissal in 1910, after conflicts with the trustees' Chairman, J. P. Morgan. In 1909 Fry designed and built a house at Guildford, Durbins, where he hoped his wife would recover, but she became permanently insane and spent the rest of her life in a home. All his life Fry wrote her loving letters. His sister Joan* looked after her brother and his children, Pamela and Julian. He refused the directorship of the Tate Gallery, and in 1910 his career was apparently at a dead end.

Fry was a recognised expert on Italian old masters, yet he had gradually been taking more interest in modern French art. Although his own moderately successful paintings were in a subdued, traditional style, the colour and style of Cézanne, Van Gogh, and others attracted him and he was evolving the theory that the emotional significance of visual art lies in the form more than the content, and should be immediately accessible to the spectator. He resigned from the New English Art Club, and felt rather alone in his views until his chance meeting with Clive and Vanessa Bell** on a train from Cambridge, in January 1910. In Clive he found a fellow-enthusiast for French art and Vanessa, whom he already knew slightly, persuaded him to speak to her Friday Club. When in the autumn of 1910 the Grafton Galleries in London asked Fry to put on an exhibition, he already had half Bloomsbury as a committee; Desmond MacCarthy* was Secretary and went with Fry to Europe to collect the paintings.

The exhibition of 1910–11, "Manet and the Post-Impressionists", introduced Cézanne, Van Gogh, Gauguin and Matisse* to a British public that reacted with fear and hostility. "Daubs", "bunglers", "lunatics", and "a pornographic show" were among the milder comments; some saw the exhibition as part of a revolutionary movement including Irish Home Rulers, suffragettes and striking miners. But the Bloomsbury painters, Vanessa Bell and Duncan Grant* adopted the new styles, and Fry became the artistic leader and father-figure of the group. He also needed female companionship and encouragement, and this was soon supplied. First there was a brief affair with Lady Ottoline Morrell,* who was on the exhibition committee, then during a visit to Turkey with the Bells in April 1911, Fry was able to nurse Vanessa Bell back to health after a miscarriage and the couple fell in love. Although both found other partners later, their affection remained strong.

Fry's own painting now showed the Byzantine influence of his Turkish trip joined with the Post-Impressionist style, notably in the Borough Polytechnic murals (1911), a joint effort with other artists, including Grant and Etchells.* His one-man show in 1912 was praised by the critic Robert Ross for having made "quite English what proceeds from France", and removed "the unpleasant atmosphere" of Van Gogh or Matisse. Fry's autumn exhibition at the Grafton Galleries, however, was aimed at giving the British public "another electric shock". His original plan was for a show of modern English art, but Rothenstein* and the older members of the New English Art Club refused to collaborate and the younger set had not produced enough work. When the second Post-Impressionist exhibition opened in October 1912, it was dominated by Matisse and Picasso* in the French section; the Russian section, chosen by Anrep,* included Goncharova and Larionov. Clive Bell selected the English painters mainly from the Bloomsbury circle, and these were criticised as derivative. The exhibition as a whole provoked shock and horror again, but made Fry the chief authority on Post-Impressionism. He developed further his theory of "significant form", a phrase first used by Bell in his book *Art*, published in 1914. As he explained in a letter to his mother, freedom to express ideas mattered more to him than power, wealth or position, for which he lost all ambition after his wife's illness.

Fry had always been interested in applied art, painting on walls and furniture, and designing his own house. Contact with impecunious young artists made him feel that such work could benefit producer and consumer alike, and so in December 1912 he began to appeal for capital to start the enterprise. By April 1913 he could afford to rent 33 Fitzroy Square, where the Omega Workshops opened on 8 July. His rule of anonymity for the artists led to a quarrel with the egotistic Wyndham Lewis★ over the design of a room for the *Daily Mail* Ideal Home exhibition in 1914, but the Omega continued without Lewis and his friends, being largely managed by Nina Hamnett★ and her husband. Its products were faithfully bought by Bloomsbury and its fringes, and Fry succeeded in his aim of getting commissions for complete decorative schemes. He also learnt pottery and enjoyed the experience of working with other artists. The First World War had little impact on Fry; he did some relief work with his sister Margery (*supra*) and the Quakers in France, and consoled himself for the loss of Vanessa Bell to Grant with the friendship of Philippa Strachey★ and new styles of painting. A collage begun as a joke, *German General Staff*, was hailed as a patriotic picture, and another consisted of bus tickets, but on the whole he was striving for a greater reality and simplicity in his work. He started a notable series of portraits of his friends, and organised further exhibitions of British artists in 1917–18, in Birmingham and at the Omega Workshops. Nina Hamnett, who had some success in these shows, was his mistress for a short time.

After the war he sold Durbins, and took a house in Camden Town for himself and Margery, decorating it in bright colours. Next year he wound up the Omega, made an extended painting tour in France and wrote *Vision and Design*. It contains the definitive expression of his aesthetic theory of the importance of form, but is also an extensive survey of art outside the main European tradition. Unfortunately the work he showed that year seemed dry and academic, and disappointed the expectations aroused by his writings. From 1920 Fry spent much of each year in France. While undergoing treatment at a clinic in Nancy, he met and loved a fellow-patient, Josette Coatmellec, but she proved mentally unstable and in 1924 shot herself. In a state of acute depression he told Virginia Woolf that his last chance of happiness was gone. Painting once more brought him relief, and his pictures recovered their colour and directness.

In the last ten years of his life Fry wrote eight more books, among them *Transformations* (1926), which contains the strictest version of his theory that form outweighs subject-matter. *Cézanne, a Study of his Development* was published in 1927. He found time to lecture, help Keynes★ start the London Artists' Association, and paint more fluently than before. He acquired his final companion, Helen Anrep,★ in 1926, and they lived happily together in 48 Bernard Street, near Russell Square, until his death. Fry's inquiring mind turned to new ideas and inventions; he had long been nicknamed the "White Knight" by Bloomsbury because of the varied and useful contents of his pockets. At a birthday party at Charleston he appeared in this character, and delighted the children with his wonderful collection of odds and ends. In 1928 he bought a car, which he found would go anywhere "on No.1 gear", and in 1931 he took a half share with Charles Mauron★ in an old farmhouse in Provence. His public lectures on art filled the Queen's Hall, Langham Place, and he began to paint commissioned portraits, as well as those of his friends and himself. His aesthetic theories changed again; in 1933 he allowed some importance to the subject of a picture after all. In the same year he was offered the Slade professorship at Cambridge, and produced unorthodox ideas about the lack of "sensibility" in Greek art and the "vitality" of primitive art.

In September 1934 Fry had a fall at home, was taken to the Royal Free Hospital with a broken pelvis, and died two days later of heart failure. He was cremated and his ashes, in an urn decorated by Vanessa Bell, placed in King's College Chapel vault.

F. Spalding, *Roger Fry* (London, 1980)
Letters of Roger Fry, ed. D. Sutton (London, 1972)

GARNETT, Angelica (1918–), daughter of Vanessa Bell★ and Duncan Grant:★ born Helen Vanessa Bell at Charleston, Sussex, on Christmas Day, 1918. Although her parentage was well known in Bloomsbury circles, Angelica herself only learnt that Clive Bell★ was not her father in 1937. During the first weeks of her life she nearly died through wrong feeding and bad doctoring, and she remained thin and delicate as a young child. Great anxiety was caused in April 1924, when Angelica and her nurse were knocked down by a car, and her parents waited for several hours at the hospital before learning that her injuries were not serious. She suffered another serious illness shortly afterwards, increasing Vanessa's over-protective attitude to her daughter.

Angelica enjoyed her childhood at Charleston and in the south of France, where she spent her first holiday in 1921 at St Tropez; from 1927 the family had a villa at Cassis. Admiring adults surrounded her; she had two fathers, and a pseudo-grandfather in Roger Fry (*supra*), two much older brothers, Julian★ and Quentin,★ and a devoted aunt, Virginia Woolf,★ who made her an allowance. At her own request, in 1929 she became a boarder at Longford Grove School, Essex, where she was allowed to drop all subjects except English, French and history. She acted, learned the violin and piano, and once a week copied paintings in the National Gallery. Friends whom she made at school were unable to break into the charmed circle of Charleston; only cousins or children of other Bloomsbury families, like her earliest friend Judith Bagenal, felt really at home there.

At Easter 1935, Angelica left school, visited Rome with her mother and in the following winter stayed in Paris. On her return to England she began studying at Michel Saint-Denis' London Theatre Studio and appeared in student productions, but in 1938 she gave up acting to enter the Euston Road Art School. By now David Garnett* had fallen in love with her. He had the advantage of long familiarity with the family, and provided the refuge she needed after Julian's death in 1937. Vanessa was never so distressed by their affair as Grant or Virginia Woolf, who thought Garnett too old and too bound up with their own past. All accepted the situation when the couple began to live together in a farmhouse at Claverham, near Charleston, for the winter of 1940–1, after Garnett's wife died. While at Claverham Angelica collaborated with Vanessa and Grant in the paintings for Berwick Church, and visited her aunt Virginia in March 1941, for the last time before her suicide.

In spite of even greater parental opposition, Garnett and Angelica were married in 1942; Vanessa was reconciled to the idea by the arrival of four granddaughters, Amaryllis (1943), Henrietta (1945) and the twins Nerissa and Frances (1948). During the war the Garnetts lived mainly in London, but after 1945 returned to Garnett's home, Hilton Hall in Huntingdonshire. Angelica often accompanied her parents on holiday, and was with them on their last trip to Roquebrune in 1960. After Vanessa's death next year Angelica, now separated from Garnett, spent much time with Grant at Charleston, and when he died in 1978 she began to live there again. She now lives and works in the south of France, and has lectured in the U.S.A. on Bloomsbury. Angelica Garnett is on the committee of the Charleston Trust, and has taken an active part in the restoration of Charleston House.

Angelica Garnett, *Deceived With Kindness* (London, 1984)

GARNETT, Constance (1862–1946), translator, mother of David Garnett (*infra*): born Constance Black, daughter of a Brighton solicitor and granddaughter of Peter Black, naval architect to Tsar Nicholas I. Constance was a shy, delicate girl, who suffered from a tubercular hip until she was seven, but she was also a brilliant student. After her mother's death in 1875 she went to boarding-school and won a scholarship to Newnham College, Cambridge at seventeen. She gained a first class in the Classical Tripos and was bracketed top of the list. Constance became a governess, then librarian of the People's Palace in London. She shared a flat with her sisters, one of whom, Clementina, worked at the British Museum and so knew Richard Garnett, the Assistant Keeper of

Printed Books. Constance accompanied Clementina to tea with the Garnetts some time in 1886, met Edward Garnett,* and eventually married him in 1889; their only son David was born in 1892.

Constance began to learn Russian during her pregnancy, at the suggestion of one of her husband's Russian friends; the Garnetts befriended many Russian exiles in the 1890s, including Serge Stepniak and Prince Kropotkin. In January 1894 Constance travelled to Russia alone, carrying funds collected in England for famine relief along with secret letters to anti-Tsarist factions in Russia. She went as far as Nijni Novgorod (Gorki) and visited the Tolstoys at Yasnaya Polyana. From 1894 onwards Constance began to publish her translations from the Russian; she had completed at least seventy volumes by 1930, and was the first to translate the major works of Dostoevsky and Chekhov into English. Her work on *War and Peace* (1904) so strained her already weak eyes that she had to employ a secretary to read the Russian text to her. Yet in the same year she visited Russia again, taking the twelve-year-old David with her and teaching him enough of the language for conversation.

In 1907 Constance was invited to interpret for Lenin at the Russian Social Democratic Conference in London, but excused herself on the ground of unfamiliarity with Marxist terms. She remained shy and retiring, and lived a mainly private life in the country until her peaceful death in 1946, on the eve of her eighty-fourth birthday.

GARNETT, David (1892–1981), writer: born at Brighton, only child of Edward and Constance Garnett;** by 1893 he had already received the nickname "Bunny" that stuck for the rest of his life. From 1896 the Garnetts lived in a secluded country house, The Cearne, in Surrey, and David was educated partly at home by his determinedly anti-establishment parents, and partly at private schools. Writers who later became famous and Russian exiles were among the family's friends, while David himself played from the age of five with the daughters of Sydney Olivier (see OLIVIER, Noel). With his mother he spent the winter of 1898–9 at Montpellier and the summer of 1904 in Russia; he learnt both French and Russian conversationally. That autumn Constance Garnett took a flat in Hampstead, so that David's education might continue at University College School, and later at the London Tutorial College. At the latter he befriended several revolutionary

Indian students, and in 1909, according to his own account, joined in a plot to rescue one of them from prison; his father saved him from serious trouble. Yet he managed to pass matriculation and in October 1910 entered the Royal College of Science, Kensington. From 1911 he specialised in biology, and his discovery of a new species of fungus in 1914 earned him a scholarship for a fifth year's research in botany. In 1913 he moved with his father to Pond Place, Kensington.

Garnett, now a large, fair, handsome young man with blue eyes and a habit of turning his head to look directly at an interlocutor, had begun to lead a conventional college life, even to the extent of wearing a bowler hat. However, through the Olivier girls he met Rupert Brooke,* with whom he stayed at Grantchester in the summer of 1910, and so was introduced to some younger members of the Bloomsbury circle, notably Geoffrey Keynes,* and Adrian Stephen.* He began attending card-parties at Stephen's Brunswick Square rooms, after meeting him again at a fancy-dress ball. The older members of Bloomsbury, the Bells** and the Woolfs,** rather despised Garnett, partly because he always came in his only decent suit, full evening dress, while Duncan Grant* and he positively disliked each other. Garnett had many other friends and diversions; he visited Russia in 1911 and Munich, where he met D. H. Lawrence,* in 1912, and yet he longed to be admitted to the ideal society of Bloomsbury.

At the start of the First World War Garnett tried in vain to join the R.A.M.C. with Geoffrey Keynes before resuming his studies and his social life. His friendship with Francis Birrell* developed when they started a play-reading society, the Caroline Club, and in November he met Mark Gertler* and Carrington,* but his real acceptance by the Bloomsbury group came at Christmas 1914; he and Birrell were invited to join Lytton Strachey's* party at The Lacket in Wiltshire. During the course of a long Boxing Day walk, Grant and Garnett discovered that their mutual dislike had disappeared and they soon became inseparable. This was Garnett's only love-affair with a man, and it did not exclude many encounters with girls, some of whom he took to Grant's studio to avoid using the Pond Place flat when his father was at home. He became more familiar with Maynard Keynes* and Vanessa Bell, and stayed early in 1915 at West Wittering with Grant and Vanessa, both of whom painted his portrait. These new friendships estranged him from Lawrence, who was violently opposed to both Birrell and Grant.

The war put an end to Garnett's research, with which he was now bored in any case, and in June 1915 he and Birrell went to France with the Friends War Victims Relief Mission, an experience recounted in *The Flowers of the Forest*. Conscription began soon after he returned to England in January 1916. To forestall their call-up Grant and Garnett went to farm on their own at Wissett Lodge, Suffolk, and Vanessa Bell soon joined them. Here Garnett started bee-keeping, an activity he pursued all his life. Later in the year a tribunal declared that the two men could not be exempt from military service if they were self-employed. The household decided to move to Charleston in Sussex, where Grant and Garnett could work for a local farmer.

In October 1916 Garnett went ahead to see his future employer; accompanied by Barbara Hiles (Bagenal*) and Carrington he broke into nearby Asheham House, the Woolfs' country home, for a night's lodging (see CARRINGTON). This exploit and his manner of excusing it did not endear him to Virginia as a neighbour. Nevertheless Grant, Garnett and Vanessa were settled at Charleston by the end of 1916 and remained there until the war was over. Their triangular relationship and the hard labour on the land proved something of a strain, especially in the second winter, and Garnett despaired of his own abilities. Cheered by conversations with Keynes and Strachey, however, he began his writing career with *The Kitchen Garden* (1918), a version of an old French gardening book. On Christmas Day 1918, Vanessa's baby by Grant was born, and Garnett, who had returned to Charleston to see Vanessa through, is reported to have said that he would marry the small Angelica (Garnett*) when she grew up, Meanwhile he had to make some money and wrote a bad novelette, *Dope Darling*, under the name of Leda Burke; the first edition of 15,000 was sold out.

Late in 1919, after Garnett had gained some experience as a bookshop assistant, he and Birrell started a shop of their own on the ground floor of 19 Taviton Street, a communal house in Bloomsbury. One of the other inhabitants, Rachel (Ray) Marshall became Garnett's wife in 1921, and her sister Frances (Partridge*) was taken on as assistant in the following year. Birrell and Garnett furnished their shop with tables bought cheaply in the closing sale of the Omega Workshops, sold all their friends' books and kept a good secondhand stock. Although they were totally unbusinesslike, they were well patronised by Bloomsbury and its connections, until in 1923 they acquired a partner with money and were able to move to Gerrard Street. In the same year Garnett published *Lady Into Fox*, illustrated with woodcuts by his wife. It was the first of his "fable" novels; the background and animal characters are observed with a naturalist's eye, the humans treated less sympathetically, but all is written in a clear, vigorous, deceptively simple style. The book won both the Hawthornden and the Tait-Black prizes in 1923, a year in which Garnett became a partner in the Nonesuch Press, and his son Richard was born. Another son, William, arrived two years later.

Success, which also attended *The Man in the Zoo* (1924), encouraged Garnett to sell his share of the shop and buy Hilton Hall, a handsome but cold house in Huntingdonshire. There he entertained Bloomsbury visitors, devised a new dining-club called "The Cranium" with Birrell, and in 1925 produced what many considered the best of his early novels, *The Sailor's Return*. However, from 1929 Ray's recurring cancer threatened the family's happiness, though she seemed to recover from the first attack.

Garnett began learning to fly that year, an activity approved by his new friend T. E. Lawrence; he flew solo in 1931. In 1932 he visited the U.S.A. in search of background for *Pocahontas* (published 1933). With the help of Keynes, who also made him an allowance for his sons' education, Garnett became Literary Editor of the *New Statesman* from November 1932 until 1935; he wrote the magazine's "Books in General" page for another five years after that. Needing to live in London again, he took a flat in Endsleigh Street, and was at last elected to the Bloomsbury Memoir Club in 1933. *Pocahontas* was a Book Society choice, enabling its author to buy a half share in an aeroplane, and the following year a holiday cottage in Swaledale, Yorkshire. Garnett's arrival in his own plane sometimes alarmed Old Bloomsbury, especially on the afternoon in August 1933 when he landed at Charleston from Ham Spray and caused Roger Fry* to take avoiding action by driving his car into the gatepost.

His flying experiences led Garnett to write a memorandum early in 1939 on the siting of new airfields, and when war came in September he was invited to join the Intelligence department of the Air Ministry as a Flight Lieutenant. By now he had begun his love affair with Angelica Bell, and after his wife's death in 1940 they lived together in a farmhouse at Claverham, near Charleston. Angelica's parents accepted the situation, though Grant was angrier than Vanessa, but the couple's marriage in 1942 caused another breach. The wedding was attended only by the Partridges and Garnett's younger son, and Garnett himself was not welcomed at Charleston again until 1943, when Angelica was expecting her first child. Four girls were born to them, but they were separated in the 1960s.

After 1945 Garnett returned to writing full-time, although he also ventured into publishing again with Rupert Hart-Davis in 1947. As well as producing his autobiography he did a good deal of editing; he was already responsible for an edition of T. E. Lawrence's letters (1938), and now edited Peacock's novels (1948), his own correspondence with T. H. White (1968), and Carrington's letters (1970). He was still primarily a novelist, however; his last published novel *Up She Rises* (1977), is a fictional version of his great-grandmother's life. *Great Friends* (1979), a collection of biographical sketches, was his final work.

In 1952 Garnett was made a C.B.E. and in 1956 a Fellow of his old college, now Imperial College. His home in later years was Le Verger de Charry, a farmhouse near Cahors, and he died in France on 16 February 1981.

David Garnett, *A Rabbit in the Air* (London, 1932), and three volumes of autobiography, *The Golden Echo, The Flowers of the Forest, The Familiar Faces* (London, 1953, 1955, 1962)

GARNETT, Edward (1868–1937), publisher's reader, writer, father of David Garnett (*supra*): born in London, son of Richard Garnett, Keeper of Printed Books in the British Museum Library. The six Garnett children played in the museum, but were forbidden to run about on the Reading Room roof. After leaving the City of London School at sixteen, Edward did nothing for two years; he then met Constance Black (Garnett*), fell in love and got a job with the publisher Unwin, first as a packer, later as a reader. The Garnetts settled in a newly-built house, The Cearne, Limpsfield Chart, in Surrey in 1894. Garnett left Unwin's in the late 1890s, was briefly with Heinemann, and then spent a whole summer unemployed, feeding his family mainly on mushrooms. From 1901 to 1914 he was with Gerald Duckworth.* He served with the Friends Ambulance Corps in Italy during the First World War, and after 1918 worked for Jonathan Cape.

Edward Garnett had a great gift of discovering talent; he strongly recommended Virginia Woolf's* first novel, *The Voyage Out*, to Duckworth's in 1913. Many writers who stayed at The Cearne were later famous, among them Conrad, Galsworthy and D. H. Lawrence,* and Russian exiles from the Tsarist régime were also guests there. Garnett established a literary circle in London which met for lunch on Tuesdays at the Mont Blanc restaurant, Soho, and

was also a welcome visitor in Bloomsbury circles. Before 1918 he
wrote essays, reviews and two novels, but thought most highly of
his four relatively unsuccessful plays. The last of these, *The Trial of
Jeanne d'Arc*, written in 1912, was on the point of production when
Shaw wrote *St. Joan*. Garnett, seeing himself always as an
anti-establishment figure, rejected all honorary degrees for his
work, even refusing to become a Companion of Honour. He died
suddenly in 1937.

GERTLER, Mark (1891/2–1939), painter: born in London, son of
Louis and Golda Gertler, Jewish immigrants from Przemysl,
Galicia. Failing to make a living on their first visit, the Gertlers
returned to Galicia to keep an inn, but came back to London in
1896 and lived in great poverty in one Whitechapel room, though
Louis Gertler eventually established himself as a furrier. Mark went
to Hebrew school and state elementary schools, where he learned
English. From his first sight of the local pavement artists he began
to copy them, drawing for hours on the paving-stones in the
back-yard. When he left school in 1906, friends helped him take the
art course at the Regent Street Polytechnic, but his examination
results at the end of the year were not good and his parents could
not afford the fees. A job with a glass painting firm enabled Gertler
to continue at evening classes, and by 1908 his oil painting was good
enough to win the Bronze Medal in the National Art Competition.
However, he failed the annual drawing examination, and his health,
undermined by his slum childhood, began to give way under the
strain of working day and night. Gertler applied for help to the
Jewish Educational Aid Society and was invited to show his work to
William Rothenstein.* On 3 October 1908 he took his paintings to
Rothenstein's house; ten days later he was starting at the Slade
School of Art, supported by Rothenstein and a grant from the Aid
Society.

At the Slade Gertler was very successful, winning a scholarship in
his first year. His friend C. R. W. Nevinson (1886–1946, official
war artist) introduced him to a wider social and artistic circle, and
he began exhibiting with Vanessa Bell's* Friday Club and the New
English Art Club. From 1909 he had been painting his own family
and environment, and won praise in 1911 for *Jews Arguing* at the
Friday Club and *Golda*, a portrait of his mother, at the N.E.A.C.
Among Nevinson's Slade friends was Dora Carrington,* with
whom Gertler gradually fell in love. In 1912 he left the Slade and set

up his own studio on the top floor of his brother Harry's house. Although he felt the influence of Post-Impressionism like all his generation, Gertler tried to keep the realism of his working-class Jewish origin alive in his painting, and so was less fashionable than some artists. He was short of money until in 1913 he met a patron of the arts, Eddie Marsh, and the writer Gilbert Cannan.* Marsh made him a temporary allowance, while Cannan became a friend and introduced him to Lady Ottoline Morrell.* From September 1915 Gertler was virtually resident painter at Garsington, and through the Morrells met Lytton Strachey* and the Woolfs;** the Bells and Duncan Grant (*infra*) he knew already. In the same year he acquired a Hampstead studio and another useful patron in Montague Shearman.*

By 1916 Gertler had arrived sufficiently to be included in *Who's Who* and have a novel, *Mendel,* written about his life by Cannan. One of his most famous pictures, *The Merry-go-round* (Tate Gallery), was finished that autumn, but he was advised not to show it with the London Group of artists immediately for fear of condemnation by patriotic critics; some of Gertler's work had already been described as "Hunnish" and "indecent". The painting was included in the London Group's show in 1917, however, the first time that Gertler exhibited with the group. In the same year Carrington, whom he had at last persuaded to become his lover, deserted him for Strachey. This seemed a double betrayal as Gertler had encouraged the friendship, seeing Strachey as a harmless go-between, and on 14 February 1918 he attacked Strachey in the street. Keynes* intervened, no great harm was done and Gertler apologised the week after. He remained on reasonable terms with the Woolfs, showing Virginia his studio in July and staying at Asheham in September, though neither he nor his painting found great favour with her. Omega Workshops went on showing his work.

After the war Gertler drifted further away from Bloomsbury, but retained his link with the Morrell family and occasionally saw the Woolfs; his commercial success began from his first one-man show in 1921. When Carrington married Ralph Partridge,* Gertler bought a gun, but it was mainly a dramatic gesture. By then he had been in a sanatorium for the winter of 1920–1 with tuberculosis, an experience repeated in 1925. He married Marjorie Hodgkinson in 1930 and their only son Luke was born two years later.

The Depression of the 1930s affected the art world, and Gertler had to teach at the Westminster Technical Institute to supplement his income. In 1934 he had an unsuccessful show, and by 1936 was back in the sanatorium; while there he tried to kill himself. On returning home he began painting with greater vigour and fluency than ever, but the art market was still uncertain as war came nearer. Estrangement from his wife, who went to live in Paris, increased Gertler's depression, and on 23 June 1939 he gassed himself in his flat.

John Woodeson, *Mark Gertler* (London, 1972)
Mark Gertler, *Letters*, ed. Noel Carrington (London, 1965)

GRANT, Duncan James Corrowr (1885–1978), painter: born in Scotland at Rothiemurchus, the Grants' family home, son of Major Bartle Grant and his wife Ethel. Duncan stayed in India with his parents until in 1894 he was sent to Hillbrow Preparatory School, Rugby, where he was a younger contemporary of his cousin James Strachey* and Rupert Brooke.* From 1899 to 1901 he attended St Paul's School, London, first as a boarder, then as a day-boy, living with his aunt Lady Strachey* and her family. As he was intended for the army, he went up the modern side of the school, but won no prizes except for art, and Lady Strachey persuaded her brother to let him enter the Westminster School of Art. The painter Simon Bussy,* husband of Grant's cousin Dorothy* (see BUSSY, Dorothy), encouraged and helped him with advice; to him Grant owed his regular habit of starting work first thing every morning. He learned little at the Westminster, but spent the winter of 1904–5 in Italy, copying the masters, and in February 1906 was able to go to Paris to Jacques-Emile Blanche's school, La Palette. Here he concentrated on drawing and studying French art, though not yet the most modern variety.

By 1907 Grant had decisively rejected the love of his cousin Lytton Strachey* and was beginning a relationship with Keynes,* to whom Strachey had introduced him. They spent Easter together in Paris, when Grant also met the Bells** and Adrian* and Virginia Stephen (Woolf*); he knew Vanessa Bell* already from her Friday Club. In London Grant shared rooms with Keynes, from 1909 in Fitzroy Square; they moved into the Stephens' communal house, 38 Brunswick Square, in 1911. Grant's artistic education continued with a short spell at the Slade School in the summer of 1908, and he became a frequent visitor to the studios of Matisse* and Picasso.* Meanwhile he began to exhibit at the New English Art Club (1909) and the Friday Club (1910); at the latter his *Lemon Gatherers* (Tate

Gallery) so impressed Vanessa Bell that she bought it. Influenced by the Post-Impressionists, Grant began to paint less realistically and with greater use of colour, as in his still life and flower paintings of the period. Complete abstraction did not claim him, though he declared that all good painting is abstract, and he painted many portraits of his friends, including James Strachey (1910), and Roger Fry's* daughter Pamela (1911). His pictures were shown in Paris as well as London, and he started to take an interest in applied art, collaborating with Fry and other artists in the murals for the Borough Polytechnic in 1911 and painting on walls for Fry, Keynes and Adrian Stephen. From 1913 Grant was a co-director of Fry's Omega Workshops; he not only produced wall-panels and decorated furniture for them, but also designed textiles. Next year he created his first theatrical costumes, for *Twelfth Night*, produced by Jacques Copeau in Paris (1914).

The Bloomsbury circle welcomed Grant from the first for his dark good looks, high-spirited charm and humour. At their parties he danced, sometimes in one of Nijinsky's* rôles and in later years partnering Lopokova;* he was in fact an expert Scottish dancer. Unlike most of the Bloomsbury set, he rarely spoke ill of anyone and had few enemies; the naval officers who abducted him before breakfast as a punishment for his part in the *Dreadnought* hoax were disarmed by his sweet temper and pleaded with him in vain not to go home on the train in bedroom slippers. But conventions of dress meant nothing to him, and his friends often had to lend him both money and clothes. Until 1914 Grant was still living mainly with Keynes, but was attracted to Adrian Stephen, and then to David Garnett.* At the same time Vanessa Bell's friendship and admiration of his work had drawn the two painters closer together, especially during their visit to Italy in May 1913, and she made a home for both Garnett and Grant from the summer of 1915. The arrival of conscription in 1916 meant that both men had to work on the land as conscientious objectors. They started out at Wissett Lodge in Suffolk, a farm left by an aunt of Grant's to Major Grant, who helped them despite disapproving of his son's pacifism and "your friend Garbage". Vanessa Bell joined them and in 1917 moved them all to Charleston House; this was to be Grant's country home until the year before his death, and for a brief period he and Vanessa were lovers. Their daughter Angelica (Garnett*) was born at Christmas 1918.

Throughout the war Grant continued to paint as much as possible, and with Vanessa decorated the interior of Charleston. In 1915 he had been commissioned to design costumes for Jacques

Copeau's production of *Pelléas et Mélisande*, but as a "pacifist anarchist" was refused permission to land in France; he completed his designs for the New York opening of the play in 1917. Early in 1918 he obtained the catalogue for the sale of Degas' collection and persuaded Keynes to acquire many of the pictures for the National Gallery.

After the war Grant had a studio in Hampstead and from 1920 at 8 Fitzroy Street, where Vanessa eventually joined him. His painting still showed great use of colour, but was solider and less fanciful than his earlier style. Except for the war years of 1939–45 his work was regularly exhibited from his first one-man show in February 1920 until 1977; he and Vanessa Bell dominated the London Group of Artists and the London Artists Association in the 1920s and 1930s. With Vanessa, he accepted commissions for interior decoration, including Keynes' rooms at King's College, Cambridge (1922); Mrs Ethel Grant, widowed in 1924, agreed to embroider many of their needlework designs. In the 1930s the two artists began to create textile patterns and paint ceramics for commercial firms. Grant also produced some jackets and illustrations for his friends' books, although this formed a greater part of his output after 1945. In 1923 he began designing for ballet with *Togo, or the Noble Savage* for Massine's* small company, which included Lopokova; his last ballet décor was the Camargo Society's *Swan Lake*, Act II (1932). Two plays in 1925, *Son of Heaven* by Lytton Strachey and *The Pleasure Garden* by Beatrice Mayor, were also designed by Grant. From 1935 until 1936 he was working on the decorations for the *Queen Mary*, that were eventually rejected by Cunard. Commissioned work suited Grant well, as it provided income without forcing him to the hated course of selling his pictures; he preferred to put them aside in the hopes of later improvement, but usually forgot them. His old friend Keynes eased his existence by making him an allowance from 1937.

Early in 1927 Grant, staying at Cassis in the south of France with his mother and aunt, had a severe attack of pneumonia; Vanessa Bell hastened to his side and after his recovery they began what was to be the first of their regular summer visits. Next year they had their own villa, *La Bergère*, which they decorated like Charleston. Despite this settled domestic and working partnership, Grant never ceased to find young men attractive, but most of his friends could happily be accommodated within the permanent relationship with Vanessa; his support was vital to her after her son's death in 1937 and her sister's suicide in 1941. In the Second World War Charleston was their only home, at first sheltering also Grant's mother and aunt. Their London studios were destroyed in the bombing. Both Grant and Vanessa were upset by Angelica's affair with David Garnett and subsequent marriage in 1942, but were later reconciled to Garnett. Grant spent some of the summer of 1940 as official war artist in Plymouth, and he and Vanessa worked together on the paintings in Berwick church (1940–3). They had one other joint commission, for a school dining-room at Tottenham, unveiled by Keynes in 1944. During the war Grant painted his best-known portrait of Vanessa (1942, Tate Gallery) and several Charleston interiors and landscapes.

After the war the two painters still shared Charleston and holidays in France, but Grant was often alone in their London flat; for part of the time he was looked after by a young poet, Paul Roche ("Don") whom he met in 1946 and whom he often used as a model. Grant was still fulfilling commissions; in 1956 he produced his first designs for an opera, Blow's *Venus and Adonis* at Aldeburgh, and from 1955 to 1959 decorated the Russell Chantry at Lincoln Cathedral (Roche modelling the Christ). In 1950 he refused to be made C.B.E., but painted St Paul's in its blitzed surroundings immediately after the war at the request of Queen Elizabeth, now the Queen Mother; she bought his two St Paul's pictures and two later works. The Tate Gallery gave Grant a retrospective exhibition in 1959.

Next year Vanessa and Grant spent their last holiday in France together. When she died in April 1961, Grant drew her on her deathbed. At his request Roche, who had left for a post in the U.S.A. in 1954, returned; though he now had a wife and family he devoted much time to his friend. Grant's curiosity for new experience and new scenes to paint was as strong as ever, as was his love of good food and drink. With Roche he visited Turkey twice, Scotland and Tangier, and at the age of eighty-three took a studio in Morocco for two months of 1968. At home in Charleston he entertained serious students of his and Vanessa's art to tea; the charm of their host worked on them still though the house was collapsing visibly round him. During the Tangier trip in 1975 Grant nearly died of pneumonia, and two years later, after his final show, he moved to the Roche home at Aldermaston. In April 1978 he flew to Paris for the Cézanne exhibition, and on his return painted his last picture, a flower piece. Duncan Grant died on 9 May 1978, and was buried in Firle churchyard beside Vanessa Bell. A memorial service was held in St Paul's Cathedral on 27 June. Much of his decorative work is well seen in the restored Charleston

House, and many of his paintings are in the Tate Gallery, though not always shown.

Paul Roche, *With Duncan Grant in Southern Turkey* (London, 1982)
Richard Shone, *Bloomsbury Portraits: Vanessa Bell, Duncan Grant and their circle* (London, 1976)

H

HAMNETT, Nina (1890–1956), painter: daughter of an army officer, her maternal grandfather was William Archdeacon, surveyor of Western Australia. Nina was educated at the Royal School, Bath, then at art schools in Portsmouth (1903) and Dublin (1905). In London she attended the same Kensington art classes as Vanessa Bell★ had done and ended up at the London School of Art. After a trip to Russia with a fellow student in 1909, Nina tried a stage career, but got no further than one job in the chorus at the Aldwych, so decided to try to make a living by art. She took a room in Grafton Street, Bloomsbury and went home to her parents in Acton when she was hungry.

Nina met other young artists including Carrington★ and Mark Gertler,★ and the sculptor Henri Gaudier-Brzeska, who used her as a model for a torso now in the Victoria and Albert Museum. Walter Sickert★ took an interest in her work and it began to be exhibited, but to earn extra money she asked Roger Fry★ for a job at the Omega Workshops and was paid two or three pounds a week for batik work. During the winter of 1913–14 she went to Paris, frequented the artists' cafés wearing an Omega shirt of blue, orange and black designed by Fry, and became a friend of Modigliani. In July 1914 she began living with Roald Kristian, known then as (Count) Edgar de Bergen, a Scandinavian artist. When war began in 1914 the couple were arrested as Germans; Nina was released to return home, but had to go back to France later for Kristian. Eventually they left for England together, were married and settled in an attic in Camden Town. Both went to work at the Omega, and were largely responsible for maintaining the enterprise from 1916. Kristian, however, neglected to register with the British police and so was arrested, sentenced to three months in prison and deported back to France; Nina had her last letter from him just after the end of the war. Her career as a painter was greatly helped by the shows Fry organised in 1917–18, and she became his mistress, moved into the house where he was living in Fitzroy Square and stayed at his Guildford home, Durbins. For a little while she was part of the Bloomsbury circle, dining in Soho with the Woolfs,** and attending Shearman's* Armistice night party. Her strong, realistic paintings, including *A Landlady*, shown at the Omega in 1918, attracted critical praise. She exhibited with the London Group, and in 1918 taught the art class of the Westminster Technical Institute. Most of the time she was horribly bored, and in March 1919 she returned to her old friends in Paris.

For the next seven years Nina Hamnett lived and worked in France; in February 1926 she met Diaghilev* in Monte Carlo, and, by her own account, whistled English sea-shanties to help Georges Auric compose the ballet *Les Matelots*. Later that year she went to London for an exhibition of her work, and remained for the rest of her life in England, though she often visited France. A critic of her 1927 show still called her a "Bloomsbury artist", but by then she lived in St Pancras and saw little of her old contacts. Boxers and sailors were among her friends, and many of her subjects were found in London pubs, where she spent most of her spare time. In 1956 she fell from an upstairs window on to railings below and died not long after. Her two volumes of autobiography, *Laughing Torso* (1932) and *Is She a Lady?* (1955) are entertaining if unreliable records of a flamboyant artist's life.

Denise Hooker, *Nina Hamnett, Queen of Bohemia* (London, 1986)

HAWTREY, Ralph George (1879–1975), economist and civil servant: born in London, the son of George Procter Hawtrey, and educated at Eton and Trinity College, Cambridge, where he enjoyed distinguished academic success, particularly in Mathematics, and was elected an Apostle. So sharp was his intellect that even as an undergraduate he could engage both Moore* and Bertrand Russell* in arguments over logic and metaphysics. His later career never lived up to the promise of these early years, for he entered the Civil Service in 1904 and, after twelve months at the Admiralty, he joined the Treasury where he remained until the end of the Second World War, holding from 1919 to 1945 an important policy-making post as Director of Financial Enquiries. Between 1913 and 1961 Hawtrey wrote twenty-one books on economics, the best-known being *The Gold Standard in Theory and Practice* (1927). He was at times highly critical of the theories of Keynes,★ an old friend. For two years, 1946–8, Hawtrey was President of the Royal Economic Society. He was created a Companion of the Bath in 1941 and received a knighthood in 1956.

At Cambridge Hawtrey was a friend of Thoby Stephen,★ Saxon Sydney-Turner★ and Lytton Strachey,★ whom he introduced into the Apostles in 1902. Virginia Woolf★ remembered, twenty years later, "gallopading round the room with Hawtrey" at the Trinity May Ball of 1900. He appears to have been one of the "young men" who joined the Stephen family at Carbis Bay in Cornwall in September 1905 and was an early member of the Bloomsbury group, arguing earnestly over literary aesthetics with his friend Thoby's younger sister as once he had disputed philosophy with Moore and Russell. He was more musical than were the Stephen family and in 1915 married Hortense Emilia d'Aranyi (1887–1953), one of three great-nieces of the Hungarian violinist, Joseph Joachim, who were touring England as concert musicians when war broke out in 1914. Marriage severed most of his Bloomsbury contacts.

HIGGENS, Grace, *née* Germany (1904–83), Charleston house-keeper: a tall, handsome girl, daughter of a smallholder in Banham, Norfolk, who came to work for Vanessa Bell★ in Gordon Square in 1920. She accompanied the family to Charleston in the summer, and to St Tropez in 1921, when she began learning French. Her main duty was to look after the small Angelica (Garnett★) and by 1927 she was her recognised nurse on the family's first trip to Cassis. There she continued her French lessons and received two proposals from the pastrycook's son, who very properly began by approaching her employer. She was an excellent cook and from the autumn of 1929 cooked at 50 Gordon Square for Clive Bell,★ and also at Vanessa's studio in Fitzroy Street when the Bells entertained together. The most exciting event there for Grace was a party for Queen Victoria's granddaughter, Lady Patricia Ramsay. In 1934 she married a Sussex man, Walter Higgens, and the couple lived all the year round at Charleston, where their son John was born. Higgens acted as gardener until the Second World War. Although the house was inconvenient and the pay low, Grace and Vanessa developed a relationship of mutual confidence, not interfering in each other's spheres of action. Their chief disagreement was over the old-fashioned kitchen, but after 1945 Vanessa was at last persuaded to cover the concrete floor with linoleum and install an Aga cooker. Grace was one of the few to attend Vanessa's funeral in 1961, and kept Charleston going for Duncan Grant* until she retired to nearby Ringmer in 1970. Her contribution to the comfort and charm of the house was such that she was called "the angel of Charleston". A memorial plaque to her may be seen in the restored Charleston kitchen.

HILLS, John Waller (1867–1938), solicitor and M.P.: came from a Cumberland family, his father being a judge who leased Corby Castle, near Carlisle, from the Howards. Jack Hills was at Eton with George Duckworth* but subsequently became a classicist at Balliol College, Oxford. As a young solicitor, living in Ebury Street, Victoria, he fell in love with George Duckworth's sister, Stella (*infra*). She rejected a proposal of marriage at St Ives in the summer of 1894, but Hills was encouraged to pursue the courtship by her mother, Julia Stephen,* and was accepted by Stella in August 1896, fifteen months after Mrs Stephen's death. Jack and Stella were married at St Mary Abbots, Kensington, on 10 April 1897, after they had agreed to live at 24 Hyde Park Gate, so as to be close to Leslie Stephen* and his four children. Stella died 100 days after her marriage; and in the autumn Hills travelled north with her step-sisters, Vanessa (Bell*) and Virginia (Woolf*), for a week with his parents at Corby Castle. By the summer of 1900, when he escorted both girls to Henley Regatta, their step-brother George feared (rightly) that Vanessa was falling in love with Hills. Although marriage with a deceased wife's sister was possible on the continent, it remained illegal in England; but it is unlikely that Hills, who had political ambitions, would have wrecked his career with anything so romantic, however deep his genuine, and enduring, attachment to Vanessa. He treated the Stephen family well, ensuring that until 1931 they received interest on the investments from Stella's marriage settlement.

Although in later life Hills settled down as a country gentleman he did not disapprove of the Bloomsbury "Thursday evenings" so strongly as his brothers-in-law; his Toryism never made him a boorish philistine. As a young man he had interested the Stephen children in the collection of moths and butterflies and once, before her father's death, convinced Virginia that he would write a play in collaboration with her. He was, to some extent, the original of her

Mr Dalloway. In middle age "Waller"—as "Jack" had become—still read, with interest, the younger poets. Despite suffering from a stutter he was elected Conservative-Unionist M.P. for Durham City in January 1906 and remained in parliament until 1922, returning to the Commons from 1925 until his death. As well as being a solicitor—a partner in Halsey, Lightly and Hemsley—he was a Director of the Midland Railway Co. from 1910 to 1922. He was commissioned in the Durham Light Infantry in 1914 and, as Commanding Officer of the regiment's 20th Battalion, was wounded in September 1916 and invalided home. In 1929 he was sworn a Privy Councillor; two years later he married again, his second wife being Mary Grace Ashton. But his health gave way in the spring of 1938 and he died on Christmas Eve, leaving in his will legacies to his first wife's surviving half-sisters and half-brother.

HILLS, Stella, *née* Duckworth (1869–97), wife of John Waller Hills (*supra*): was the second child and only daughter of Herbert and Julia Duckworth and therefore a sister of George and Gerald Duckworth** and a half-sister of the Stephen children—Vanessa (Bell*), Thoby,* Virginia (Woolf*), Adrian*—all of whom felt great affection for her. On her mother's death in May 1895 she dutifully tried to look after her stepfather, Leslie Stephen,* and his sons and daughters, of whom the eldest (Vanessa) was only sixteen. She had rejected Jack Hills* as a suitor when he joined the Stephens on holiday in Cornwall in 1894 but, while the family was staying at Hindhead in August 1896, she accepted his proposal—a romantic episode frequently recalled by her young half-sister, Virginia. It was agreed that the Hills would continue to live in Hyde Park Gate, close to the Stephens. But within a fortnight of her marriage (10 April 1897) Stella contracted peritonitis. Although "out of danger" early in May, she collapsed a month later, dying on 19 July.

HOLMES, Charles John (1868–1936), Director of the National Gallery: the son of an Anglican clergyman with a parish in Cornwall. He was educated at Eton before going up to Brasenose College, Oxford, as a Classics scholar in 1887. His feeling for the countryside made him a skilled landscape painter, conventional in technique, and he became an art historian, particularly interested in Rembrandt. Late in 1903, the year in which he married Florence

Hill Rivington, Holmes was appointed co-editor of the new *Burlington Magazine,* a post he held for five years and in which he collaborated closely with Roger Fry.* He was Slade Professor of Fine Art at Oxford (1904–10) and Director and Keeper of the National Portrait Gallery (1909–16), receiving a commission in the Royal Navy soon after the outbreak of war. From 1916 until retirement at the age of sixty he was Director of the National Gallery; in 1921 he received a knighthood.

Although puzzled by the Post-Impressionists, Holmes was not a hidebound traditionalist and in 1910 joined Fry, Clive Bell,* Ottoline Morrell* and MacColl* on the committee of the Contemporary Art Society. In the spring of 1918 he accompanied Keynes* to Paris for the sale of the Degas collection. Prices were low, for the city was under bombardment at the time. Holmes purchased for the nation works by Corot, Delacroix, Ingres and Manet but missed an El Greco and, to Bloomsbury's indignation, rejected several Cézannes, returning to London with a quarter of his grant unspent. From its first inception in April 1926 Sir Charles gave vigorous support to the project for pavement mosaics at the National Gallery, discussing their design in detail with Boris Anrep,* whom he commissioned to execute the work.

Holmes, Charles, *Self and Partners (Mostly Self)* (London, 1936)

HUTCHINSON, Mary, *née* Barnes (1889–1977), was a daughter of Sir Hugh Barnes, whose wife was born Winifred Strachey, a first cousin of Lytton Strachey.* Early childhood in India was followed by schooling in England at Effington, with her grandparents looking after her in the holidays. In 1910 she married the barrister St John Hutchinson, who became a King's Counsel and a Trustee of the Tate Gallery. Mary Hutchinson was a close confidante of Strachey, to whom she once seemed "the only sympathetic person in London"; and it was Strachey and Grant* who introduced her to Bloomsbury. Some of the group thought her tongue-tied but marriage brought self-assurance and sharpened her conversational responses. Lytton Strachey and his friends enjoyed the Hutchinsons' hospitality at River House in Hammersmith before the First World War and at their principal Sussex home, Eleanor House in West Wittering, near Chichester. When the Hutchinsons moved from Hammersmith to Regent's Park their new house was decorated with murals by Duncan Grant* and Vanessa Bell.* In

Anrep's* mosaic pavement at the National Gallery, Mary Hutchinson is represented as the Muse of Erotic Poetry but her literary interests were, in fact, more conventional: she was the author of *Fugitive Pieces*, a collection of stories accepted by the Hogarth Press in the early spring of 1926 but, to her irritation, not published until June 1927. Clive Bell* was in love with her for some ten years, a passionate relationship tolerated by Clive's wife and Mary's husband. She was determined to be accepted as the chic hostess of a salon rather than as an intellectual, although she was more intelligent and perceptive than her friend and social rival, Ottoline Morrell.* She had a deep appreciation of the painting and literature of modern France and was especially interested in the theatre, becoming an early champion of the works of Samuel Beckett. In her later years she warmly supported the Royal Shakespeare Company and, at the age of seventy, gave her backing to a new avant-garde literary and artistic quarterly magazine *X*. Her son Jeremy is the life peer and distinguished barrister, Lord Hutchinson of Lullington.

HUXLEY, Aldous Leonard (1894–1963), novelist and essayist: born at Godalming in Surrey. He was a grandson of the biologist T. H. Huxley (1825–1895), younger brother of the zoologist Sir Julian Huxley (1887–1975), a great-nephew of Matthew Arnold, and a nephew of the novelist Mrs Humphry Ward (1851–1920). Aldous Huxley was educated at Eton and Balliol College, Oxford, where he took his degree in English in 1915. At the age of seventeen he was attacked by the disease of the cornea known as keratitis, which frustrated his hopes of following an academic or scientific career. Poor eyesight also ruled out military service in the First World War: Huxley worked briefly in 1916–17 on the Garsington farm and taught at Eton before joining the staff of the *Athenaeum*, under Middleton Murry.* He first met Virginia Woolf* in April 1917 and, for the next five years, he often met the "Bloomsberries" socially, especially Lytton Strachey,* the Bells** and the Woolfs. But he never regarded himself as part of Bloomsbury and his closest links were with Garsington: it was there that he had met Maria Nys, the Belgian refugee whom he married in 1919.

After publishing three books of verse and a collection of short stories, Huxley brought out his satirically Chekhovian country-house novel *Crome Yellow* in 1921: Ottoline Morrell* was a model for Priscilla Wimbush; Carrington* for Mary Bracegirdle; Gertler* for the painter Gombauld. *Antic Hay* in 1923 was set in post-war London, but Chelsea rather than Bloomsbury. *Point Counter Point* (1928) had D. H. Lawrence* disguised as Rampion and Middleton Murry as Burlap. By then Huxley was living mainly in Italy; he crossed to southern France to complete *Brave New World* (1932). He visited Mexico and central America in 1934 before writing *Eyeless in Gaza* (1936). Thereafter he settled in California, interesting himself in the psychology of hysteria (*The Devils of Loudun*, 1952), in mysticism, and in experiments with hallucinatory drugs.

I

ISHERWOOD, Christopher William Bradshaw (1904–86), novelist: born at Wybersleigh Hall, Cheshire, the son of an army officer killed in the First World War. He was educated at Repton and Corpus Christi College, Cambridge, and wrote two early novels, *All the Conspirators* (1928) and *The Memorial* (1932), which owe much in style to Forster★ and Virginia Woolf,★ who greatly admired his work. Life in Berlin as a private tutor of English led Isherwood to write the highly successful *Mr Norris Changes Trains* (1935). This was published by the Hogarth Press, as were three of his other early novels. The sales of the Hogarth edition of his *Sally Bowles* (1937) particularly gratified the Woolfs. Isherwood travelled widely in Europe and China, generally with his friend from preparatory schooldays, W. H. Auden (1907–73). With Auden, too, he left for the United States in January 1939, the year in which his *Goodbye to Berlin* was published. He worked on Hollywood film scripts for M.G.M., settled in Santa Monica, and became an American citizen in 1946. A literary career begun in the afterglow of Bloomsbury ended in devotion to Vedanta and Hindu philosophy. But his *Christopher and his Kind* (1976) reverted to reminiscences of homosexual affairs in early manhood.

J

JAMES, Henry (1843–1916), novelist: born in New York, settled in Europe in 1875 and, during the twenty years he lived in London, was a friend of Leslie Stephen;* the Stephens' children, fascinated by what Virginia Woolf* called the "humming and hawing" of his table-talk, believed they could remember once seeing the great man tilt his chair gradually backwards until he slipped out of it in the middle of a complex sentence, which he duly completed on the floor. The principal theme of "the Master's" novels and short stories was the impact of European traditions on nineteenth-century American culture. In 1898 he moved to Rye in East Sussex and lived at Lamb House for most of the following eighteen years, although he retained a home in Cheyne Walk, Chelsea. He became a British subject in 1915 and was awarded the Order of Merit eight weeks before his death (in Chelsea). His neighbour in Rye, Mrs Fanny Prothero, lived in Bedford Square during her visits to London and in 1905–6 brought reports to him of the Thursday "At Homes" at 46 Gordon Square. He was shocked at such unconventional behaviour. In a paper called "Old Bloomsbury", which Virginia Woolf read to the Memoir Club in the winter of 1921–2, she described how "Henry James, on seeing Lytton and Saxon at Rye, exclaimed to Mrs Prothero, 'Deplorable! Deplorable! How could Vanessa and Virginia have picked up such friends? How could Leslie's daughters have taken up with young men like that'?"; and he developed a strong antipathy to Clive Bell.* But Henry James thought highly of Desmond MacCarthy,* who visited him at Chelsea after the outbreak of war, and his influence on the Bloomsbury novelists was considerable.

V. Woolf, *Moments of Being*, ed. Jeanne Schulkind, and including the "Old Bloomsbury" Memoir (London, 1976)

K

KELLY, Gerald Festus (1879–1972), painter: born in Camberwell, London, where his father was a vicar. He was educated at Eton but was said to be delicate and, after three years there, was sent to South Africa to build up his strength. On the voyage out to Capetown some water-colours were praised by a fellow passenger who was an architect and Kelly decided that he wished thereafter to concentrate on developing his artistic gifts. His father, however, insisted he should go up to Trinity Hall, Cambridge. At university he neglected his academic studies but won a Reading Prize and showed enthusiasm for the theatre. Rather than risk having a son who was an actor, his father agreed that, in the autumn of 1901, Kelly should go to Paris to study painting. His skill with oils was so outstanding that his first completed work was hung. Late in February 1904 Clive Bell,★ who had recently arrived in Paris, visited Kelly at his studio in the Rue Campagne Première in Montmartre. Kelly helped improve Bell's technique and introduced him to French and British artists and to the novelist Arnold Bennett. When Leslie Stephen's★ daughters Vanessa (Bell★) and Virginia (Woolf★) passed through Paris in May 1904 they met Clive Bell and Kelly, whose enthusiasm for art and music impressed them. Despite these Bohemian early years, Gerald Kelly later became an orthodox and conventional painter; he was elected an R.A. in 1930, served on the Royal Fine Art Commission from 1938 to 1943, and was President of the Royal Academy from 1949 to 1954, receiving a knighthood in 1945, the year in which Sir Gerald painted state portraits of King George VI and Queen Elizabeth.

C. Bell, *Old Friends, Personal Recollections* (London, 1956)

KENNEDY, Richard Sylvester (1912–), publisher's apprentice: nephew of the architect, George Kennedy (1882–1954), a friend often consulted by the Woolfs.** Slow scholastic progress forced Richard Kennedy to leave Marlborough at the age of sixteen. His uncle's influence enabled him to begin work in May 1928 as an apprentice assistant to Leonard Woolf at the Hogarth Press, with a salary of £1 a week. He was employed by the press for two years before he was accepted for a course in journalism at University College, London, and he is mentioned on several occasions in Virginia Woolf's diary. More than forty years later Kennedy published an account of this period in his life in the form of a diary. *A Boy at the Hogarth Press* (London, 1972). This irreverent book does not claim to be an accurate chronicle, but it has amusing passages, notably an account of a Bloomsbury cricket match.

KEYNES, Geoffrey Langdon (1887–1982), surgeon and bibliophile: born in Cambridge, the brother of Maynard Keynes (*infra*). He was educated at Rugby School, where he was a close friend of Rupert Brooke,* and at Pembroke College, Cambridge. At the university he shared Brooke's interest in acting and in 1907 was a founder-member of the Marlowe Society, becoming Secretary in the following year; among his other friends were Duncan Grant* and the mountaineer, George Mallory.* In 1909 Geoffrey Keynes gained first-class honours in the Natural Science Tripos and in 1910 began his distinguished medical career at St Bartholomew's Hospital, London, where he became a house surgeon three years later. At this period he was living about a mile from the hospital, on the top floor of 38 Brunswick Square, above Leonard and Virginia Woolf.** When she took an overdose of veronal, on 9 September 1913, Keynes drove speedily to St Bartholomew's for the stomach-pump which enabled her life to be saved.

He kept in close touch with Brooke and the "Neo-Pagans" while he was in London, but on the outbreak of war he enlisted in the R.A.M.C., eventually becoming a surgical specialist with the British Expeditionary Force on the Western Front, with the rank of Major. In 1917 he married Margaret Darwin, a granddaughter of the great scientist and younger sister of Gwen Raverat;* there were four sons of the marriage. After the war, Keynes returned to St Bartholomew's Hospital, with an interest in the development of blood transfusion, on which in 1922 he published an important monograph. His distinguished medical career included three years as Hunterian Professor at the Royal College of Surgeons (1923, 1929 and 1945) and six years as Senior Consultant Surgeon in the R.A.F., with the acting rank of Air Vice-Marshal (1939–45). He was knighted in 1955.

The Bloomsbury group respected him as a bibliophile. He remained loyal to the memory of his old friend, Brooke, whose letters he edited for publication in 1968. But he was, like his brother, a natural collector and he built up a remarkable library, originally in London and later at his Suffolk home, Lammas House, Brinkley, near Newmarket. As early as 1914 he completed a bibliography of John Donne, later publishing bibliographies of several other English authors, including William Blake, Thomas Browne, William Hazlitt and John Evelyn. In all Keynes wrote three studies of Blake, on whose life and works he became the greatest modern authority. His range of interests was considerable; he helped Sir Francis Meynell design sixteen books for the Nonesuch Press; and, in the 1920s and 1930s, he was a patron of the sculptor, typographer and illustrator, Eric Gill. Most remarkably, Keynes used his knowledge of Blake to prepare a detailed synopsis for Ninette de Valois's "masque for dancing", *Job*, which was first mounted at the Cambridge Theatre, London, in July 1931 to music by Vaughan Williams and with the scenery and costumes designed by Gwen Raverat. From 1942 to 1966 Sir Geoffrey was a Trustee of the National Portrait Gallery, serving as Chairman for the last eight years of this period. His prize-winning biography of William Harvey was published in his eightieth year; and he was ninety-four when his memoirs, *The Gates of Memory*, appeared.

KEYNES, John Maynard (1883–1946), economist: born in a comfortable Victorian House (6 Harvey Road) in Cambridge, the son of John Neville and Florence Keynes. His father, a Lecturer in Moral Science (including Economics) became University Registry and his mother, a graduate of Newnham College, was Cambridge's first woman councillor and Mayor (1932–3). He had a sister Margaret (1885–1970), who in 1913 married the physiologist and Nobel Prize winner, A. V. Hill (1886–1977), and a younger brother, Geoffrey (*supra*).

Maynard was a precocious child, whose health was delicate. From St Faith's Preparatory School in the Trumpington Road, he gained a scholarship to Eton College (1897), where he won a succession of academic prizes, rowed a good deal, showed skill at the "Wall Game", and tentatively experimented with homosexuality. His diary entry for 2 February 1901 is a vivid account of Queen Victoria's funeral as witnessed by the Eton boys.

"I've had a good look round the place and come to the conclusion that it's pretty inefficient" was Keynes' initial reaction to King's College, Cambridge, where he went to read mathematics in 1902. During his long association with the college, lasting until his death, he was to remedy much of the inefficiency without losing the affection for King's that first drew him there. He made several friends in college, but also became intimate with the Trinity set that was the basis for the later Bloomsbury group, especially Lytton Strachey* and Leonard Woolf.* In February 1903 Keynes was elected an Apostle, an unusual honour for a freshman. He distinguished himself academically and as a speaker in the Union, of which he became President (1905). Outside his own syllabus he took up the study of economics, but he decided to leave Cambridge for the Civil Service and from October 1906 to June 1908 was at the India Office. He then returned to Cambridge to work for a prize Fellowship.

Although Keynes lived in a service flat in Westminster he remained in close touch with his Cambridge friends, particularly his brother Apostles. He was drawn closer to the Bloomsbury group by his relationship with Lytton Strachey's cousin, the painter Duncan Grant,* whom he first met in 1905 and visited in Paris at Easter, 1907. For four years they went on holidays together—to the Orkneys, to Greece, to North Africa; and when Grant took a flat at 21 Fitzroy Square in November 1909 Keynes had a room there as his London *pied-à-terre*. For the rest of his life Keynes kept a Bloomsbury residence, though often as part of a commune. In 1911 he and Grant moved to 38 Brunswick Square, the house taken by Adrian Stephen* and his sister Virginia (Woolf*). When the lease expired in September 1914, he went into rooms for four months and then rented 3 Gower Street. Here he shared the house with John Sheppard,* Gerald Shove,* two girl art students (Dorothy Brett* and Dora Carrington*) and Katherine Mansfield* and John Middleton Murry.* Keynes' final move was to take over 46 Gordon Square from the Bells** (1916).

His professional life was centred on Cambridge after 1908 as an economics lecturer; he was elected a Fellow of King's College in March 1909. He wrote for *The Economist* and in 1911 became editor of *The Economic Journal*. His India Office work was not wasted, as he produced papers on Indian economics, served on the Royal Commission on Indian Currency and published *Indian Currency and Finance* (1913). At the start of the First World War he was called in by the Treasury as an adviser and negotiator. His position became more important as the war went on, and in 1917 he paid his first official visit to the U.S.A. When conscription was introduced in January 1916, Keynes disapproved of the measure but did not resign from the Treasury in protest, as his pacifist Bloomsbury friends had expected. He was able to help Grant, the Strachey brothers and David Garnett* to obtain exemption from military service; but ambivalent feelings over his own position may have increased the tension and exhaustion that later broke his health. From October 1916 onwards he found refuge frequently at Charleston with Vanessa Bell and Duncan Grant, for whom he retained a deep—if less passionate—affection.

He became disillusioned with the Allied statesmen who thrashed out the peace settlement. As Principal Treasury Representative at the Paris Peace Conference, he played a great part in the financial negotiations with defeated Germany, but on 7 June 1919 he resigned. Within five months he had completed his famous *The Economic Consequences of the Peace*, written largely at Charleston and published on 12 December in that same year. Technically the book was an economist's attack on the folly of imposing heavy reparations on a defeated country, but the most memorable feature of Keynes' work was the vivid pen portraits of President Woodrow Wilson and Georges Clemenceau, the French Prime Minister.

Keynes returned to Cambridge, giving up his lectureship, but taking on greater responsibility in college, eventually becoming Bursar of King's (1924). He went on expressing his views on the policy of German reparations in newspaper articles, but became a government adviser again in 1923 when Baldwin was Prime Minister for the first time.

His personal life underwent a great change after the war. He had begun to show an interest in women, attracted by the art students in the Bloomsbury circle. When Diaghilev's* Russian ballet returned to England in 1919, Keynes appeared as the regular escort of the ballerina Lydia Lopokova.* She moved into Gordon Square, living at first in the Bells' house, and in 1925 they were married. They immediately paid the first of three visits to Russia, where Lydia's sister and brothers were still working in what had formerly been the Maryinsky ballet. On this occasion Keynes represented Cambridge at the bicentenary of the Leningrad Academy of Science. He wrote

A Short View of Russia, later published by the Hogarth Press, after the trip. The Keynes acquired a house at Tilton, Sussex, and divided their time between the country, Bloomsbury and Cambridge.

In the inter-war years Keynes' professional activities were balanced by increased involvement in the arts. He was elected a Fellow of the British Academy (1929), served on the Economic Advisory Council (1930) and made two lecture tours of the U.S.A. (1931, 1933). He published *The Revision of the Treaty* in 1922, and in 1925 a series of newspaper articles criticising the Chancellor of the Exchequer for linking too closely Wall Street and the City of London by returning to the Gold Standard became, in book form, *The Economic Consequences of Mr Churchill.* In the same year his *A Treatise on Money* foreshadowed the more comprehensive economic analysis of his *The General Theory of Employment, Interest and Money* (1936). His belief that protracted unemployment could occur "involuntarily" unless governments took practical measures to create employment caused long-lasting feuds with other economists. He had also been active in the City of London from 1919 and was a director of several insurance companies.

Long before his marriage to Lydia, Keynes had been interested in theatre and ballet. After the end of the Diaghilev company in 1929 he helped her in her new career as an actress and in the formation of the Camargo Society (1930), one of the roots from which British ballet grew. Keynes' most ambitious artistic project was to found a theatre at Cambridge. He launched the Arts Theatre as a private company, largely with his own money, on a site leased from King's College, and it opened in February 1936 with a gala by the Vic-Wells Ballet. In 1938 Keynes made over his shares to a trust set up to administer the theatre for the university and town of Cambridge.

Keynes was also a great collector of books and pictures. In 1918, on Duncan Grant's advice, he secured a Treasury grant to buy paintings for the National Gallery at the Paris sale of Degas' collection. Keynes bought for himself as well, most notably a Cézanne still life. Later he added paintings by Picasso,★ Braque, Sickert★ and Matisse★ and helped to form the London Artists' Association. After his marriage Keynes kept up with the Bloomsbury group, although its women members were sometimes critical of Lydia. Vanessa Bell disliked the marriage and Virginia Woolf was scathing about the couple's prospects and contemptuous of Tilton hospitality, with its poor dinners and broken-springed lodging chairs. Yet Keynes was financially generous to several old friends and gave Grant an income for life. Eventually Lydia was accepted even into the Memoir Club, to whom on 9 September 1938 Keynes read a paper, "My Early Beliefs", an exposition of the origins and early days of the Bloomsbury group.

From September 1939 onwards Keynes bombarded the government with memoranda on the financing of the war effort, and in 1940 published *How to Pay for the War*. Although he had suffered a coronary in 1937, and was never strong again, he became adviser to Kingsley Wood, Chancellor of the Exchequer in Churchill's government. He visited the U.S.A. six times under wartime conditions for financial negotiations. During the war Keynes was made a Director of the Bank of England (1941), a peer (Baron Keynes of Tilton) in 1942, and High Steward of Cambridge (1943). In 1944 he attended the Bretton Woods Conference and took part in the Lend Lease Stage II negotiations, and in 1945 helped to negotiate a post-war American loan, all in the U.S.A.

Back in Britain, Keynes became chairman of C.E.M.A. (Council for the Encouragement of Music and the Arts) and prepared for its transformation into the Arts Council after the war. As a result he was greatly involved in the reopening of the Royal Opera House, Covent Garden, in February 1946 and the establishment of the Covent Garden Trust. The opening performance (the ballet *Sleeping Beauty*) was still in Keynes' mind when he spoke next month at the conference to set up the International Monetary Fund and the World Bank, in Savannah, U.S.A. He would have preferred less American domination of the two institutions and hoped that "no malicious fairy, no Carabosse" would curse them at their birth. The U.S. Secretary of the Treasury resented the word "fairy" rather than "malicious".

Keynes left Savannah in a pessimistic frame of mind; the voyage home in the *Queen Mary* was rough and the ship filthy from use as a troop ship. Keynes had suffered a small heart attack in 1944 and became very weak during the journey. Nevertheless he wrote one more memorandum for the government, on the Savannah Conference, and was pleased to add further honours to the D.Sc. Cambridge had just given him; he was elected a Fellow of the Royal Society and accepted appointment to the Order of Merit, though he did not live to receive it. By April 1946 Keynes seemed to have recovered but at Tilton, on Easter Sunday morning, he suffered a fatal heart attack. He was survived, not only by Lady Keynes, but by both parents.

R. Harrod, *John Maynard Keynes* (London, 1951)
R. Skidelsky, *John Maynard Keynes, Hopes Betrayed 1883–1920* (London, 1983)
C. H. Hession, *John Maynard Keynes* (New York, 1984)

KOTELIANSKY, Samuel Solomonovich (1882–1955), "Kot": Russian translator born in the Ukraine, of Jewish parentage, educated at the University of Kiev. He came to London in the winter of 1910–11 on a three months' scholarship to study economics and remained in England for the rest of his life, his family being wiped out during the Revolution. In 1914 he was employed by the Russian Law Bureau in London, but he made a career for himself as a translator of the Russian classics, especially Tolstoy, Gorky, Dostoyevsky and Chekhov. He was a friend of Gertler★ (and thus of Carrington★) and he was introduced to the Woolfs★★ by Katherine Mansfield★ and Middleton Murry★ in the summer of 1917. He was a reader for the Cresset Press and worked for Murry on *The Adelphi*, but his English was eccentric and his major translations were given an elegant polish by Katherine Mansfield (Chekhov letters), by the Woolfs, and by other leading literary figures of the day. He much admired D. H. Lawrence★ and, at the end of July 1918, tried to arrange a meeting between Lawrence and the Woolfs but was rebuffed by Virginia Woolf, who does not seem to have appreciated Kot's fear of friendlessness in alien London. In all, the Hogarth Press published eight of his Russian translations; there was close collaboration between Koteliansky and Virginia Woolf on *Tolstoi's Love Letters* and on his translation of A. B. Goldenveizer's *Talks with Tolstoi*, both published by Hogarth Press in 1923, while translation of the Hogarth's edition of Maxim Gorky's *Reminiscences of Tolstoy, Chekhov and Andreev* (1934) is jointly attributed to K. Mansfield, Koteliansky and L. Woolf. Koteliansky was a formidable personality, sternly critical of frivolous pursuits, powerfully built, with an intense gaze through bloodshot eyes. To Leonard Woolf he seemed "a major Hebrew prophet", while D. H. Lawrence thought him "a bit Jehovah-ish".

L

LAMB, Henry Taylor (1883–1960), painter: third son of Sir Horace Lamb, F.R.S., born in Australia, brought up in Manchester where his father was Professor of Mathematics in what became (1903) Manchester University. He was educated at Manchester Grammar School and the medical school of the university, but gave up medicine for art and in 1905 eloped to London with a local girl, Nina Forrest, known as Euphemia, whom he married in 1906. His brother Walter Lamb (*infra*) asked his Cambridge friend Clive Bell★ to look up the runaways, and so Lamb met Clive's fiancée Vanessa Stephen (Bell★) who was just forming her "Friday Club" for artists. Vanessa's sister, Virginia (Woolf★) was fascinated by Nina Forrest, but never liked Lamb, though she may have sat unsuccessfully for him later on.

The main influence on Lamb's painting was Augustus John, whose Chelsea Art School he attended, and whose flamboyant velvet suit, beard and hat he copied to enhance his own golden good looks. He was a friend of John's first wife, and in love with the second, Dorelia, for twenty years, though not to the exclusion of other women. By 1907 the Lambs had split up, and Lamb was attending the art school, La Palette, in Paris; a fellow-student was Duncan Grant★, but his greatest new friend was Boris Anrep;★ Anrep, along with the Diaghilev Ballet, opened his eyes to Russian art. In 1908–9 he returned to London, and was living in Fitzroy Street with Helen Maitland (Anrep★), and exhibiting his work with Walter Sickert's★ group. But Lamb would never be bound to any group and was equally hostile to art galleries and critics, perhaps the reason why his first one-man show was not till 1922. He particularly disliked the theories of Roger Fry★ and Clive Bell, the "false aesthetics of the Clive-Fry coalition" as he called them. In 1912 he quarrelled with Bell, who, he said, had borrowed the wrong Lamb painting for the second Post-Impressionist exhibition, and again in 1913 over Bell's rejection of a picture by Stanley Spencer. As late as 1 April 1927 he tricked Fry into accepting complimentary tickets for a non-existent piano recital of his own, a reference to Fry's opinion that Lamb was a better pianist than painter.

Yet Lamb had good friends in Bloomsbury; he painted Leonard Woolf* and rode with him, and shared a love of music and concert-going with Saxon Sydney-Turner.* All three went to Russian classes together in 1912. He was most familiar with Lytton Strachey,* who pursued him amorously in vain, for Lamb was a determined heterosexual. Their friendship survived some disastrous holidays, in Brittany and the Lake District; Lamb was fond of simple, not to say rough, food and accommodation, but Strachey needed his comforts, and both men had weak stomachs. From 1909 they had a curious three-way relationship with Lady Ottoline Morrell,* whose Peppard cottage Lamb used as a country studio. Strachey was involved in Lamb's quarrel with Rupert Brooke* about Katherine Cox* at the beginning of 1912 and later that year the two friends joined in the protest over the ban on Epstein's memorial to Oscar Wilde in Père Lachaise cemetery, Paris. In 1911 Lamb began his great painting of Strachey, for which he made many drawings. It was finished at the end of August 1914.

Unlike most of Bloomsbury, Lamb was not a pacifist. In September 1914 he volunteered as a medical orderly, first at Guy's Hospital, then in France. By 1916 he was commissioned in the R.A.M.C. He served in Palestine and Macedonia, was awarded the Military Cross and became an official war artist. Although he shed most of his earlier connections with Bloomsbury after the war, David Garnett* sat for him, and he was still friendly with Strachey and a confidant of Carrington,* whom he met first in 1925. Lamb was now accepting many commissions for portraits. He had already painted his father for Manchester University (1913), and in 1926 undertook Pernel Strachey's* portrait for Newnham College, Cambridge. He lived out of London, first at Poole, then from 1928 in his own house at Coombe Bissett. In this year he married Lady Pansy Pakenham, sister of the sixth Earl of Longford, whom he had met two years before; she was twenty years younger than himself. Inevitably their friends were of her generation. These included the Partridges,** so the Lambs continued visiting Ham Spray after the deaths of Strachey and Carrington. Apart from the official portraits, which included an unfinished Neville Chamberlain (1938), Lamb painted mainly Pansy and their children (two daughters and a son). In the Second World War he was once again a war artist. Towards the end of his life he developed arthritis and died after a short illness brought on by cortisone treatment. His major war pictures are in the Imperial War Museum and his great portrait of Lytton Strachey in the Tate Gallery, though in neither case are they permanently on display.

K. Clements, *Henry Lamb, the Artist and his Friends* (Bristol, 1985)

LAMB, Walter Rangeley Maitland (1882–1961), Secretary of the Royal Academy: second son of Sir Horace Lamb, F.R.S., Professor of Mathematics at Manchester University, and older brother of Henry (*supra*). He was educated at Manchester Grammar School and read Classics at Trinity College, Cambridge (1902–5). He interspersed lecturing in Classics at Cambridge with two years, 1907–9, as assistant master at Clifton College, Bristol, then in 1913 was appointed Secretary of the Royal Academy. This post he held until 1951.

At Cambridge Lamb was one of the group that included Clive Bell,★ Lytton Strachey★ and Leonard Woolf.★ He contributed to their collection of verse, *Euphrosyne* (1905), and visited Virginia Stephen (Woolf★) in Fitzroy Square and on holiday in Dorset. His half-hearted courtship of Virginia was at first taken seriously, though it was largely conducted through Bell until July 1911. Virginia's letter of 21 July describes their long walk in Richmond Park, during which Lamb explained that he would like to be in love with her, given time and a greater knowledge of her character, but that it was very difficult as she lived in "a hornet's nest". Lamb's declaration and his subsequent rather more passionate letters set the hornets buzzing; Virginia was furious with Bell and the affair ended with Bell and Lamb never speaking to each other again, an outcome assisted by their disagreement in artistic matters.

Bloomsbury, in fact, made Lamb their butt. Strachey had already nicknamed him "The Corporal", because of his officious behaviour, and as he grew into his position at the Royal Academy, he became more and more a laughing-stock. In his elegant house at Kew Green he entertained royalty, then trotted round to Hogarth House to tell the Woolfs the latest sayings of the King or Princess Victoria. Virginia Woolf's diaries give the sharpest picture of his life as what Leonard Woolf called a "superior footman". After the First World War such intimacy as he had with Bloomsbury ended.

Yet Lamb was a conscientious official, showing none of his brother's impatience with the establishment. His services were rewarded at home with the K.C.V.O. (1943) and in Europe with the Belgian Medal of King Albert (1920) and the French Légion d'Honneur (1950). In 1927 he was married at last, to Rose Brooks of Chicago, whose portrait his brother Henry painted. He published works on Thucydides and on the Royal Academy, and translated Plato and Lysias in the Loeb editions.

LAWRENCE, David Herbert (1885–1930), novelist, poet and painter: born in Eastwood, Nottinghamshire, the fourth child of a miner and a schoolteacher and educated at Nottingham High School and University College, Nottingham, although suffering in his boyhood from bad health and considerable poverty. He taught at an elementary school in Croydon before eloping in 1912 with Frieda Weekley, whom he subsequently married. His literary career had begun in 1911, with the publication of his first novel, *The White Peacock*. Between 1913 and 1930 he wrote seven major novels, four volumes of verse, three volumes of short stories, some literary criticism, and some personal narratives in the form of travel books. He was a rather less successful painter, an exhibition of his pictures at the Warren Gallery, London, being raided by the police in July 1929 after complaints of obscenity by an anonymous informer. His literary work outraged conventional moralists by its vividly explicit style; in Britain and the United States *Lady Chatterley's Lover* could not be published in unexpurgated editions for thirty years after his death. Some of the hostility was Germanophobe in origin: Frieda Lawrence was a first cousin of the German air ace, Baron von Richthofen; Lawrence himself was consumptive and was therefore exempted from military service; but little attempt was made to understand the dilemmas of husband and wife, who were hounded throughout the First World War.

Although the Bloomsbury group sympathised with Lawrence in his difficulties with censorship and officialdom, in general they found him personally antipathetic and thought his style unattractive. The aversion was reciprocated; Lawrence derided Bloomsbury's intellectualism and its reverence for purely aesthetic values. Early in his literary career Lawrence had received encouragement from Edward Garnett★ and, in 1912, David Garnett★ joined Lawrence and his wife in Bavaria and in walking the Tyrol. Through David Garnett and Ottoline Morrell,★ Lawrence met other members of the Bloomsbury group over the following three years, but rarely made himself agreeable. He was exceptionally rude to Duncan Grant* about his paintings when invited to his studio. When David Garnett and Francis Birrell* were guests of the Lawrences at their cottage at Greatham on the South Downs over the weekend of 17–18 April 1915, Lawrence took an irrational dislike to Birrell. On the following day, he wrote to Garnett telling him never to bring Birrell to see him again and abusing Duncan Grant, Keynes,* and the Stracheys, all of whom he denounced as members of Garnett's "set". Seven months later, at a party given by Dorothy Brett,* Lytton Strachey and the Lawrences observed each other "for several hours" without seeking formal introduction or exchanging words. Lawrence and his wife dined with the Bells in Gordon Square, but the Woolfs declined an invitation from Koteliansky* (who greatly admired Lawrence) to meet him in 1918, and the Lawrences avoided the Bloomsbury group at the famous Armistice Night party given by Shearman.* It was, however, on that occasion that Garnett and Lawrence, who had not spoken to each other for three years, met for the last time. Subsequently Virginia Woolf* carefully noted down the two occasions upon which she saw Lawrence: in a shop at St Ives; and on the station platform at Civitavecchia. Never, however, did she engage him in conversation. After his death—from tuberculosis at Vence in March 1930—Virginia Woolf modified her views, blaming Middleton Murry* for having discouraged her from reading *Sons and Lovers* during Lawrence's lifetime and thereby appreciating his genius. But she was not consistent in her retrospective critical comments.

D. Garnett, *The Flowers of the Forest* (London, 1955)

LEHMANN, (Rudolf) John Frederick (1907–87), poet, editor, general author, and publisher: born at Bourne End, Buckinghamshire, the son of the barrister, journalist and Liberal M.P., R. C. Lehmann (1856–1929), and an American mother; and the brother of Rosamund Lehmann (*infra*). He was educated at Eton, where he was a King's Scholar, and at Trinity College, Cambridge. Among his closest friends at the university were Julian Bell* and "Dadie" Rylands.* A book of Lehmann's earliest verses was published in Edinburgh in 1929 and Rylands drew the attention of Leonard and Virginia Woolf** to his poetry a year later, at a time when they were looking for a new manager for the Hogarth Press. Lehmann served in this capacity from January 1931 to September 1932, the second summer being clouded by difficulties with Leonard Woolf, largely over trifling economies. Nevertheless he introduced a number of younger authors to the press, notably his friend, Isherwood.* Lehmann's collection of poems, *A Garden Revisited*, was published by the Hogarth Press in 1931 and he stimulated Virginia Woolf into writing her critical study, *A Letter to a Young Poet* (1932).

After leaving the press, Lehmann spent several years abroad, mainly in Vienna, where he had a flat until the eve of the Second World War. Contact with continental writers helped him when, in 1936, he founded and edited *New Writing*. His novel, *Evil was Abroad* was published in 1938 and was followed a year later by *Down River*, essentially a travel book. In April 1938 he returned to the Hogarth Press, of which he was a partner and general manager until 1946. The Hogarth Press assumed responsibility for *New Writing* until 1940 when Allen Lane agreed that Lehmann should produce a *Penguin New Writing*, reprinting some earlier material but containing much that was new as well. There were forty issues of *Penguin New Writing* before it was wound up in 1950. By then Lehmann had left the Hogarth Press, for in 1946 he became Managing Director of John Lehmann Ltd. He held this post for six years, but he continued to write essays of literary criticism and poems before becoming founder-editor from 1954 to 1961 of *The London Magazine*, a monthly literary magazine which aimed to reach "the common reader" and avoided being "university based". He wrote three volumes of autobiography: *The Whispering Gallery* (1955), covering the period down to the Second World War; *I Am My Brother* (1960), the years from 1939 to 1946; and finally, *The Ample Proposition* (1966). In 1970 he completed an interesting "historical portrait" of Holborn and edited the *Selected Letters of Edith Sitwell*. He wrote *Virginia Woolf and her World* in 1975 and five years later a study of Rupert Brooke* and his legend. A detailed account of Lehmann's relations with Leonard and Virginia Woolf followed in 1978; at Cyril Connolly's suggestion, Lehmann called the book, *Thrown to the Woolves*. On two occasions he was a visiting professor in the United States. In 1964 Lehmann was made a Companion of the British Empire.

LEHMANN, Rosamond Nina, Lady Milford (1905–), novelist, elder sister of John Lehmann (*supra*): was educated at Girton

College, Cambridge, and used the university as a setting for her first, highly successful, novel, *Dusty Answer* (1927), an evocation of the thought processes through which an adolescent intellectual matures to womanhood. Two later novels, *Invitation to the Waltz* (1932) and *The Weather in the Streets* (1936), were also concerned with the loss of a young girl's innocence, culminating in a failed marriage and an abortion; while *Note in Music* (1930) caused a sensation by its treatment of homosexuality. Rosamond Lehmann and her second husband, the left-wing painter Wogan Philipps (born 1903, succeeded his father as the second Baron Milford in 1962) were friends of Lytton Strachey* and Carrington,* were frequent visitors to Ham Spray House, and attended Bloomsbury parties in the early 1930s. Virginia Woolf* much admired her earlier novels; in 1933 the Woolfs were guests at the Philipps' Oxfordshire home. Rosamond Lehmann also wrote short stories, a play (*No More Music*, 1939), and several later novels. An autobiographical statement of her spiritual experiences seen against certain episodes in her earlier life was published in 1967 as *The Swan in the Evening*.

LEWIS, Percy Wyndham (1884–1957), painter and writer: born on a yacht off Fundy, in Maine, his father being American and his mother British. He was educated at Rugby School and the Slade School of Art. Most of the years 1901 to 1909 he spent in France but, on his return to England, he had short stories published in *The English Review* and exhibited avant-garde paintings with the Camden Town Group in 1911. He worked closely with Fry* and the Bells** for a couple of years; his paintings (which showed the influence of cubism) were included in the second Post-Impressionist exhibition; and he was prominent in the earliest Omega Workshop undertakings at 33 Fitzroy Square. But Lewis had a quarrelsome nature: he clashed with Sickert* over the foundation of the London Group; and in October 1913 Lewis drafted an indignant round-robin letter in which a small group of younger artists accused Fry of securing for Omega collectively commissions which were intended for individual Omega painters (notably Lewis and Etchells*) and of concentrating too much on aesthetic "Prettiness". Lewis' secession from Omega was followed by the establishment of his own movement, "Vorticism", which believed it was reflecting in art the impact of modern technology. Lewis was joint Editor, with Ezra Pound, of a periodical *Blast, the*

Review of the Great English Vortex which lasted for only two issues (1914–15) and he organised the sole exhibition of British vorticist art in 1915. A year later he enlisted in the Royal Artillery and served in France, subsequently becoming an official war artist.

A satirical novel, *Tarr*, appeared in 1918 and he continued to combine the writing of satires and literary criticism for another thirty-seven years. His magazine, *The Enemy* (three issues only, 1927–9), contained some challenging and perversely right-wing articles, all written with able clarity by Lewis himself. It was in his *The Apes of God* (1930) that Lewis made the first of several sustained and vicious attacks on the Bloomsbury group. He moved steadily towards Fascism in art and politics, painting a portrait of Hitler as early as 1931 and thriving on a paranoia which intensified his intellectual isolation during the 1930s and 1940s. *Men without Art*, published in October 1934, went to great lengths to emphasise the insignificance of Virginia Woolf's achievements, setting a fashion in snide criticism which worried her unduly over the following years.

Lewis spent the Second World War out of favour in America and Canada but returned to England in 1945 and was art critic of *The Listener* from 1946 to 1951 when his eyesight began to fail. *Blasting and Bombardiering* (1937) and *Rude Assignment* (1950) were autobiographical. His paintings displayed in the Tate Gallery show the originality of a creative genius stifled by a destructive desire to shock and confound his contemporaries.

J. Meyers, *The Enemy* (London, 1980)

LOPOKOVA, Lydia Vasilievna (1892–1981), dancer, actress: born in St Petersburg, daughter of Vasili Lopukhov, usher at the Alexandrinsky Theatre, and his Estonian-Scottish wife. Lydia, her elder sister Evgenia, and her brothers Andrei and Feodor were all educated at the Imperial Ballet School. Evgenia and Andrei became distinguished dancers at the Maryinsky (later Kirov) Theatre, while Feodor was also a choreographer and ballet master, credited with inventing the overhead lift in *pas-de-deux*. Lydia first appeared on the Maryinsky stage at the age of eight, and after her graduation in 1909 danced there until the following April. She had just been promoted to *coryphée* when she joined Diaghilev's* company in Paris. So great was her excitement at the prospect of appearing there that she fainted on arrival at the Gare du Nord.

Lydia danced several solo parts, notably in *Prince Igor,* and the lead in *The Firebird,* her youthful, snub-nosed charm and tremendous elevation delighting the French critics. Instead of returning to Russia, she left for the U.S.A. with her sister and brother Feodor, and stayed there, acting as well as dancing and appearing in music halls, until the Diaghilev company toured New York in 1916. Lydia rejoined them, married the business manager Randolfo Barocchi, and toured with the company through North and South America in 1917, dancing with Nijinsky* for the last time. The following year she made her first appearance in England, and enchanted British audiences with her lively performance in Massine's* *The Good-Humoured Ladies;* she had an even greater success as the Can-Can dancer in his *La Boutique Fantasque* (1919). In October 1918 she was introduced to Maynard Keynes* at the Sitwells,** and met him again at Shearman's* party on Armistice night.

At the beginning of July 1919, Lydia suddenly disappeared from England, turning up in a musical comedy in New York two years later; what she did in the interval was never disclosed. Back with Diaghilev, she danced on his 1921 tour, and appeared in the autumn as the Lilac Fairy and Aurora in his great London production of *The Sleeping Princess.* Keynes sat in the stalls nearly every night, and began to pay Lydia serious attention when she remained in London after the closure of the ballet in February 1922. He became her financial adviser and tried to integrate her into Bloomsbury.

From the first Lydia was a favourite with Duncan Grant,* and both Vanessa Bell* and he painted her portrait. However, when she lived in Gordon Square below the Bells her ebullient chatter interrupted Vanessa's work, and she moved on to shake James Strachey's* house while practising *entrechats.* Keynes was still unsure about his course of action, and some of his friends warned him against marriage, Vanessa in particular feeling it would be impossible to bring a new member permanently into the Bloomsbury circle. Virginia Woolf* also prophesied doom for Keynes, and Lytton Strachey* harped on the dissimilarity of the couple's intellect. But Lydia was deeply in love, and felt she could appreciate Keynes' genius without understanding economics; "for me it is just like Bach!" she said. When her first marriage was annulled, she and Keynes were married on 25 August 1925 and went at once to visit the Lopukhov family in Russia. Further Russian visits took place in 1927 and 1928. Meanwhile Keynes took a lease of Tilton, a farmhouse near Charleston in Sussex, as well as keeping on 46 Gordon Square.

During the period 1922–5 Lydia appeared mainly with Massine, sometimes in ballets designed by Grant, but in October 1925 she returned to "Big Serge", as she called Diaghilev, and appeared for the last time with his company in June 1927. Her unpaid performances at Bloomsbury parties have become legendary, whether she sang pathetic Victorian ballads, or danced with her husband the famous "Keynes-Keynes", first seen in 1926 and the subject of a cartoon by Vanessa. Other frequent partners were Grant and the young Frederick Ashton. Although Vanessa and Virginia still had reservations about the newcomer, there was much mutual entertaining in the country, and it became a tradition for Bells and Woolfs to visit Tilton at Christmas.

As Mrs, later Lady, Keynes Lydia was a decided success in the world outside Bloomsbury. With her active encouragement Keynes took greater interest in theatre and ballet administration. They both worked for the Camargo Society, founded in 1930 to keep ballet going in Britain. Keynes was Treasurer, while Lydia was on the committee and danced, creating the rôles of the Milkmaid and Tango in Ashton's *Façade* for the society (1931). She also danced Swanhilda in *Coppélia* with the infant Vic-Wells Ballet in 1933. As a child in Russia, Lydia had acted in drama, and when she and Keynes founded the Arts Theatre, Cambridge (1936), she played leading parts in Ibsen's *A Doll's House* and *The Master Builder*. Her strong Russian accent detracted from her performances, but was no hindrance to her B.B.C. talks, mainly on Russian ballet music or literature. A narrator in Tolstoy's *War and Peace*, broadcast in 1943, was her last dramatic part.

Keynes had his first serious illness in 1937, and from then Lydia devoted herself to his health; they took a flat in Cambridge so that she could stay with him there and she accompanied him on his journeys to the U.S.A. during and after the Second World War. Lydia charmed foreign statesmen and financiers as she had all her audiences, though she was quite uninhibited in her remarks; till his dying day Keynes never knew what she might say next. When that day came in 1946, Lydia took ten years to recover completely from her loss. She kept on her three residences, but in London and Cambridge saw more of the ballet and theatre world than she did of Old Bloomsbury. E. M. Forster* remained a good friend, and she still entertained Leonard Woolf* once a year at Tilton, but only occasionally visited Charleston. By 1960 she lived entirely in the country and after four years in a nursing home died on 8 June 1981.

Lydia Lopokova, ed. Milo Keynes (London, 1983)

MacCARTHY, Dermod (1911–86), paediatrician: born in Chelsea, London, son of Desmond and Mary MacCarthy,★★ godson of Hilaire Belloc. Although almost a child of Bloomsbury, and eventually a member of the Memoir Club his mother had started when he was nine, MacCarthy's career took him into a different world. Educated at Gresham's School, Holt and St Bartholomew's Hospital, he qualified in 1937 and became a paediatrician at Great Ormond Street Children's Hospital (1939–42), but broke off to serve in the R.N.V.R. until 1945. After the war MacCarthy helped set up children's units in hospitals throughout the country, and was consultant paediatrician to a group of hospitals around Aylesbury, Buckinghamshire from 1948 till his retirement in 1975. He was also honorary physician to the Institute of Child Psychology. In 1947 he married Marie-France Geoffroy-Dechaume, a heroine of the French Resistance awarded the Croix de Guerre; they had four sons.

MacCarthy's sensitive imagination gave him an insight into the terrors of hospital life for children. He was a pioneer of the movement to free small patients from restrictions and allow their parents to stay with them, supporting the National Association for the Welfare of Children in Hospital from its foundation in the 1950s. In 1974 he became President of the paediatric section of the Royal Society of Medicine, and in 1982 was given the James Spence Medal, highest award of the British Paediatric Association. MacCarthy spread his reforming ideas through personal contacts, for, like his father, he wrote little. Just before he died in 1986, however, he completed a book that recalled his childhood, *Sailing with Mr Belloc*.

MacCARTHY, (Charles Otto) Desmond (1877–1952), literary journalist: born in Plymouth, into an Anglo-Irish banking family, and educated at Eton before going up to Trinity College, Cambridge, in 1894 to read History. He was elected an Apostle two years later, early winning recognition as a gifted conversationalist. In the summer of 1897, however, he was seriously ill with asthma, could not sit for his final examinations, and had to be content with an aegrotat. He began his journalistic career as a freelance contributor to *The Spectator* and was the shrewdest critic of Shaw's early plays at the Royal Court. In 1904 he became engaged to Mary Warre-Cornish (*infra*), whom he married at Eton in July 1906, with Virginia Stephen (Woolf★) and her brother among the guests. The following year his Shaw reviews were published in book form and he became editor of the *New Quarterly*. His literary skills and his charm as a raconteur enabled him to become a friend, not only of G. E. Moore★ and Bertrand Russell,★ but of Thomas Hardy and of Henry James,★ and he was an early champion in England of the plays of both Ibsen and Chekhov. At the same time he was induced by Roger Fry★ to become his secretary and business agent for the first Post-Impressionist exhibition, for which he wrote an introduction to the programme. From 1913 to 1919 he contributed to the *New Statesman,* although he served with the Red Cross, attached to the French army, in 1914–15. From 1920 to 1927 he was the *New Statesman's* literary editor, moving over to the *Sunday Times* in 1928 as senior literary critic.

MacCarthy, whose clubbable tastes were socially catholic, always refused to regard himself as a member of Bloomsbury; it was not his part of London, for he spent many years in Chelsea and later beside the Thames at Hampton. But he was reading a paper to the Friday Club as early as January 1906, he became a founder-member of the Memoir Club in 1920, and he was present at many parties in Fitzroy Square. Moreover the group whom his wife called "Bloomsberries" constantly encouraged him to realise the literary ambitions of which he talked by writing a novel. This he did not; nor did he write any great single work of criticism. By temperament he was indolent, and conversation remained his greatest gift: Virginia Woolf noted that when she met him on 27 February 1937, there followed seven hours of non-stop talk between them. Nevertheless MacCarthy's collected reviews and essays fill ten volumes and his judgement was much respected. He was knighted in 1951 and his old university bestowed an honorary doctorate on him in June 1952. But his health gave way while he was at Cambridge; he died two days later.

MacCARTHY, Mary Josefa (Molly) (1882–1953), writer: born Mary Warre-Cornish, daughter of a housemaster at Eton College, and his wife Blanche (Ritchie), sister-in-law of Lady Anne Ritchie.* Molly was the penultimate child of eight, five girls and three boys, all musical and literary, and spent her childhood at Eton (from 1893 in the Vice-Provost's house), educated by governesses and her eldest sister Margaret. Most of her education came from reading, but she spent a year as a day-girl at an Anglican convent, then went to Northlands School, and was "finished" with a few months in France and a year in Germany (1901–2).

She had many German admirers, and a proposal from an army officer, but returned fancy free to enjoy the social life of Eton and London with her sisters. Their frequent escort was Desmond MacCarthy (*supra*), a friend of their brothers at Eton and Cambridge. In 1904 Molly and Desmond became engaged, but six weeks later Molly had a serious and unexplained breakdown, the story of which she told in a paper to the Bloomsbury Memoir Club in 1934. She convalesced at the seaside and had to be rescued by her mother and Desmond MacCarthy from her nurse, an addict who tried to dose her patient with the drugs she took herself.

The MacCarthys were married on a "happy and baking hot August" day, according to Molly (in fact 10 July 1906) and during their honeymoon Desmond introduced his wife to Thomas Hardy, on the first of many visits. Their married life began in part of a farmhouse at Ampton in Suffolk, where they entertained contributors to the *New Quarterly*, of which MacCarthy had just become Editor; their visitors included G. E. Moore,* G. Lowes Dickinson,* and Lytton Strachey.* But Molly also enjoyed driving about the country in a governess-cart, making friends in the village. In London the MacCarthys went often to the theatre and were enthusiasts for Granville Barker's productions, Shaw and Ibsen. They were "liberals—but not socialists", though Molly was involved to some extent in the Women's Suffrage movement and was friendly with Belloc and Dick Sheppard, the anti-establishment vicar of St Martin's-in-the-Fields; she met him first when he was Rector of Livermere in Suffolk. Unlike so many of her friends, Molly MacCarthy remained a Christian and, towards the end of her life, a practising one.

The two older MacCarthy children, Michael (*infra:* 1907) and Rachel* (1909), were born in Suffolk, but the family moved in 1910 to 25 Wellington Square, Chelsea, after Desmond and Molly had spent three months in South Africa. Molly also accompanied her husband and Roger Fry* on their trip to Paris to arrange the first

Post-Impressionist exhibition, and met Picasso.* It was after the MacCarthys settled in London that they began to meet regularly the group whom Molly christened "Bloomsberries" and to attend their evenings. Their last child, Dermod,* was born in 1911, but help in the house was plentiful and the notes Molly made for her memoirs are full of theatres, "Fancy Dress parties" (a great Bloomsbury favourite) and activities of the kind described as "Clive Bell* and going about". The MacCarthys also visited Lady Ottoline Morrell* in "fantastical Bedford Square".

The war years were harder, with the children and many of their friends in the country, and the death of Molly's parents and brother Gerald. Yet some time in 1918 Molly started a Bloomsbury Novel Club, with the idea of getting her husband to write the great novel everyone predicted for him and which never appeared. After a year she transformed it into the Memoir Club, with herself as "Secretary and drudge" a post she held until 23 January 1946. The first meeting was at 25 Wellington Square on 4 March 1920.

As well as writing papers for the club, Molly MacCarthy published a novel, *A Pier and a Band* (1918) and several non-fiction works: *A Nineteenth Century Childhood* (1924); *Fighting Fitzgerald* (1930, on four eighteenth-century eccentrics); *Handicaps* (1936, a study of disabilities overcome by the famous); *Festival* (1937, essays and stories). Her life became an increasing struggle against deafness caused by otosclerosis; after her daughter Rachel's marriage she had another complete breakdown and spent Christmas 1932 in a nursing-home. By 1945 she could hear nothing at all when in a group of people. Between the wars the MacCarthys had often let their Chelsea house to save money, and from 1940 they did so permanently, moving to a flat in Garrick's Villa, on the Thames at Hampton. Here Molly wrote *Dire Februaries*, a Memoir Club paper on the London air raids.

Both the MacCarthy sons were married by the end of the Second World War and Molly enjoyed visiting her children and grandchildren, but was increasingly worried about her husband's health, and was with him when he died in Cambridge on 7 June 1952, two days after receiving an honorary degree. Molly moved into a smaller flat in Garrick's Villa and, after a heart attack, died peacefully on 28 December 1953.

Elizabeth F. Boyd, *Bloomsbury Heritage: their Mothers and their Aunts* (London, 1976)

MacCARTHY, Michael (1907–73), farmer: born at Ampton in Suffolk, the eldest child of Desmond and Molly MacCarthy.** He was no academic, but became an enthusiastic farmer (mainly sheep and goats) in Argentina, South Africa and England.

MacCARTHY, Rachel, Lady David Cecil (1909–82), the second child and only daughter of Desmond and Molly MacCarthy:** born in Suffolk, but spent her childhood and youth in London or near Oare in Wiltshire. She enjoyed amateur theatricals and was popular not only with the younger Bloomsbury set but with other literary figures in London as well. Among close friends were Ralph and Frances Partridge** and Jane Bussy.* Her father, who seems to have thought her immature, was surprised in September 1932 by her engagement to Lord David Cecil.* The couple were married at St Bartholomew's, Smithfield, on 13 October 1932, Virginia Woolf* writing a sourly anti-clerical account of the wedding in her diary. In the 1950s Lady David wrote a nostalgic novel of London in the 1920s; it was published under her maiden name and called *Theresa's Choice* (1957).

MacCOLL, Dugald Sutherland (1859–1948), painter and gallery director: born in Glasgow, the son of a Presbyterian minister, and educated at Glasgow Academy, University College School in Hampstead, and University College, London, before becoming a Classics scholar at Lincoln College, Oxford, in 1881, where a year later he won the Newdigate Prize for verse. He travelled widely in Italy and Greece, developing his appreciation of classical art and the Italian renaissance. He was himself a water-colour painter and, on settling in London, became art critic of *The Spectator* (1890–6) and subsequently of *The Saturday Review* as well as lecturing on art history at University College, London. He encouraged young British painters to join him on expeditions in France to absorb the essence of later Impressionism: in 1894 he led a party who were based on La Roche Guyon and in 1895 he was near Fécamp, on the coast of Normandy. Roger Fry* visited MacColl on both these occasions. A year later MacColl helped establish the New English Art Club. By now he was held in awe in London as an interpreter of the Impressionists; his critical judgement continued to be respected in Britain for another fifty years. He was Keeper of the Tate Gallery

(1906–11) and of the Wallace Collection (1911–24). He was eighty-six when he won the James Tait Black Prize for his biography of his friend, the painter Wilson Steer (1860–1942).

In 1896 MacColl married Andrée Zabe (died 1945), a friend of Roger Fry. MacColl was an early and constructive critic of Fry's paintings and theories, and collaborated with Fry in safeguarding the integrity of the *Burlington Magazine* in the winter of 1903–4. Three articles concerning Fry (published in 1912, 1919 and 1928) were reprinted in MacColl's, *Confessions of a Keeper* (1931). Literary Bloomsbury he held in respect, but he thought artistic Bloomsbury light-weight. MacColl's poems were published in 1940. He died at Hampstead in December 1948.

MALLORY, George (1887–1924), mountaineer: was born in Cheshire, the son of a country rector. He was educated at Winchester and Magdalene College, Cambridge, subsequently teaching history at Charterhouse from 1911 to 1915 (and again after the war). In January 1916 he was commissioned in the Royal Artillery and fought for two years in the Ypres salient. He first climbed in the Alps at the age of seventeen but did not tackle Himalayan peaks until 1921, returning to Everest a year later. In June 1924 he was lost on the slopes of Everest, together with his friend, A. J. Irvine; many people believed they had reached the summit of the mountain before being swept away in a blizzard.

At Cambridge Mallory, who enjoyed an intellectual argument, was a close companion of Jacques Raverat* and Geoffrey Keynes,* his physique being much admired by the university's coterie of homosexual aesthetes, especially Lytton Strachey.* Over such matters Mallory appears to have been a hearty innocent. He was a Fabian socialist, an oarsman, college representative for the university's Woman's Suffrage Association, and a keen actor, playing two roles in the famous production of *Dr Faustus* of November 1907 in which his friend Brooke* was Mephistopheles. Strachey introduced Mallory to his cousin, Duncan Grant,* for whom he agreed to pose as a nude model for several paintings. While teaching at Charterhouse in the summer of 1913 Mallory supervised the production of a single-copy literary magazine, *Green Chartreuse*, for which he persuaded Duncan Grant to come to the school and paint posters, exhibited at the cricket pavilion. Strachey, too, stayed with him at Charterhouse over the weekend of 23–24 May 1914, Mallory subsequently commenting to his fiancée, with some surprise, on his guest's apparent dislike of schoolboys. Mallory stayed with Simon Bussy* and his wife for several months at Roquebrune in the winter of 1909–10. Although he never became a Bloomsbury habitué, Virginia Woolf* remembered him: "a divine undergraduate", with bad teeth, but "a head like a Greek God".

Mallory's tenuous contact with Bloomsbury ended with his marriage in July 1914. But he chose Virginia Woolf's *Night and Day* to read on his final voyage out to India, before the fatal assault on Everest. His brother, Air Marshal Sir Trafford Leigh-Mallory (1892–1944), commanded the Allied air forces in the invasion of Europe in 1944; he was killed, together with his wife, on 14 November 1944 in an air crash near Grenoble.

D. Robertson, *George Mallory* (London, 1972)

MANSFIELD, Katherine (1888–1923), writer: born Katherine Mansfield Beauchamp in Wellington, New Zealand, daughter of Harold Beauchamp, educated at Wellington Girls' High School (1898–9) and Miss Swainson's private school (1900–3). Bespectacled and stammering herself, Katherine suffered comparison with her beautiful mother and four sisters. A young 'cellist, Arnold Trowell, stimulated her interest in music and desire for European culture, and she persuaded her parents to take her to England. With her sisters, Charlotte and Vera, Katherine completed her education at Queen's College, Harley Street from 1903 until 1906. Although Arnold Trowell was now available in Europe, Katherine enjoyed sentimental female friendships more, notably with Ida Baker, who repaid her with a lifetime of devotion. After her return to New Zealand, Katherine took a secretarial course at Wellington Technical College and began to write sketches for Australasian newspapers. She was so bored and unhappy that her parents agreed to let her make her career in England, and in 1908 she left New Zealand for ever.

Katherine, staying in London with the Trowells, fell in love with Arnold's twin brother Garnet, but when she became pregnant by him she married an older man, the singer George Bowden, whom she left very soon after the wedding. Her mother arrived to take her to Germany for the birth of a stillborn baby, a grim experience which provided material for several stories, and Katherine's first published book *In a German Pension* (1911). A brief return to Bowden resulted in a second pregnancy and an abortion. After another operation her lungs were affected for the first time by disease, diagnosed as pleurisy.

Katherine had now become a very attractive woman, with a cool, mysterious façade that concealed her emotions, unless she lost control in sudden rage. In 1911 she met John Middleton Murry,* who came to live in her London flat next year. The couple soon became lovers, and shared a dozen different homes between 1912 and 1914; they often quarrelled and lived separately, sometimes finding other partners. Murry was a friend of D. H. Lawrence,* and at the Lawrences' wedding in 1914 a fellow guest, the artist Mark Gertler,* introduced Katherine to some of the Bloomsbury circle. Ottoline Morrell* also "took her up" and Katherine stayed frequently at Garsington. For a time in 1916 she and Murry lived in the heart of Bloomsbury, sharing Keynes'* house, 3 Gower Street, with Brett* and Carrington.* Although Virginia Woolf* sometimes called her "common", she and Katherine had a real friendship, not without some mutual envy; their recurring ill-health made for sympathy, their similar literary objectives for rivalry. Virginia once said that Katherine Mansfield's was the only writing she could be jealous of, but Katherine envied her Leonard Woolf's* constant support.

Katherine's own illness, not recognised as tuberculosis until 1917, grew worse, and between 1914 and 1922 she consulted twenty-two doctors, some charlatans and all useless. She tried a warmer climate, but the war and Murry's dislike of living abroad made this difficult. The couple spent the winter of 1915–16 happily in Bandol, but when Katherine returned there next year with Ida Baker, she was cold and depressed, and came home after suffering a first haemorrhage. In May 1918, after her marriage to Murry, Katherine tried Cornwall and the Riviera with Ida again, but refused to go to a sanatorium except for a short period in the winter of 1920–1. She agreed to stay in Switzerland, where her cousin, the writer Elizabeth von Arnim lived, during 1921. Katherine's months abroad were tormented by jealousy of Murry's relations with other women, even her friend Brett, whom she had charged to "look after the little lad", and she began to dislike Ida Baker. In 1922 she joined the mystic Gudjieff's Institute at Fontainebleau, but his dominating methods failed to cure her, and she died at Fontainebleau in 1923.

Katherine Mansfield continued writing until six months before her death; *Bliss* (1920) and *The Garden Party* (1922) are the best-known collections of her short stories, the genre in which she excelled; although she also published poems. After her death Murry edited her letters and journals.

Jeffrey Meyers, *Katherine Mansfield* (London, 1978)
A. Alpers, *Katherine Mansfield* (London, 1980)

MASSINE, Leonide Fedorovich (1895–1979), Russian dancer: born in Moscow and trained at the Moscow Bolshoi School before joining the Ballets Russes of Diaghilev★ in 1914, when he replaced Nijinsky★ in many dancing rôles and in the impresario's affections. In 1917 he was choreographer of *The Good Humoured Ladies* (for Lopokova★) and *Parade*. He came to London with Diaghilev in the autumn of 1918 and was present at the famous "Bloomsbury junta" party of Montague Shearman★ on Armistice night. He was responsible for the choreography of *The Three Cornered Hat* (designed by Picasso★) and *La Boutique Fantasque* (designed by Derain★), dancing in both these ballets at the Alhambra Theatre in 1919, a year in which he was lionized by the Bloomsbury balletomanes, particularly Lady Ottoline Morrell.★ A year later he choreographed *The Song of the Nightingale*, with designs by Matisse (*infra*). Massine broke with Diaghilev in 1921 and, although he returned to the Ballets Russes from 1925 to 1928, his principal works over the following forty years were for French companies; he became a naturalised French citizen in 1944, but in his later years he travelled widely, supervising revivals of his ballets by various companies, including the Royal Ballet in London. He also arranged dances for several C. B. Cochran revues. While working on these productions, in 1925, he lived in Bloomsbury which, forty years later, he remembered as "the centre of the artistic and intellectual life of London" and he particularly recalled "a delightful afternoon in Fitzroy Square with Roger Fry★ and Duncan Grant★", exchanging ideas on Cézanne, cubism and the future of the ballet. Massine principally danced character rôles and much of his choreography showed touches of inspired comedy but he was also a pioneer in choreographing ballets from existing symphonic music.

L. Massine, *My Life in Ballet* (London, 1960)

MATISSE, Henri (1869–1954), French painter: born at his grandparents' home in Le Cateau (Nord), the son of a corn chandler from Bohain. He was a lawyer's clerk in St Quentin when, in 1890, he began painting while recovering from appendicitis. By 1895 his paintings were attracting attention in Paris and he became a pupil in the studio of Gustave Moreau, where Simon Bussy* was also studying at that time. He suffered great financial hardship between 1900 and 1904, but by 1905 his experiments with rich colours assured him recognition as one of the avant-garde "wild beasts" (fauves), together with Derain,* Braque and others. Roger Fry* thought him "a very queer . . . neo neo-Impressionist" when he visited Matisse's studio at Issy-les-Molineaux in 1909 but gave prominence to Matisse in the first of the London Post-Impressionist exhibitions a year later, and his paintings dominated the second of the exhibitions, in 1911–12; he greatly influenced Grant,* the Bells** and the whole Omega experiment.

By 1912 Matisse was a celebrity in Paris, Clive Bell noticing how he rode in the Bois in brown top-boots, once falling from his horse. He was unfit for service in the First World War, from 1916 spending much of his time at Nice. Like so many other French artists of his generation he was attracted to the Ballets Russes of Diaghilev;* he visited London with the company in October 1920 for the presentation of *The Song of the Nightingale* (which he designed), but it was for him a fortnight of hard work and he saw little of his Bloomsbury admirers. Clive Bell visited him in Cimiez as late as 1951, finding Matisse in bed and painting on the ceiling with a fishing rod. Among the greatest, and more restrained, of his later works are the series of Dance murals for the Barnes Foundation in Pennsylvania (on which he worked from 1930 to 1932) and the decoration of the Chapel of the Rosary at Vence, which was built between 1949 and 1951. He died at Nice in November 1954 after struggling for thirteen years against a debilitating illness.

A. H. Barr, Jnr, *Matisse, his Art and his Public* (New York, 1951)
L. Gowing, *Matisse* (Oxford, New York and Toronto, 1979)
N. Watkins, *Matisse* (Oxford, 1984)

MAURON, Charles (1899–1966), French scientist, critic and translator: born in Provence, near Avignon, and trained as a chemist. He was hampered in his scientific career by failing eyesight, but he possessed an acute sense of aesthetics, delighting in the fine arts, in poetry, and in prose narrative which was essentially impressionistic. Roger Fry★ first met Mauron while travelling in southern France in 1919 and was interested in the Frenchman's theories of parallel standards for literary and artistic criticism. By 1925 Fry had introduced Mauron to E. M. Forster★ and a year later—again on Fry's initiative—Mauron began to translate some of Virginia Woolf's★ *To the Lighthouse*. Over the following thirteen years Mauron translated all of Forster's major novels, some Katherine Mansfield,★ V. Woolf's *Orlando* and *Flush*, and some T. E. Lawrence. He was also the author of two studies in aestheticism, published in their English version by the Hogarth Press, *The Nature of Beauty in Art and Literature* (1926) and *Aesthetics and Psychology* (1935).

Mauron was much respected by Leonard Woolf,★ but he remained particularly the friend of Fry and Forster. From 1923 onwards Fry often stayed with Mauron and his wife (a novelist) at St Rémy-en-Provence, a small town east of Tarascon, between the Rhone and the Durance; and from 1931 Fry and the Maurons shared ownership of a farm at St Rémy which had belonged to Charles Mauron's parents. In the spring of 1929 Fry encouraged him to come to England in the mistaken belief he would be invited to give a public lecture on the poet Stephane Mallarmé (1842–98) at Oxford; instead it was delivered to an invited audience in Bloomsbury. Fry, and Julian Bell,★ collaborated with Mauron in producing a translation of Mallarmé's poems, published in 1936. Mauron thought highly of Julian Bell's intellectual promise and contributed a memoir to the volume about his brother which Quentin Bell★ edited for the Hogarth Press in 1938. Virginia Woolf, who had taken the Chair at a second Bloomsbury lecture given by Mauron in November 1929, at first found him formidable, but he won her friendship in the late 1930s when she was writing Fry's biography, not least because of his opinion of her nephew, Julian.

By 1940 Mauron, a convinced anti-Fascist, was virtually blind but he was able to survive the Vichy régime and occupation in his native Provence. When the war ended he began fourteen years of service to his local community as Mayor of St Rémy, where he died early in December 1966.

MAXSE, Katherine (Kitty), *née* Lushington (1867–1922), friend of the Stephen family: born in Cobham, Surrey, the daughter of Vernon Lushington (1832–1912), a barrister and County Court

Judge, who was a Cambridge contemporary of Leslie Stephen.★ Vernon Lushington's wife, who died when Kitty was seventeen, had been Julia Stephen's★ closest friend. The Lushingtons' town house was in Kensington Square and Kitty was therefore a frequent visitor to 22 Hyde Park Gate. To the Stephens' daughters she became "a foster mother in the ways of the world" since, as Virginia Woolf★ told the Memoir Club, she "had the reputation with us of profound knowledge and exquisite sympathy". While staying with the Stephens in Cornwall at Talland House in 1890 Kitty Lushington became engaged to Leopold Maxse (1864–1932). He, too, was a guest of the Stephens, for he was the second son of Admiral Frederick Maxse (1833–1900), once naval aide-de-camp to Lord Raglan in the Crimean War but later a radical and atheist, held in much respect by Leslie Stephen. Virginia Woolf told the Memoir Club in 1921 that "their engagement under the jackmanii in the Love Corner at St Ives was my first introduction to the passion of love". The Maxses were also friends of the French radical politician, Georges Clemenceau, with whom they often exchanged visits, and it was through Clemenceau that they met Claude Monet and other Impressionists. This world into which "the lovely Kitty Lushington" married appears to have made a deep impression on Virginia, and even more on the slightly older Vanessa (Bell★).

But Leopold Maxse was not himself a bohemian character. He was a political journalist, from 1893 the editor and proprietor of the *National Review*, a periodical which became increasingly right-wing in sentiment, outstandingly anti-German, and alarmed at the size of the Kaiser's navy as early as 1900. Maxse's sister, Violet, married Lord Edward Cecil (and after his death Lord Milner) while Kitty Maxse became a political hostess, a particular favourite with Joseph Chamberlain. Her efforts to persuade Vanessa and Virginia to shine in this society were unsuccessful, and by 1903 Virginia's comments on Kitty Maxse were extremely hostile. Mrs Maxse was "already screaming against Bloomsbury" in 1904, Gordon Square being so unfashionable an address after Hyde Park Gate; and a year later she was highly critical of the appearance of the young men who came to the earliest of the Thursday evenings. In 1911 Virginia was rebuked by Lady Robert Cecil★ for having treated Kitty Maxse so badly, and there was little further contact between the Bloomsbury group and the Maxses; Kitty did not like the style which Virginia Woolf perfected in her novels. Leopold Maxse was one of the chief journalists who attacked the Liberals over the Marconi scandal in

1912–13; subsequently he became strongly opposed to the League of Nations. His health was poor and he relied heavily on the support of Kitty Maxse as a hostess. In October 1922 she injured herself fatally in a fall on the stairs of their home, 33 Cromwell Road, London.

When Virginia Woolf began writing *The Voyage Out* in 1908 she told her sister that the character who became Clarissa Dalloway was "almost Kitty verbatim". Rewriting, however, may have blurred the portrait, while the Mrs Dalloway who gave her name to the novel finished in 1924 seems to represent the author herself as much as the prototype depicted sixteen years before.

MOORE, George Edward (1873–1958), philosopher: born in London, son of Dr Daniel Moore and brother of the poet Thomas Sturge Moore, educated at Dulwich College (1881) and Trinity College, Cambridge (1892), reading Classics in Part I of the Tripos. In 1894, the year when he became an Apostle, he changed to Moral Sciences for Part II, obtaining a first in both parts. Bertrand Russell* encouraged the move and the two met regularly in Cambridge for discussion, though they gradually came to disagree. The award of a Trinity prize Fellowship in 1898 allowed Moore to concentrate on philosophy and complete his most famous work, *Principia Ethica* (1903).

Moore stressed the importance of asking the right questions rather than constructing a system of answers. The rational questioner will discover that goodness, an indefinable quality discernible by intuition and common sense, belongs in the highest degree to the appreciation of beauty in art and nature and to personal affection; states of mind alone are good in themselves and therefore worth pursuing for their own sakes. Other things may be good in relation to their aims, and right actions are those which lead to a preponderance of good over evil. "Moorism" was enthusiastically received in Cambridge; it seemed to replace outmoded obligations with standards that gave an individual the freedom to pursue his own "good" and that of his friends. Keynes* later maintained that Moore's followers had adopted the ethical and aesthetic principles of his philosophy, but ignored his views on right conduct (*Two Memoirs*, 1949). Lytton Strachey* certainly equated "personal affection" with homosexual love.

After his departure from Cambridge in 1904, Moore lived in Edinburgh until 1908, trying to understand and review Russell's

Principles of Mathematics, then moved to Richmond with his sisters. He succeeded Keynes' father as Lecturer in Moral Sciences at Cambridge, and in 1925 was appointed Professor of Philosophy and a Fellow of Trinity. In 1916 he married Dorothy Ely, who came to his 1915–16 lectures while at Newnham, and they had two sons. Moore had no strong views on the war at first, but by 1916 he was definitely in opposition and helped formulate arguments for the tribunals of his conscientious objector friends, including Strachey and Norton.* He did not suffer for his opinions professionally, for in 1918 he became a Fellow of the British Academy and was editor of *Mind* from 1921 until 1947. When he resigned his professorship in 1939 Moore lectured at Oxford, and was visiting professor at several American universities from 1941 to 1944. He received the Order of Merit in 1951, and died at Cambridge in October 1958.

Moore's published works are *Ethics* (1912), *Philosophical Studies* (1922) and *Some Main Problems of Philosophy* (1953). Although he also wrote many important articles, his thought spread through the Bloomsbury group and their contemporaries from discussions at meetings of the Apostles and from his Easter reading parties. Desmond MacCarthy* was his best friend, and Leonard Woolf* had great affection for him, considering him a major influence on Virginia's* work. She read *Principia Ethica* in 1908 and mentioned Moore in her first novel, *The Voyage Out*, but did not meet him until his visit to Asheham in 1914. They remained friends, though Virginia later wondered why they had respected him so greatly in their youth. The answer must lie partly in Moore's own sweetness of character, the innocence and lovable absurdities that made Leonard Woolf compare him to Socrates in his pursuit of the truth.

Paul Levy, *Moore: G. E. Moore and the Cambridge Apostles* (London, 1979)

MORRELL, Ottoline Violet Anne, *née* Cavendish-Bentinck (1873–1938), society hostess: born in London, fifth child of Lieutenant-General Arthur Bentinck, who died when Lady Ottoline was aged four. Two years later her step-brother succeeded a distant cousin as Duke of Portland and much of her childhood was spent at the family seat, Welbeck Abbey. As a young woman she travelled widely, especially in Italy, and briefly sampled university education both at St Andrew's and at Somerville College, Oxford. She met Philip Morrell (*infra*) in 1900 and married him at

St Peter's, Eaton Square, on 8 February 1902. They lived at first in Grosvenor Road, on the southern fringe of Westminster, but when her husband entered the Commons in January 1906 they moved to 44 Bedford Square. This was their Bloomsbury home until 1915, when they established themselves east of Oxford at Garsington Manor, purchased by Philip Morrell in March 1913.

Life at Bedford Square began tragically for Lady Ottoline. She gave birth to twins, a boy and a girl, on 18 May 1906: the girl (Julian) survived, but became the Morrells' only child, for the boy died three days later. By 1908 Lady Ottoline was mainly concerned with establishing her ascendancy in London society as a literary and political hostess. As she was prepared to seek out the unfamiliar, if instinct told her it possessed qualities she could admire, she took the initiative, towards the end of the year 1908, in coming to a Thursday "At Home" of Virginia Stephen (Woolf★) in Fitzroy Square, with Augustus John and his wife as her companions. Lady Ottoline enjoyed good conversation, shared Bloomsbury's interest in contemporary art, and possessed the wealth to give it her patronage; already she had entertained Clive and Vanessa Bell,★★ whom she first met in the previous spring. Soon most of Old Bloomsbury were welcomed at her Bedford Square parties, where they mingled not only with the artists of "Chelsea" but with "Westminster" as well—mainly Philip Morrell's Liberal colleagues, including Winston Churchill. Personal taste inclined her to champion the rebellious and unconventional in music, painting and books. Her dress, too, was eccentric, "window-curtaining clothes", complained Henry James★ after enjoying her company in early May 1912. It was natural for her that summer to draw into her circle the artistic invaders associated with Diaghilev★ and the Ballets Russes.

She had passionate love affairs with Augustus John and Henry Lamb★ and a more protracted relationship with Bertrand Russell.★ Lytton Strachey★ found her fascinating, and spent most of November and December 1910 with her (and with Lamb) at the Morrells' cottage in Peppard, near Henley. Thursday evening receptions continued at Bedford Square in the first winter of war: by now Lady Ottoline was including among her guests young writers such as David Garnett★ and T. S. Eliot,★ the artists Gertler,★ Carrington★ and Brett,★ and also D. H. Lawrence★ and his wife, whom she treated with a generosity ill-repaid. She gave hospitality to refugees from France and Belgium, and helped equip a field hospital, but she regarded the war as a tragic mistake and consistently supported pacifists hounded by London's flag-waving patriots. By the summer of 1915—when Strachey, Duncan Grant★

and Vanessa Bell were among the first guests at Garsington—she was presiding over what was not so much an anti-war salon as a liberal, cultural retreat-house, with mullioned windows looking out towards a hedged garden, where the peacocks shrieked. Conscientious objectors, including Gerald Shove* and Clive Bell, were allowed to work in the fields of the Garsington farm. At the same time Lady Ottoline remained on friendly terms with the Prime Minister, Herbert Asquith, who had petted her when she first came to London, before her marriage. On the last Sunday in May 1916—three days before the battle of Jutland—the Prime Minister, Lytton Strachey, Carrington, Lady Robert Cecil,* Bertrand Russell and Maynard Keynes* were all at Garsington, taking tea on the lawn.

Lady Ottoline was constantly welcoming new friends to her community: writers like W. B. Yeats, Aldous Huxley,* Siegfried Sassoon, André Gide, Katherine Mansfield* and Middleton Murry;* progressive churchmen like Dick Sheppard of St Martin's-in-the-Fields and Charles Gore, the Anglo-Catholic Bishop of Oxford from 1911 to 1919. After the war Garsington attracted young undergraduates from neighbouring Oxford, some of whom like Ritchie* and Senhouse* were particularly welcomed into the Bloomsbury set. Three Garsington guests caused her distress: Pearsall Smith* by malicious gossip, and the novelists Lawrence and Huxley who ridiculed her way of life, thinly disguised, in *Women in Love* (1920) and *Crome Yellow* (1921). By 1926 she was growing tired of country-house life at Garsington and at midsummer in 1927 she returned to London, holding court, generally on Wednesday evenings, at 10 Gower Street, Bloomsbury, for the last eleven years of her life. As early as 1926 she had begun work on her memoirs, sending some extracts to Virginia Woolf for her comments, and she continued to work on them in the early 1930s, but they were published posthumously, in two volumes. In the spring of 1928 she was seriously ill with what appears to have been a dental infection and became deaf, but she recovered much of her old social vigour. She suffered a stroke in May 1937 and died in a clinic at Tunbridge Wells on the following 21 April. A moving tribute to her by Virginia Woolf in *The Times* of 28 April 1938 is reprinted in *The Diary of Virginia Woolf* (Vol. V, appendix 2).

R. Gathorne-Hardy (ed.), *Ottoline*, Vol. I, *The Early Memoirs* (London, 1963) and Vol. II, *Ottoline at Garsington, 1915–1918* (London, 1974)

S. J. Darroch, *Ottoline* (London, 1976)
C. J. Heilbrun (ed.), *Lady Ottoline's Album* (London, 1976)

MORRELL, Philip Edward (1870–1943), lawyer: born in Oxford, a member of an Oxfordshire brewing family, although his father was a lawyer and his mother was the daughter of an Oxford head of college. He was educated at Eton and Balliol College, Oxford, becoming a solicitor. In February 1902 he married Lady Ottoline Cavendish-Bentinck (*supra*). He was elected Liberal M.P. for the Henley division of Oxfordshire in 1906 but lost the seat in January 1910. Eleven months later he was returned as M.P. for Burnley, a constituency he represented until he retired from politics in 1918. Morrell was one of the few M.P.s who spoke out against British entry into the First World War, arguing on 3 August 1914 that no country could claim to be defending civilisation if it were fighting in alliance with so repressive a system of government as Tsarist Russia. His subsequent sympathy with the pacifist cause cost him much support in his constituency.

In March 1913 Morrell had purchased Garsington Manor, five miles south-east of Oxford, originally a Tudor house. During and after the war he was a gentleman-farmer at Garsington, providing accommodation and work in his fields for several conscientious objectors. He did not, however, understand the economics of farming, his losses contributing to his wife's decision in 1927 to return from Oxfordshire to London. Philip Morrell was a good host, both in Bloomsbury and at Garsington, playing a pianola, encouraging the writers—particularly Aldous Huxley★ and Lytton Strachey★—and tolerating his wife's extravagant gestures as patroness of a modernism he often failed to comprehend. He had marital infidelities of his own, fathering his secretary's son in 1917. At one time he had hoped to be an actor and he maintained a lively interest in literature and the arts after his wife's death, but his only book was an edition of *Leaves from the Greville Diary*, published two years after the Morrells left Garsington. He died in the first week of February 1943.

MORTIMER, (Charles) Raymond Bell (1895–1980), author and literary critic: educated at Malvern College and Balliol College, Oxford. As he was rejected on medical grounds for service in the

First World War, he found work in the hospital at Cannes, later returning to England and accepting a temporary post at the Foreign Office. He became a lifelong friend of Harold Nicolson★ and Edward Sackville-West★ and, by the autumn of 1923, was a holiday companion of Maynard Keynes★ and Rylands★ in Dorset, where he met the Woolfs★★ for the first time. By the following spring he was accepted as a regular member of "new Bloomsbury", having moved his home from Chelsea to Gordon Square. In 1927, on Virginia Woolf's initiative, he joined the *New Statesman*, becoming the paper's Literary Editor from 1935 to 1947; he was also literary and drama critic of *Vogue*. He modelled his style on Desmond MacCarthy★ (whom he was to succeed as principal critic on the *Sunday Times* in 1949). Mortimer enjoyed travelling: he was with Nicolson in Teheran, Clive Bell★ in Berlin, and Lytton Strachey★ and Roger Senhouse★ in Copenhagen. But his great love was France, especially its cuisine and its paintings. In his youth he was accepted into the Roman Catholic Church, although he never joined the circle of convert literary zealots. He was a connoisseur of old masters who also gained amusement from reading about the eccentricities of nineteenth-century divines and found solace in music.

Mortimer's output of books was small: *Channel Packet* in 1942; *Manet's Bar aux Folies-Bergère* in 1944; and, in the same year, a brief assessment of his friend Duncan Grant★ for The Penguin Modern Artists series. So demanding were his critical powers that he refused to allow publication of his own Clark lectures, given at Cambridge soon after the war, on *Five Dissident Voices* in Victorian England. His Francophilia gained Mortimer the Légion d'Honneur and he was created C.B.E. in 1955.

C. R. B. Mortimer, *Try Anything Once* (London, 1976)

MURRY, John Middleton (1889–1957), journalist and critic: born in Peckham, his father being a copy clerk in the War Office. From a local state elementary school he gained a scholarship to Christ's Hospital, subsequently going up to Brasenose College, Oxford, where he became Editor of an avant-garde periodical, *Rhythm*, in 1911, a year before he graduated. At Oxford he was a friend of the novelists Joyce Cary and Michael Sadleir. After settling in London Murry continued to edit *Rhythm* for a year, while also contributing to the *Westminster Gazette*. *Rhythm*, however, lost him money and by 1913 he was a bankrupt.

Murry met Katherine Mansfield* while still an undergraduate; she became his mistress in 1912 and eventually, in 1918, the first of his four wives. Their relationship was often tempestuous, and her admirers—notably Koteliansky*—deplored Murry's lack of consideration for his companion's health and sensitivities. Murry's friendship with D. H. Lawrence,* from 1913 onwards, was also stormy, although close during the early years of the war. He met Lytton Strachey* in 1915 and, early in 1916, was introduced by Waterlow* to Virginia Woolf.* By then he was a member of the Morrell* circle at Garsington. He moved into Bloomsbury in the autumn of 1916, sharing an apartment with Katherine Mansfield at 3 Gower Street, Maynard Keynes,* Carrington,* Brett,* Shove* and Sheppard* living on other floors of the same house. His first novel, *Still Life*, was published in that year, but he was able to write only in the evenings as he was employed by the War Office during the day, primarily to compile an abstract from foreign newspapers. He remained an undischarged bankrupt until 1921 and was glad to continue his work at the War Office even after the Armistice. In 1919 he became Chief Censor and in 1920 received an O.B.E. for his services to military intelligence. His duties did not, however, prevent his completing a study of Dostoyevsky, published on the eve of the Russian Revolution.

From 1919 to 1921 Murry was the last editor of *The Athenaeum*, with Virginia Woolf, Strachey, and T. S. Eliot* among his contributors. It was during this period that Murry published *The Evolution of an Intellectual* (1920) following it up with a literary study of *The Problem of Style* in 1922. By now Virginia Woolf, who admired the clarity of his mind a few years earlier, had decided that Murry belonged to the pretentious literary "underworld" of what she regarded as spurious intellectuals. Murry, however, enjoyed considerable stature as an authority on English literary style: he was a guest lecturer at both Oxford and Cambridge; and in 1923 he founded a new monthly journal, *The Adelphi*, which for the seven years of his editorship tended to strike Lawrentian attitudes in criticism. A growing poetic delight in metaphysical romanticism isolated Murry from Bloomsbury: a *Life of Jesus* (1926) was followed in 1932 by *The Necessity of Communism* and five years later by *The Necessity of Pacifism*. At the same time Murry frequently paid homage to the memory of his first wife, who had died in 1923: reminiscences and editions of her letters helped create an image of Katherine Mansfield at variance with his treatment of her during her lifetime. Inconsistencies continued throughout Murry's later life: the Christian pacifist who was editor of *Peace News* from 1940 to 1946 could also write *The Free Society* (1948), which virtually called for a preventive war against the Soviet Union. He completed, in all, more than forty books, his final study—*Love, Freedom and Society*—appearing only two days before his death. In *Who's Who* Murry listed his profession as "author and farmer", for he spent his last years in the rich agricultural country around Diss, in Norfolk, dying in hospital at Bury St Edmunds on 13 March 1957.

F. A. Lea, *John Middleton Murry* (London, 1959)

N

NICOLSON, Harold George (1886–1968), diplomat and author: born in Teheran where his father (later the first Lord Carnock) was acting head of the British Legation, He was educated at Wellington College and at Balliol College, Oxford, and entered the diplomatic service in 1909. He was in the British delegation to the Paris Peace Conference in 1919 and later undertook important duties at Teheran and Berlin. In October 1913 he married Vita Sackville-West★ at Knole and was the father of two sons, Benedict (1914–78), the art historian, and Nigel (born 1917), publisher and author. Harold Nicolson left the diplomatic service in December 1929 to have greater freedom to pursue the literary career which had already produced biographical studies of Tennyson, Byron, Verlaine and Swinburne and the nine semi-fictitious character sketches of *Some People* (1927). He wrote biographies of his father, an account of Curzon's later years, studies of peacemaking in 1919 and in 1814–15, and the official biography of King George V (1952), an undertaking which earned him a knighthood. He sat in the Commons as National Labour M.P. for West Leicester from 1935 to 1945 and, as Parliamentary Secretary to the Ministry of Information, was in 1940–1 a junior minister. Three volumes of extracts from his diaries were edited by his younger son (1966–8).

Harold Nicolson was never a member of the Bloomsbury circle. He strongly disliked Lytton Strachey★ but respected the Woolfs.★★ In January 1929 he was perplexed by the behaviour of Virginia and Leonard Woolf, Vanessa Bell★ and Duncan Grant★ whom he sought to entertain when, with his wife Vita, they came to Berlin. He tolerated the brief physical relationship in the long friendship which bound Vita and Virginia, not least because he was himself at times in love with young men.

J. Lees-Milne, *Harold Nicolson, a Biography* (2 vols, London, 1980; 1982)

NIJINSKY, Vaslav (1889–1950), Russian male dancer: born at Kiev, both his parents being dancers. He graduated from the Imperial Ballet School at St Petersburg in 1907 and was the sensational star of that season, as he was also when he danced with the Diaghilev company in Paris for the first time two years later. When in 1911 he resigned from the Maryinsky Theatre after conflicts with the management, Diaghilev* established his touring Ballets Russes as an independent company based upon Nijinsky's gifts, not only as a dancer but as a choreographer, notably of *L'après-midi d'un faune* (1912) and *Le Sacre du Printemps* (1913). Nijinsky's sudden marriage to the Hungarian dancer, Romola de Pulszky, in September 1913 ended his homosexual relationship with his impresario, and Diaghilev at once severed all links with Nijinsky. The emotional conflict was so intense that Nijinsky's mind began to waver. A brief attempt at running a company of his own in 1914 ended in failure. He rejoined the Diaghilev company for a North American tour in 1916–17 but his mind became so deranged that, on his return to Europe, he suffered a total breakdown. Much of his remaining thirty-four years of life was spent in mental hospitals. He died in London.

Nijinsky danced in England in 1911 and in the following summer was socially lionized, particularly—but not exclusively—by Lady Ottoline Morrell.* Richard Buckle's researches suggest that it was on 12 July 1912 that Nijinsky and Bakst* were so impressed by the sight of Duncan Grant* and Adrian Stephen* playing tennis in a London square that they used this vignette of Bloomsbury life in their joint ballet *Jeux*, presented in Paris in May 1913. Lytton Strachey* greatly admired his dancing, especially in *Petrushka*, but was disappointed when he met him and, after his marriage, thought him a "cretinous lackey". Less subjective critics more charitably deplored the tragic illness which so swiftly doused his flame of artistic creativity.

R. Buckle, *Nijinsky* (London, 1971) and *Diaghilev* (London, 1979)

NORTON, Henry Tertius James (1886–1937), mathematician: a wealthy Etonian who went up to Trinity College, Cambridge, in October 1905 and showed outstanding intelligence, his contemporaries rating him alongside Bertrand Russell,* with whom he could creditably sustain an argument. "Harry" Norton was elected an Apostle in 1906, became a lifelong friend of Lytton Strachey,* and was a member of the Bloomsbury group by the summer of 1908. Virginia Woolf,* in a memoir printed in *Moments of Being*, recalled him as "the essence of all I meant by Cambridge; so able; so honest; so ugly; so dry . . . scowling in his pince-nez, yellow and severe against a bank of roses and carnations". He became a devoted admirer of Vanessa Bell,* accompanying the Bells and Roger Fry* to Turkey in 1911. Later he was attracted to Carrington* and to Alix Sargant-Florence (Strachey*). During the First World War he was a conscientious objector. He joined Lytton Strachey for several holidays and, as he continued to enjoy a considerable private income, made him several loans, putting up the money from which the Mill House, Tidmarsh, was purchased. In 1918 Strachey dedicated *Eminent Victorians* "to H.T.J.N.".

Norton was elected a Fellow of Trinity in 1910 and began to seek to advance the theory of numbers which Georg Cantor had developed in the late nineteenth century. Papers by Norton were printed in *The Proceedings of the London Mathematical Society* for 1917 and 1928; but no great work appeared. Norton had long suffered from alternations of excitability and despair. He designed the walled garden at Charleston with mathematical precision, but in November 1920 collapsed completely, spending most of that winter in Gordon Square receiving treatment from the psychological specialist consulted by the Woolfs in 1912 and 1915. Although Norton was well enough to resume his mathematical studies, he never triumphed over his sense of inadequacy and by the 1930s wished only to retire into obscurity.

OLIVIER, Noel (1892–1969), doctor; youngest of the four beautiful daughters of Sydney (later Lord) Olivier, who was Governor of Jamaica, the first Labour peer, Secretary of State for India, and Laurence Olivier's uncle. Noel was educated at Bedales School and the London School of Medicine for Women. Two older sisters went up to Newnham College, Cambridge, Margery (1887–1974) in 1907, and Daphne (1889–1950) in 1910. They belonged to Rupert Brooke's★ "Neo-Pagan" circle, and included their sisters Brynhild (1887–1935) and Noel in their bathing and camping parties, with their childhood friend David Garnett.★ Noel was loved by Brooke, Adrian Stephen★ and James Strachey,★ and Adrian's sister Virginia (Woolf★) was sure that she would have made him a wonderful wife. Noel's affair with James Strachey, begun after Brooke's death (1915), lasted until 1938.

In 1917 Noel Olivier qualified as a doctor, and early in 1919 helped save the life of the new-born Angelica Bell (Garnett★), by sending her friend, Dr Marie Moralt, to replace the Bells' out-of-date practitioner. Noel married Dr Arthur Richards of Llanelli in 1921, at St Martin's-in-the-Fields. They had three children, Benedict, Angela, who compiled the index volume of James Strachey's translation of Freud, and Virginia, named for her "godmother" Virginia Woolf.

Margery Olivier suffered periods of dementia, during one of which she is said to have chased her father with a carving-knife. Brynhild married Hugh Popham, late of King's College, Cambridge and a friend of the Bloomsbury men, in 1912; their daughter Anne Olivier is the wife of Quentin Bell.★★ Daphne, a teacher, married Cecil Harwood in 1925, and had three sons and a daughter.

P

PARTRIDGE, Frances Catherine (1900–), writer: born Frances Marshall in Bedford Square, London, youngest daughter of the architect William Marshall, educated at private schools and Bedales. Through her mother, a suffragist, she knew Marjorie and Philippa Strachey,** and the Rendel* family; her older sister Judy later married Dick Rendel. In 1908 her father retired to the country house he had designed for himself at Hindhead, Surrey and Frances went to school with Julia Strachey,* with whom she often stayed in the holidays, while Julia, as a boarder, spent her Sundays with the Marshalls. Frances followed Julia to Bedales in 1915, and in 1918 went up to Newnham College, Cambridge. Ballroom dancing and music were her favourite pastimes at college; her dancing partners included the future Lord Mountbatten, and she sang in the Bach Choir. By the time she left Cambridge in 1921, her father had died and her mother moved to 27 Brunswick Square, Bloomsbury.

The following year David Garnett,* who had married her sister Ray, gave Frances a post in his bookshop. Here she met the Bloomsbury circle coming in to buy books, and soon began to be invited to their parties, and to spend weekends at Charleston or the Mill House, Tidmarsh. Clive Bell* was particularly interested in her, but so was the Woolfs'** young assistant Ralph Partridge (*infra*, see also CARRINGTON and STRACHEY, Lytton) who delivered books to the shop from the Hogarth Press. Frances and Partridge began living together in 1926, first at 41 Gordon Square, then in Great James Street, where they rented a room in the house Garnett shared with the Nonesuch Press. Frances continued to work in the bookshop until 1928, when she started helping Partridge with the research he was doing for Strachey. After the deaths of Strachey and Carrington in 1932 the couple lived mainly at Ham Spray House, and were married in 1933. (Lytton) Burgo, their only son, was born in 1935.

Frances Partridge's memoirs describe her happy country life from 1939, with few anxieties apart from Burgo's education and her husband's health. The Partridges made Ham Spray a centre of entertainment for old and young Bloomsbury, enjoying visits from the Garnetts,★ the Bells★ and Duncan Grant.★ Of Frances' own circle, Julia Strachey was a particularly welcome and frequent guest. Virginia Woolf, although kind to the young couple after the tragedies of 1932, held slightly aloof and deplored in her diary and letters the changes at Ham Spray. After Partridge's death in 1960, Frances sold the house and returned to London. Her son married Henrietta Garnett and died suddenly in 1963.

As well as her autobiographical works, Frances Partridge produced many translations from French and Spanish authors, and a life of Julia Strachey based on her friend's memoirs, *Julia* (1983).

Frances Partridge, *A Pacifist's War* (London, 1978); *Memories* (London, 1982); *Everything to Lose* (London, 1985)

PARTRIDGE, Reginald Sherring (1894–1960), son of William Partridge of the Indian Civil Service, educated at Westminster School and Christ Church, Oxford (1913). From 1914 to 1918 he served in France, Belgium and Italy, ending the war as a Major with the Military Cross and bar and the Croce de Guerra. He was twice wounded and once buried alive. Back at Oxford he gained a distinction after a shortened English course (1920) although he was originally a classicist. Much time was spent rowing, but he refused selection for the university boat.

Partridge's life was re-shaped when, in July 1918, his pre-war college friend, Noel Carrington, introduced him to his sister (Carrington★). She invited him to Tidmarsh and he soon fell in love with her. Although he affected to despise her companion, Lytton Strachey,★ and disagreed with his views, gradually the two men became great friends. Strachey was attracted by the obstinately heterosexual Partridge's good looks; he contributed much to his intellectual development and dubbed him "Ralph"—the name stuck. Carrington and Partridge became lovers during a Spanish holiday in 1919; he moved into the Mill House a year later, but she would not marry him.

In October 1920 the Woolfs** engaged Partridge as a part-time assistant at the Hogarth Press. Although initially successful he failed in the end to satisfy Leonard's exacting standards, like all Hogarth employees. Virginia blamed him, in March 1921, for muddling the publication date of *Monday or Tuesday*, thereby, as she thought, losing her the expected reviews; a party he gave to celebrate Strachey's *Queen Victoria*, published that same month, did not raise his standing with the Woolfs. Nevertheless he made Virginia his confidante over Carrington's behaviour. Although Virginia thought he would be a "despotic" husband, she encouraged a marriage in order to preserve the status quo at Tidmarsh. The couple were married in May 1921, but another crisis arose a year later over Carrington's affair with Gerald Brenan.* Strachey forestalled an explosion and reconciled Ralph to Brenan but failed to keep him at the Press. When Partridge finally left Hogarth in March 1923 he became Strachey's secretary and agent, supplementing his income by learning bookbinding.

By now Partridge had met Frances Marshall (*supra*) and by 1923 was pursuing her with the intensity he sought Carrington. Yet he still felt deeply attached to Strachey and Carrington, both of whom had come to depend upon him; their new home, Ham Spray House, was bought in 1924 in Ralph's name and partly with a legacy from his father. After much anguish Ralph and Frances agreed to live together during the week in rooms at 41 Gordon Square, James Strachey's* home. Every weekend Partridge would go down to Ham Spray, sometimes on his own. This arrangement worked well enough until Lytton Strachey's last illness in the winter of 1931–2. When Carrington's nerves gave way, Partridge remained at Ham Spray to support her and to organise the household. He frustrated her first suicide attempt on 20 January 1932, the eve of Strachey's death, and tried thereafter to ensure her time was occupied. But while he was in London on 11 March she shot herself; he returned with Frances and David Garnett* only to see her die. The double bereavement agonised him so intensely that Frances feared for his life; but a long trip to France, revisiting the battlefields, put the more recent horrors in proportion. In 1933 he married Frances Marshall and settled down again at Ham Spray.

They had begun research in 1928 for Strachey's projected *The Greville Memoirs*. When Roger Fulford took over the editing, the Partridges remained responsible for the index, working on it until 1937. During the Second World War Partridge, now a convinced pacifist, was exempted from military service after taking his case to an appeal tribunal. From the late 1940s, he reviewed crime novels and history for the *New Statesman* and, after visiting Broadmoor, he became interested in abnormal criminology, his book *Broadmoor* appearing in 1953. But from 1956 he suffered from heart disease and he died suddenly at Ham Spray House on 30 November 1960.

PICASSO, Pablo Ruiz (1881–1973), artist: born in Malaga but first showed his artistic talents in Barcelona from 1898 onwards, settling in Montmartre in April 1904. His search for an angular style which could express his revolt against naturalism led him in the spring of 1907 to display a huge and incomplete canvas of five female nudes to his friends, who nicknamed this sensational work *Les Demoiselles d'Avignon*. Within eighteen months Picasso—like his friend, Georges Braque—was beginning to experiment with cubism in a major revolt against the traditions which had dominated representional art for the past six centuries.

The first Englishman to appreciate the significance of Picasso's work was Roger Fry* who selected two pre-cubist oils—*Nude Girl with Basket of Flowers* (1905) and *Portrait of Clovis Sagot* (1909)—for his first Post-Impressionist exhibition, which opened in November 1910. Two years later Fry included thirteen Picasso paintings and three drawings in the second Post-Impressionist exhibition, some of those chosen being analytically cubist in form. During the war Picasso broadened his cultural interests by associating with Diaghilev* and the Russian ballet and he did not come to London until July 1919, twelve months after his marriage to the dancer Olga Khoklova, who was the daughter of a senior Tsarist army officer. Picasso was responsible for the décor of the ballet *The Three Cornered Hat*, which opened at the Alhambra Theatre on 22 July 1919. Husband and wife, who stayed at the Savoy Hotel, were fêted by London society: Picasso (and Derain*) were guests of Roger and Margery Fry* at Dalmeny Avenue and met other "Bloomsberries" at a dinner given jointly by Clive Bell* and Keynes* in Gordon Square; and the Picassos were entertained by the Morrells* at Garsington. In 1922 Clive Bell wrote a preface for the catalogue of the first major exhibition of Picasso's work in London; members of the Bell family* and Duncan Grant* visited Picasso's studio in Paris on several occasions, notably in 1937 when they were awed by the massive canvas on which he sought to capture the tragedy of *Guernica*. Picasso's friendship with Lydia Lopokova,* dating from 1918, survived the break-up of his marriage in 1935; they met again in November 1950 on his only other visit to Britain. He died at Mougins, near Cannes, in April 1973.

R. Penrose, *Picasso, His Life and Work* (3rd edn, London, 1971)

PLOMER, William Charles Franklyn (1903–73), novelist, poet and biographer: born, of English parents from Pinner, in Pietermaritzburg, and educated at Rugby School up to the age of fifteen when, for health reasons, he returned to South Africa. There, in his early twenties, he wrote a bitterly satirical novel, *Turbott Wolfe*, which he sent to the Hogarth Press; Leonard and Virginia Woolf★★ so liked his work that they published the novel in 1926. He spent two years teaching in Japan and returned to England in April 1929, being immediately welcomed into the Bloomsbury circle, where he remained a particular friend of the Woolfs. A book of his poems, *The Family Tree*, was published by the Hogarth Press in the autumn of 1929 and his novel about Japan, *Sado*, in 1931. Plomer also wrote a biography of Cecil Rhodes, which appeared in 1933, several more volumes of poetry and collections of short stories, and four librettos for Benjamin Britten, his *Gloriana* (1953) owing much of its character to Strachey's *Elizabeth and Essex*. He became best known in England for editing the three volumes of *Kilvert's Diary* (1938–44). During the war he worked at the Admiralty. In 1963 he received the Queen's Gold Medal for Poetry and in 1968 was created C.B.E.

PROBY, Granville (1883–1947), barrister: the son of an army officer. He was a friend of Maynard Keynes★ at Eton, where he was known as Hamilton, his father subsequently changing the surname to Proby by deed poll. He went up to Trinity College, Oxford, in 1902 and was called to the bar of the Middle Temple. Occasionally he entertained Keynes' friends at Oxford, notably Lytton Strachey.★ From 1907 to 1944 he was Clerk of the House of Lords. When the Memoir Club was established in 1920 his name was among those whom Molly MacCarthy★ proposed as founder members, but he never joined the group. From 1926 to 1935 he was joint Editor of the *Victoria County History of Huntingdonshire;* he became High Sheriff of Cambridgeshire and Huntingdonshire in 1935, and was Lord Lieutenant of Huntingdonshire in 1946. He was made a Companion of the Bath two months before his death.

RAVERAT, Gwendolen Mary, *née* Darwin (1885–1957), painter and wood-engraver: born in Cambridge, the elder daughter of the Professor of Astronomy, Sir George Darwin, and a granddaughter of the great scientist, Charles Darwin; her mother was an American, born Maud du Pay in Pennsylvania. Gwen Darwin received her basic education at home from a governess, but learnt Latin and German with her brother, Charles, and in 1901 went at her own request to a boarding-school. By 1907 she was studying painting at the Slade School but she retained close links with Cambridge, appearing with Rupert Brooke★ in the Marlowe Society's *Comus* of 1908 and becoming a friend of the Stephen family★ and of Jacques Raverat (*infra*). Her sister married Geoffrey Keynes.★ Gwen Darwin was recognised as a painter of talent but she learnt carving from her sister-in-law, Elinor Darwin, and this soon became her speciality. She exhibited from 1912 to 1940 and in 1920 was accepted as one of the original members of the Society of Wood-Engravers. She married Jacques Raverat in May 1911 and was the mother of two daughters. After her husband's death—and having suffered disappointment in her love for another French painter—she spent much of her life at Harlton, near Cambridge. With the backing of her friend Virginia Woolf★ she secured a post with *Time and Tide;* her reminiscences of childhood, *Period Piece,* were published in 1952.

RAVERAT, Jacques Pierre (1885–1925), French painter: born in Provence but educated in England at Bedales before going to the Sorbonne and to Emmanuel College, Cambridge, as a mathematician. At the university he became one of the "Neo-Pagan" disciples of Rupert Brooke★ and was a friend of Geoffrey Keynes★ and of the mountaineer, Mallory.★ Through the Neo-Pagan circle he met "Ka" Cox,★ to whom he was greatly attracted, and Gwen Darwin (*supra*), whom he married on 27 May 1911. Virginia Stephen (Woolf★) was a guest at their wedding; her letters show slight jealousy of their attachment, mingled with admiration for Raverat as a handsome, strong-minded, anglicised French intellectual.

Raverat's principal relaxation, painting, had increasingly absorbed his interest by 1909, and after his marriage it dominated his life. The Raverats settled near Vence in the Alpes-Maritimes but he remained a member of the New English Art Club, with whom he exhibited in the summer of 1918. He renewed his friendship with the Woolfs, by letter, in 1922 and for three years Virginia Woolf maintained with him a curious correspondence in which serious comparative analysis of the artistic satisfaction derived respectively from writing and from painting alternated with gossip about post-war Bloomsbury. In these last years Raverat suffered from disseminated sclerosis, bravely seeking to continue his painting with brushes tied to his hands. At last, on 7 March 1925, paralysis claimed his life. He greatly admired Virginia Woolf's skills as essayist and novelist and, in his last dictated letter to her, praised *Mrs Dalloway*, which she had sent him in proof.

RENDEL, Frances Elinor (Ellie) (1885–1942), daughter of Lytton Strachey's★ eldest sister Elinor and James Rendel. She was educated at Kensington High School for Girls in the 1890s, becoming very friendly with Ray Costelloe (Strachey★), whom she introduced to the Strachey family circle. In 1904 Ellie went up to Newnham College, Cambridge, and after taking her degree spent the year 1908–9 at Bryn Mawr College, U.S.A., together with Ray. The two friends became active in the Women's Suffrage movement, first in America, then on speaking tours of England. However, Ray's love affair with Ellie's uncle, Oliver Strachey,★ greatly disturbed Ellie. When she and Ray visited Corfe Castle at Easter 1911, and found Oliver staying there too, she became temporarily blind, so that Ray had to lead her about the village.

Despondency about her future and Ray's marriage led to a nervous breakdown, but on her recovery Ellie decided to train as a doctor. She studied medicine at London University (1912–15), and served during the war as a dresser with the Scottish Women's Hospital in Romania (1915) and as an X-ray operator in the Balkans

(1917). From 1921 Ellie was in general practice, and became Virginia Woolf's* doctor, delaying the completion of *The Waves* by being an hour and a half late for an appointment on 4 February 1931. Although Ellie did not attend Lytton Strachey officially, she was present during his last illness to interpret the specialists, and give her own mistaken diagnosis of typhoid. She continued in practice until the year of her death.

RITCHIE, Lady Anne (1837–1919), daughter of William Thackeray (1811–63), and "Aunt Anny" to several of the Bloomsbury group. Leslie Stephen's* first wife was her sister Minny (Harriet), his second wife her own friend Julia (Stephen*); she was godmother to James Strachey,* and married Molly MacCarthy's* uncle.

Anny Thackeray's mother became insane in 1840, and the two girls were brought up by their grandparents in Paris until 1846, when their father fetched them home to educate them himself. Anny was by now a bright, determined child, who "fights every inch of her way", according to her grandmother. She grew up accustomed to the society of authors, and Thackeray encouraged her to write, publishing her first story in his *Cornhill Magazine* in 1860. When their father died the sisters were lent a cottage at Freshwater, Isle of Wight, by their friend Julia Margaret Cameron, the photographer and aunt of Julia Jackson (later Stephen). On their return to London they lived together in Kensington, until in 1867 Leslie Stephen married Minny and joined the household. Through him Anny met the new literary generation, and became friendly with Henry James,* Hardy and Meredith.

After Minny's death in 1875, Anny, Leslie and his daughter Laura* moved to Hyde Park Gate. Two years later, and much against Leslie's wishes, she left to marry Richmond Ritchie, seventeen years her junior and just down from Cambridge. The marriage was a success, and the Ritchies had two children, Hester, who attended Mlle Souvestre's* school with the Strachey girls, and William. Anny continued to visit the Stephen family, however, and her cheerful astringency was particularly welcome to them during the gloomy years when Leslie Stephen, once more a widower, was dying of cancer. She made her own Freshwater cottage available to the Stephens, warmly approving of their new home in Bloomsbury after Leslie's death in 1904.

Through all the changes in her life, Anny went on writing, producing six novels, memoirs, and essays on the famous literary figures she had known—Tennyson, the Brownings, Ruskin and Mrs Gaskell. In 1894 she began the complete edition of her father's works with biographical introductions to each volume; it was finished in 1898 and was followed by a centenary edition in 1911. Lady Ritchie (Richmond was knighted in 1907) survived her husband's death (1912), living long enough to vote among the first enfranchised women in the 1918 election. In her obituary in *The Times Literary Supplement* of 6 March 1919, Virginia Woolf described her as "a true artist", and painted an affectionate portrait of "Aunt Anny" as the novelist Mrs Hilbery in *Night and Day*, published later that year.

Winifred Gérin, *Anne Thackeray Ritchie* (Oxford, 1981)

RITCHIE, Philip Charles Thomson (1899–1927), barrister: was the eldest son of the second Baron Ritchie of Dundee. He was educated at Magdalen College, Oxford and was called to the bar in Lincoln's Inn. While an undergraduate he became an occasional guest at Garsington where, in 1923, he met Lytton Strachey★ who was much attracted by him, subsequently sending him love poems and entertaining him at Ham Spray House; it was Ritchie who introduced Roger Senhouse★ to Strachey. By February 1925 Ritchie was in the chambers of Charles Sanger★ in Lincoln's Inn and was a regular participant in Bloomsbury parties. He contracted severe tonsillitis in the summer of 1927 and underwent a tonsillectomy which was followed a few days later by a haemorrhage and eventually by septic pneumonia, from which he died in mid-September.

ROBERTSON, Ainslie John (1880–1954), businessman: born in Harrow, the son of the Reverend James R. Robertson, who by the turn of the century was vicar of Whittleford in Cambridgeshire. Ainslie Robertson was educated at Winchester College, going up to Trinity College, Cambridge, in October 1899 as a Pensioner. He was elected to a Classics scholarship in 1901 and subsequently gained first-class honours in the first part of the Classics Tripos. His career thereafter was entirely in commerce: he was Assistant Secretary of the Booth Steamship Co., 1905–18, and then Manager, 1918–20. For seven years he was a Liverpool fruit-broker and

President of the Fruit-Brokers' Association in 1925–6, before ending his career as Managing Director of the Hurricane Smock Co., 1928–40, and retiring to Goring-on-Thames. In 1904 he had edited a collection of his father's poems, *Arachnia*, but his greatest recreational interest was in music; he was Chairman of the Liverpool Philharmonic Society in 1926–7 and again in 1934–6. He married Phyllis Roughton in 1910; their son, James Robertson (born 1912) gained distinction as a conductor and opera director in Britain, Canada and New Zealand.

Ainslie Robertson joined Clive Bell,★ Lytton Strachey,★ Leonard Woolf,★ and Saxon Sydney-Turner★ as a founder-member of the reading club (Midnight Society) established at Trinity College in January or February 1900 and regarded by Bell—in his book, *Old Friends*—as the prototype for Bloomsbury's Thursday evenings. Strachey, in particular, appears to have found the tall, cherubic-faced Robertson agreeable but he does not seem to have remained in this select group for long, possibly because of his Anglican religious background. He is unlikely to have come to Gordon Square although Virginia Woolf,★ in her Memoir Club paper of 1921–2 on "Old Bloomsbury", mentions him as the butt of a Strachey joke.

His younger brother, Sir Dennis Robertson (1890–1963), was a pupil of Keynes★ who subsequently became a Fellow of Trinity, Professor of Economics at London, adviser to the Treasury and President of the Royal Economic Society from 1948 to 1950. By 1931 he was highly critical of Keynes' theories but the two men were friends and colleagues throughout much of the 1920s, giving Dennis Robertson that fringe contact with Bloomsbury which his brother, Ainslie, never possessed. Sir Dennis, a good actor as an undergraduate, took the role of head eunuch in Strachey's *A Son of Heaven* when it was performed at the Scala Theatre in 1925.

ROTHENSTEIN, William (1872–1945), painter and art historian: born in Bradford, the son of Moritz Rothenstein (1836–1914), a prosperous wool merchant who had emigrated from Hanover in 1859, and his wife, Bertha (1844–1913), daughter of a Jewish banker from Hildesheim. "Willie" was educated at Bradford Grammar School, the Slade School and the Académie Julian in Paris, maintained by generous grants from his affluent parents. While in Paris he was able to observe the work of Degas and Toulouse-Lautrec, and he was prominent among the British artistic expatriates; he knew not only Sickert,* MacColl,* Walter Steer and Roger Fry* but an older generation, including Whistler and Oscar Wilde. By 1893 he was back in England, sketching at Oxford and in Chelsea. As a young artist of twenty he visited 22 Hyde Park Gate and sketched Leslie Stephen's* wife, for he was a friend of her son, George Duckworth.* He remembered Julia Stephen's* beauty and her daughters "looking as though they had walked straight out of a canvas by Watts or Burne-Jones"; but his drawing offended Mrs Jackson (Julia Stephen's mother) who, as he recalled, in her indignation rose from her sickbed, "came heavily downstairs, and the piece of her mind which she gave me was a solid one".

In Chelsea others thought more highly of Willie Rothenstein's talents, particularly of his portrait drawings, and he joined the New English Art Club in 1894. Five years later he married Alice Knewstub (1870–1958), the actress daughter of Rossetti's assistant, Walter Knewstub; their elder son, Sir John Rothenstein, Director of the Tate Gallery from 1938 to 1964 and a hostile critic of the Bloomsbury artists, was born in July 1901.

William Rothenstein, although less responsive to new trends than his friend, Roger Fry, was uneasy at the conventional attitudes of the Royal Academy, declining an Associateship in December 1908; but he was also often critical of the N.E.A.C. and eager to find some new source of inspiration. In 1910–11 he became interested in Indian art and sculpture, visited the sub-continent and was therefore abroad for the first Post-Impressionist exhibition in November 1910. Before the second of these exhibitions Rothenstein had quarrelled with Fry: they disagreed over aesthetics, Rothenstein arguing that English painters could never be interested in "form for its own sake"; they held markedly different opinions on the merits of Cézanne and Matisse;* and there were misunderstandings over Fry's management of the exhibition, particularly concerning Rothenstein's Indian work. Rothenstein eventually declined to have anything to do with the exhibition and for several years there was tension between the two old friends.

This quarrel left Rothenstein cut off from the Bloomsbury artists. He shone, however, elsewhere in London society, not least in the Ottoline Morrell* galaxy. Moreover his generosity had already led him to give patronage to the Jewish Educational Aid Society and he had recognised the talents of the young Gertler,* as early as October 1908, using influence to find him a place at the Slade. Rothenstein also introduced the Bengali scholar Rabindranath Tagore to London literary and artistic circles in the late spring of 1912.

Rothenstein took the initiative in suggesting, in 1916, the official encouragement of artists who would record Britain's contribution to the war, but because of his Germanic name the French long refused to allow him to go to the Front. His own public career owed much to the support of Herbert Fisher,* who persuaded him in 1917 to become Professor of Civic Art at Sheffield University and in 1920 appointed him Principal of the Royal College of Art, even though he was without previous administrative experience. He was knighted in 1931. In later years he gave Virginia Woolf* information for her biography of Fry but she consistently refused to sit for him and, while writing amicably to him personally, continued to show a marked distaste for him in her letters to other acquaintances.

Although Sir William had suffered a heart attack as early as 1925 and spent much of the following decade writing three long volumes of memoirs, he again encouraged a war artists scheme in 1939 and saw to it that he was unofficially attached to the R.A.F. so that he could fly to numerous airfields and bases and sketch a new album of portraits even when he was approaching seventy. His *Men of the RAF* was published in 1942. The strain of these flights, however, weakened his health and he died three months before the end of the war in Europe.

W. Rothenstein, *Men and Memories* (originally 3 vols, London, 1931, 1932, 1939); abridged edn. by Mary Lago (London, 1978)

RUSSELL, Alys ("Loo") (1867–1951), first wife of Bertrand Russell (*infra*): born Alice (Pearsall) Smith, daughter of Robert and Hannah Smith, Quakers of Philadelphia, U.S.A. Educated mainly at home, she entered Bryn Mawr in 1885, the year of its foundation. Alys first met the seventeen-year-old Bertrand Russell in the summer of 1889, while staying at her parents' English home, but it was not until they met again at Cambridge in 1893 that they began the friendship that developed into love. Tales of Russell insanity spread by old Lady Russell and clear signs of recurring depressive illness in Alys' family did not deter the couple, but they decided never to have children. Their marriage took place in Quaker Meeting on 13 December 1894.

After visiting Europe and America, the Russells took a cottage near Alys' parents' home and spent every spring term in Cambridge, as Bertrand was now a Fellow of Trinity. Alys continued her work for a temperance charity though her husband had argued away the religious beliefs that first inspired her. Both were puritanically inclined and happy with a simple life, but their marriage failed because of Russell's growing dislike of his wife's relatives and his inability to remain interested in any woman for more than a few years. They stayed together, although Alys' health suffered from the strain, and even found a new common interest when Alys helped Bertrand stand as Women's Suffrage candidate in the 1907 Wimbledon by-election, but in 1911 a separation was finally agreed.

Alys went to live with her brother Logan (Smith★), at Ford Place, Sussex and later at Chilling on the Solent. Although awkward and severe with the children, she had tried to help her mother in the upbringing of her sister Mary's (Berenson★) daughters, Ray (Strachey★) and Karin (Stephen★) and she now adopted Ray's stepdaughter Julia (Strachey★). Often her home was filled with small Stracheys and MacCarthys and their friends. From 1914 Logan took a house in Chelsea, and Alys included Belgian refugees and the Labour Party among the objects of her philanthropy. She was operated on for cancer in 1917, and was completely cured by radiation treatment nine years later. After nursing her sister Mary through a breakdown in 1918, she became depressed again herself by her divorce from Russell and his remarriage (1920–1).

Although as a young woman Alys had been painted by Fry★ and William Rothenstein,★ her contacts with Bloomsbury were now only through her nieces and Julia Strachey. Her most dramatic contribution to its legends was as hostess at the Gordon Square dance on 26 June 1920, when a guest was killed falling from the roof (see STEPHEN, Adrian). She went on looking after the increasingly manic Logan until his death in 1946, despite wartime bomb damage to their Chelsea house. She then went to live with Julia, and the close of her life was made happier by a reconciliation with Bertrand Russell.

Barbara Strachey, *Remarkable Relations* (London, 1980)

RUSSELL, Bertrand Arthur William (1872–1970), philosopher: second son of Lord and Lady Amberley, who died before he was four, and grandson of the Liberal Foreign Secretary and Prime Minister, Earl (Lord John) Russell. He had a lonely education at the home of his grandparents, but at the age of eleven learnt Euclid from his older brother Frank. At first Bertrand wanted all the axioms proved; though he progressed quickly in mathematics, he never cared to take any proposition on trust.

Russell went up to Trinity College, Cambridge as a Mathematics scholar in 1890, and was elected to the Apostles society in 1892, soon becoming more interested in philosophy than mathematics. In 1893 he inherited £20,000 and proposed to the American Quaker Alys Pearsall Smith (*supra*), whom he had met four years earlier. Despite the opposition of the widowed Lady Russell, the couple were married in December 1894, and spent some time in Berlin studying political and economic theory, as Russell had obtained a non-teaching Fellowship at Trinity. Meanwhile he and Whitehead were working together on *Principia Mathematica*, the work which was to provide a logical foundation for mathematics. His attempts at a political career were unsuccessful; he failed to be elected as a Women's Suffrage candidate at Wimbledon in 1907, and was not adopted for the Liberals at Bedford in 1909 when he became openly an agnostic. This declaration also prevented Trinity from renewing his Fellowship, although they gave him a lectureship in 1910.

Poor, depressed, and no longer in love with his wife, Russell was revived by his friendship with Lady Ottoline Morrell,★ whom he met in September 1909. Their attraction was mutual, and in 1911 Russell left Alys to become Ottoline's lover, staying for long periods at her cottage at Peppard, and later at Garsington Manor. From meetings of the Apostles and through his wife's nieces, Ray (Strachey★) and Karin (Stephen★), he already knew many of the Bloomsbury group, whose ideals he largely shared. At Garsington he met them again, together with a younger generation of artists and writers.

Although Russell remained a friend of Lady Ottoline until the 1920s, their affair was on the wane when he went to the U.S.A. in 1914 to lecture at Harvard University, where T. S. Eliot★ was a favourite pupil. He returned to a Britain at war and soon arrived by a rational route at the same pacifist position as his Bloomsbury friends, joining the No Conscription Fellowship in 1915, and writing for its journal *The Tribunal*. In 1916 he escaped prison when friends arranged the payment of a £100 fine for the publication of a leaflet approved, though not written, by him. Trinity College dismissed him from his lectureship, an action which caused a split among the Fellows and in the Apostles society. As a result of an article in May 1918 on the possibility of strike-breaking by

American troops in Britain, Russell was sentenced to six months in Brixton prison, but with more privileges than the ordinary convict.

Russell's post-war career led him away from the Bloomsbury and Garsington circles. He was married three times more, to Dora Black (1921), Patricia Spence (1936), and Edith Finch (1952). He continued to write both philosophy and political and social theory, and to lecture; in 1938 he was Visiting Professor at the Universities of Chicago, and later California. A similar post was offered him at the City College, New York in 1940, but the city was legally prevented from employing him because of his "immoral" works. After two more difficult years in the U.S.A. Trinity College decided to offer Russell a Fellowship again. The British government was unwilling to arrange his passage home at first, but in 1944 Russell was once more a Fellow of Trinity, and remained one until his death.

He was now "respectable"; he received the Order of Merit (1948) and the Nobel Prize for Literature (1950), and delivered the first B.B.C. Reith lectures. He could have spent his last twenty-five years in peace at Cambridge, but peace in a larger sense had become Russell's main preoccupation. In 1958 he was President of the Campaign for Nuclear Disarmament until, finding C.N.D. too mild, he led the breakaway Committee of 100, who advocated civil disobedience. With his wife he was sentenced to two months in prison in February 1961, in his ninetieth year. Russell continued his activities, now on an international scale, until 1967.

His writings spanned seventy years, from his study of Leibniz (1900) to the third volume of his autobiography (1969). Most immediately successful of his philosophical works were *The Problems of Philosophy* (1912) and *History of Western Philosophy* (1945). Apart from the great *Principia Mathematica* (1910–13), important works include *Our Knowledge of the External World* (1914) and *An Inquiry into Meaning and Truth* (1940). His approach revolutionised the study of mathematics and philosophy.

R. W. Clark, *The Life of Bertrand Russell* (London, 1981)
A. J. Ayer, *Russell* (London, 1972)

RYLANDS, George Humphrey Wolferstan ("Dadie") (1902–), poet and Cambridge don: educated at Eton and King's College, Cambridge, where he was elected an Apostle in 1922. He became a protégé of Sheppard* and of Lytton Strachey.* By the summer of

1923 his poetry was receiving favourable comment and, with his blonde hair and liking for stagecraft, he attracted old admirers of Rupert Brooke.* Leonard and Virginia Woolf** met him for the first time at Studland in September 1923 and, at the start of the following July, he began part-time work for the Hogarth Press, lodging in Gordon Square above Vanessa Bell* and Duncan Grant.* He was a lively participant in Bloomsbury parties that year and, nearly half a century later, recalled them for a B.B.C. television documentary, of which excerpts are printed in *Recollections of Virginia Woolf by her Contemporaries*, ed. J. R. Noble (1972). The demands of the Hogarth Press on Rylands' time were so great that he only worked there for a few months, but he remained a close friend of the Woolfs and kept up his Bloomsbury contacts, in 1930 introducing John Lehmann* to the group.

Rylands became a Fellow of King's and, at various times, Dean, Bursar and Director of Studies of the college as well as a University Lecturer in English Literature. His interest in the theatre led him to direct plays for the Marlowe Society at Cambridge for more than thirty years, occasionally acting in them himself. On the death of Keynes* he became Chairman of the Trustees and Directors of the Arts Theatre, Cambridge, and subsequently a Governor of the Old Vic as well as interesting himself in long-playing recordings of Shakespeare. His Fellowship dissertation was concerned with diction in poetry and it was on *Words and Poetry* that in 1928 he published his first study. Best known of his books is the Shakespeare anthology *The Ages of Man* (1939). He became a C.B.E. in 1961 and an honorary D.Litt. at Cambridge in 1972 and in June 1987 he was appointed a Companion of Honour for his services to the arts.

S

SACKVILLE-WEST, Edward Charles (1901–65), author and music critic: son of the fourth Lord Sackville, whom he succeeded in 1962. Even as a child he showed promise as a musician; his first cousin, Vita (*infra*), claimed that she could remember his playing Wagner on the piano at Knole when he was four. At Eton and Christ Church, Oxford, he was best remembered for his skills as a pianist and in later years he occasionally accompanied Benjamin Britten in piano duets. Ill-health prevented him from following any occupation but he wrote five novels and a prize-winning biography of De Quincey. He was a collector of gramophone records and became music critic of the *New Statesman;* with his friend Desmond Shawe-Taylor he compiled *The Record Guide*, first published in 1951.

Sackville-West was still an undergraduate when Virginia Woolf* first met him, at Garsington in October 1923. Within two years he was dining in Bloomsbury and attending Bloomsbury parties. From her published letters it seems as if Virginia Woolf thought him effeminate, and she was occasionally censorious over his homosexual attachments. Quarrels came easily to him in Bloomsbury company, notably with the Woolfs and with Duncan Grant.* He shared a home near Wimborne in Dorset with Shawe-Taylor and Raymond Mortimer* and, despite his wretched health, he was able to work during the war as a B.B.C. programme director. He contributed a brief study of Graham Sutherland to the wartime Penguin Modern Painters series. In his later years he became a Roman Catholic and died in Ireland, at his home in Clogheen, County Tipperary, on 4 July 1965.

SACKVILLE-WEST, Victoria Mary ("Vita") (1892–1962), novelist, poet and creator of gardens: born at Knole, Kent, the only daughter of the third Lord Sackville (1867–1928), who had married his first cousin, Victoria (1862–1936). She possessed a romanticised sense of the Sackville past which she used to advantage in *Knole and the Sackvilles* (1922), as a background to her novel *The Edwardians* (1930) and, in a different way, in *Pepita* (1937) a study of her immediate antecedents and especially of her Spanish grandmother, Pepita Duran. "Vita" married the young diplomat Harold Nicolson★ in 1913 but, after the birth of her two sons, she allowed free range to earlier habits of mind in which she craved for masculinity, finding she was more physically attracted by women than by men. She remained, however, devoted to Harold Nicolson, their home and their children; her love affair with Violet Trefusis induced both women to leave their husbands in November 1918 and seek to live together in France; but the arrangement could not last. On 14 December 1922 Vita Sackville-West—who already knew Clive Bell★ and several other members of the Bloomsbury group—met Virginia Woolf★ for the first time; within four months she was in love with her, a passion at its height in 1925–6, although the two women remained close friends until Woolf's death in 1941. Each influenced the other's writing: Vita Sackville-West's short novel *Seducers in Ecuador*, which the Hogarth Press published in 1924, has a Woolfian allusiveness while "Vita" and her Sackville daydreams provided the inspiration for *Orlando*, the two friends seeing each other at least once a week while the book was being written.

There were other romantic attachments in Vita Sackville-West's life, notably her infatuation with Mary Campbell, the wife of the South African poet, Roy Campbell (whose Fascist enthusiasms made him hostile to Bloomsbury). But increasingly "Vita" became interested in the art of gardening and particularly in reconciling the discipline of a planned garden with the intrusion of natural wild flowers. She created gardens at Long Barn, near Sevenoaks and Knole, and in the 1930s at Sissinghurst Castle, the Nicolsons' home fourteen miles east of Tunbridge Wells; and it was a pastoral poem, "The Lands" which won her the Hawthornden Prize in 1926.

This poem was partly written in Iran, where she visited her husband while he held a diplomatic post in Teheran. She also wrote a vivid description of her journey through the desert on that occasion, in *Passenger to Teheran*. Later works included the novel *All Passion Spent* (1931), *Saint Joan of Arc* (1936), and *The Eagle and the Dove* (1943), an assessment of the two St Teresas (of Avila and Lisieux), a curious agnostic essay in spiritual incomprehension. She began writing another pastoral poem in the winter after Virginia Woolf's suicide but it was not published until four years later when, as *The Garden* (1946) it won the Heinemann Prize. These pastoral poems were much admired by the Prime Minister, Clement Attlee, and it was at his suggestion that she was created a Companion of Honour in 1947. A study of the "Grande Demoiselle", the seventeenth-century Duchesse de Montpensier, was begun in 1947 but not published until 1959, as *Daughter of France*. By then Vita Sackville-West was in poor health; she died from cancer at Sissinghurst in June 1962.

N. Nicolson, *Portrait of a Marriage* (London, 1973)
V. Glendinning, *Vita* (London, 1983)

SANDS, Ethel (1873–1962), American painter: born in Newport, Rhode Island, of wealthy parents, her mother being a society hostess and friend of Edward VII when he was Prince of Wales. Ethel Sands studied painting under Eugène Carrière in Paris from 1896 to 1900, exhibited in Paris at the Salon d'Automne from 1903 and had her first London exhibition in 1912. She worked closely with Sickert* and was a founder-member of the London Group in 1913. She shared her life, and a succession of exquisitely decorated homes, with the painter, Nan Hudson (Anna Hope Hudson, 1869–1957), a compatriot whom she met in 1894 on first coming to Paris. On the eve of the First World War the couple entertained Bloomsbury and the Chelsea artists at their seventeenth-century manor house in Newington, between Oxford and Henley. At the same time (and until 1937) Ethel Sands held court in London at 15 The Vale, Chelsea, where there were mosaics by Anrep* in the entrance hall and murals by Grant* in the dining-room. Ethel Sands, who became a naturalised British subject in 1919, much admired Virginia Woolf* both as a woman and as a writer, and she was a frequent guest in London and in France.

As a friend and pupil of Sickert, Ethel Sands had early associations with Dieppe; and after the First World War she purchased the seventeenth-century Château d'Auppegard, which was about as far along the road from Dieppe to Rouen as Charleston from Newhaven. Vanessa Bell,* although left uneasy by the showpiece tidiness of Ethel Sands' homes, crossed to Normandy several times and, with Duncan Grant, painted murals for the château loggia in the summer of 1927, restoring them in 1946 following the ravages of German military occupation. The two ladies spent most of their last years in France but Ethel Sands maintained her links with literary and artistic London to the end, respected as a generous and discreet confidante.

SANGER, Charles Percy (1871–1930), barrister: the son of a wealthy chemist from Dorking. He was a friend and contemporary of Bertrand Russell* at Trinity College, Cambridge, both men being elected Apostles in the same year (1892). He became a brilliant Chancery barrister, editing a standard legal textbook on wills as well as an English translation of Hungarian poems, an analysis of the structure of *Wuthering Heights* and a pamphlet on *England's Guarantee to Belgium and Luxembourg*. In 1905 he married Dora Pease (died 1955), a generous-hearted philanthropist with deep concern for the redemption of petty criminals. She suffered from chronic arthritis; a daughter, Daphne, was born in 1906.

Despite his growing eminence as a barrister Charles Sanger remained in close touch with the Apostles and was liked and respected by the younger "brothers" of the society, especially Lytton Strachey,* Leonard Woolf* and H. T. Norton.* He was, wrote Woolf many years later, "a saint, but a very amusing, ribald, completely sceptical saint with a first-class mind and an extremely witty tongue". Charles and Dora Sanger's first London home was near the Adelphi, south of Charing Cross, and during the halcyon years of Old Bloomsbury they entertained the Stracheys, Woolfs and their friends as well as the group associated with Ottoline Morrell* at weekly parties. It was here, in the autumn of 1910, that Charles Sanger introduced Lytton Strachey to Lady Ottoline.

Sanger was recognised and respected as a modest, intellectually brilliant and conscientious barrister. At his chambers in New Square, Lincoln's Inn, and his Chelsea home in Oakley Street he continued the generous hospitality begun off the Strand before the war. From old photographs he stands out as a small, alert man, of frail physique; in November 1929 overwork led to a physical collapse from nervous exhaustion. He died three months later.

SENHOUSE, Roger Henry Pocklington (1900–70), publisher and bibliophile: educated at Eton and Magdalen College, Oxford, where he was a close friend of Philip Ritchie* who introduced him to Lytton Strachey* at Garsington in 1924. Strachey was attracted by his smile and grey eyes and Senhouse became the last great love of his life, the recipient of passionate letters and verses. Strachey thrust Senhouse into the Bloomsbury circle, urging his old friends to be kind to his newest discovery. Virginia Woolf* thought Senhouse "pink" and "dull" and he was by nature heartier than the older generation of Cambridge aesthetes. Occasionally he would mock Strachey's intensity of passion and caused him considerable distress in the summer of 1927 by four months of apparent estrangement, but he was at Ham Spray frequently in the following winter and spent a holiday with Strachey in Paris. Senhouse preferred the company of his own generation on the Riviera on other occasions but maintained his friendship with Lytton, if in a lower key of emotional commitment than the older man would have wished.

In his will Lytton Strachey left Senhouse all his books dated before 1841 and these formed the basis of a private library which Senhouse built up at his home in Rye. In 1936 he became a founder-partner of the publishing house of Secker and Warburg. He translated Colette and, after the Second World War, was responsible for reviving English interest in Gide as well as introducing the works of Alberto Moravia to the British reading public. He died at the start of September 1970.

SHEARMAN, Montague (1885–1940), barrister and collector of pictures: born in London, the son of the High Court Judge, Sir Montague Shearman (1857–1930), several books about the Bloomsbury group confusing father and son. The younger Shearman was educated at Westminster School and Balliol College, Oxford, and was called to the bar in the Middle Temple. He was rejected by the army doctors in 1914 and joined the contraband control section of the Foreign Office, receiving the O.B.E. for his services. He remained for the rest of his life a legal adviser at the Foreign Office but he was best known as a Francophile, a connoisseur of modern art—particularly of Matisse* and Utrillo— and a patron of Augustus John and Gertler.* On Armistice Night (11 November 1918) Shearman was host at a party in his rooms at the Adelphi, between the Strand and the Thames Embankment, and there are several records of the occasion. The fullest is in *Laughter in the Next Room* by Osbert Sitwell:* he describes how he brought Diaghilev★ and Massine★ to the party and found "the Bloomsbury junta was in full session" there. He noticed the presence of L. Strachey,★ C. Bell,★ R. Fry,★ M. Gertler, Lady Ottoline Morrell,★ D. H. Lawrence,★ Keynes,★ D. Grant,★ Lopokova★ and D. Garnett;★ and Carrington★ was also present. Shearman was a close friend of the barrister St John Hutchinson, K.C. who, on Shearman's death from pneumonia in February 1940, wrote a tribute to him for *The Times*.

SHEEPSHANKS, Mary Ryot (1872–1958), educationalist: born in Harrogate, Yorkshire and educated at Liverpool High School and Newnham College, Cambridge (1891–5). From 1899 to 1913 she was Vice-Principal of the Samuel Morley Memorial College, set up in the Waterloo Road, London to provide evening classes for the workers, and in 1905 she invited Virginia Woolf★ to teach there. She managed to persuade the other Stephens, Thoby,★ Vanessa (Bell★) and Adrian,★ as well as Clive Bell,★ to help also, but they soon grew tired of the work. Virginia, however, taught English literature and composition until 1907, though she thought the lessons of little value to the recipients, an opinion apparently shared by Mary Sheepshanks. In 1914 Mary became manager of the headquarters of the Women's International Suffrage Alliance, a post she held until 1922. She lived in Hampstead Garden suburb, where Virginia Woolf continued to visit her in the 1920s.

SHEPPARD, John Tressider (1881–1968), classicist: born in London and educated at Dulwich but spent most of his life at King's College, Cambridge, as a scholar, Fellow and Lecturer in Classics (1908–33). From 1933 to 1954 he was Provost, his voice becoming well-known on the radio when the B.B.C. began broadcasting the annual Festival of Carols and Lessons from King's each Christmas Eve.

Sheppard showed academic brilliance as an undergraduate, won praise for his acting, became President of the Cambridge Union, and was elected an Apostle in February 1902 on the same day as Lytton Strachey,★ who defeated him for the Chancellor's Verse Prize. Strachey was briefly infatuated with Sheppard in 1903, the two men remaining friends for thirty years. He was a frequent visitor to Bloomsbury parties and later to Ham Spray House and

Tilton. During the First World War he worked for British military Intelligence at the War Office and lived at 46 Gordon Square, with his brother Apostle and King's man, Maynard Keynes.* He returned to classics as soon as possible after the war, his *Greek Tragedy* being published in 1920 and *The Pattern of the Iliad* a year later. A succession of studies and translations of Sophocles followed, with Sheppard warmly advocating the performance of Greek plays for modern audiences, not simply their reading as classical texts. His open lectures on Greek and English poetry were extremely popular. For much of the inter-war period he produced the triennial Greek play at Cambridge, his most famous production being the *Oresteia* in 1921. He appeared at the Scala Theatre in the two charity performances of Strachey's *A Son of Heaven* in 1925. Bloomsbury gossip credited him with gambling each season at Monte Carlo. Honorary degrees in three continents testified to his academic eminence and in 1950 he received a knighthood.

SHOVE, Fredegond, *née* Maitland (1889–1949), poet: the younger daughter of Florence Maitland, herself a sister of H. A. L. Fisher and cousin of Vanessa Bell* and Virginia Woolf.* Both Fredegond and her sister Ermengard owed their names to the Anglo-Saxon enthusiasm of their father, the great historian Frederick William Maitland (1850–1906), who was also the authorised biographer of Sir Leslie Stephen.* Fredegond maintained a regular correspondence with her Stephen cousins until she was in her late thirties and was an occasional visitor to Gordon Square on the eve of the First World War and a guest of the Morrells** at Garsington after her marriage to Gerald Shove (*infra*) in 1915. Her first volume of poems, *Dreams and Journeys,* appeared in 1918, with the Hogarth Press publishing a second collection, *Daybreak,* in 1922. But after 1923, when her husband took up his lectureship at King's, she gradually became integrated into Cambridge life, finally turning away from Bloomsbury in 1927 when she was received into the Roman Catholic Church.

SHOVE, Gerald Frank (1887–1947), economist: was educated at Uppingham School and went up to King's College, Cambridge, in 1907, a year after Brooke* but in the same year as Waley.* At the university he associated with the group of Fabian socialists with literary aspirations who called themselves the "Carbonari" and in 1909 was elected an Apostle. His inclinations were towards syndicalism, but he gradually evolved a personal philosophy based upon an assumption that the teaching of economics would illuminate the true relationship of politics to ethics. He became a friend of Lytton Strachey★ and was influenced by Maynard Keynes.★ In 1915 he married Fredegond Maitland (*supra*), a connection which brought him closer to her cousins, Virginia (Woolf★) and Vanessa (Bell★), although he was already well established in Bloomsbury society. In the First World War he was a conscientious objector, accepting work on Philip Morrell's★ farm. In 1923 he became a Lecturer in Economics at Cambridge and was elected a Fellow of King's College three years later. He was appointed University Reader in Economics two years before his death, at Old Hunstanton in the autumn of 1947. Shove wrote little; he was a teacher, interested especially in theories of value and distribution, and content to reassess the classical economists, often with a detached, ironic humour. In later years he gained strength from an undemonstrative sense of religious commitment, at variance with traditional Bloomsbury agnosticism.

SICKERT, Walter Richard (1860–1942), painter: born in Munich, the son of a Danish painter, Oswald Sickert, and his Anglo-Irish wife. The family settled in England in 1868, and from 1875 to 1877 Walter Sickert was educated at King's College, London, trying in the first instance to go on the stage. But within three years he was working as a pupil of Whistler in London. From 1883 onwards he spent much time at Dieppe, where he became friendly with Degas and, through him, with the other French Impressionists in Montmartre, particularly Pissarro. He married Richard Cobden's daughter, Ellen, in 1885. During the years 1887 to 1890 he concentrated on music-hall scenes, joining the New English Art Club (N.E.A.C.) in 1888, but he also encouraged appreciation of the Impressionists on this side of the Channel and in 1889 helped organise the "London Impressionists" Exhibition. By 1893 he was recognised as a first-rate teacher, Roger Fry★ being among his pupils that year at evening classes in The Vale, at Chelsea.

Sickert's first marriage ended in divorce in 1899. For the next six years he had lodgings on the hillside at Neuville above the harbour of Dieppe, a resort which at the turn of the century attracted chic society from Paris each season; his landlady—the red-headed chatelaine of the fish market, Madame Villain—often served as his model. In general, however, Sickert used sombre colours to depict street scenes in Dieppe and the shabbier parts of Venice. Although he maintained links with Dieppe until after the First World War, Sickert returned to London in 1905, gave classes from Whistler's old studio in Fitzroy Street and was the principal inspiration of the Camden Town Group which seceded from the N.E.A.C. in 1911. By then he was closely associated, not only with Fry but with the critic MacColl.* The Post-Impressionist exhibitions drew him closer to the Bloomsbury artists. By 1917 he was speaking, with approval, of Vanessa Bell;* in February 1919 Virginia Woolf* decided he met her ideal of a modern painter; his 1922 canvas, *The Bar Parlour*, was snapped up by that astute collector, Maynard Keynes;* and by the winter of 1925–26 he was attending Bloomsbury parties, accompanied by the French painter, Thérèse Lessore, whom he married soon afterwards. His artistic standing was higher in his sixties and seventies than before the war. He finally left London in 1938 for Bath, dying there in January 1942.

W. Baron, *Sickert* (London, 1973)

SITWELL, Edith Louisa (1887–1964), poet, critic and eccentric: the eldest child of Sir George Sitwell (1860–1943) and Lady Ida, a daughter of the first Earl of Londesborough. Edith's plain features and bookish interests made her the despair of her parents and she had an unhappy and often harsh childhood, for the most part at the family home in Derbyshire, Renishaw Hall. The tedium was relieved only by the sympathetic admiration of her brothers, Osbert (*infra*) and Sacheverell (born 1897) and, from the age of sixteen onwards, by the encouragement of her governess, Helen Rootham (died 1938). For thirty-five years Miss Rootham was Edith Sitwell's companion, the two women sharing a flat in Chelsea in 1914 and creating a London home for Edith's brothers, who were officers in the Grenadier Guards during the war.

Their mother accumulated considerable gambling debts to a London money-lender and when Sir George Sitwell refused to accept responsibility for his wife's financial problems she was arrested and, in March 1915, sentenced to three months imprisonment. It was in this same year that Edith Sitwell's first volume of poetry—*The Mother*—was published. From 1916 to 1921 Edith collaborated with Osbert on an annual verse anthology,

Wheels, which rejected the neo-Georgian lyricism popular on the eve of the war. A combination of writing talent and family notoriety ensured that, by the last months of the war, the three Sitwells were beginning to make a name for themselves in literary society. Among guests at a party of which Edith Sitwell was the hostess at Carlyle Square, Chelsea, on 10 October 1918 were such Bloomsbury luminaries as the Woolfs,** the Hutchinsons and H. T. J. Norton* and many Bloomsbury associates including Ottoline Morrell* and John Sheppard.*

Edith Sitwell cut more of the public figure in London than Virginia Woolf or Vanessa Bell,* her exhibitionism manifested by exotic dress, jewels and a turban. The Sitwell hospitality, both in Chelsea and in Italy, was accepted—and sometimes derided—by Lytton Strachey.* Virginia Woolf admired many of Edith Sitwell's early poems, although she was often puzzled by them; she was among the audience at London's Aeolian Hall on 12 June 1923 for the first public performance of *Façade*, when Edith declaimed her verses through a megaphone in syncopated rhythm to the accompaniment of William Walton's music. Two years later the Hogarth Press published her perceptive essay, *Poetry and Criticism*, as a pamphlet.

In the 1930s Edith Sitwell wrote little verse, but developed her prose style. *The English Eccentrics* in 1933 was popular, as also was her *Fanfare for Elizabeth* in 1946 and *The Queens and the Hive* in 1962. She turned to poetry again in 1941–2, deeply moved by bombing and later by the threat of nuclear destruction. In her late seventies she undertook lecture tours in America, projecting her personality as effectively as in London between the wars. In 1954 she was created a Dame of the British Empire.

SITWELL, (Francis) Osbert (1892–1969), poet, essayist, novelist and critic: born in London, the eldest son of Sir George Sitwell, to whose baronetcy he succeeded in 1943. According to the entry which Sir Osbert submitted to *Who's Who*, he was educated "during the holidays from Eton". While serving in the Grenadier Guards he joined his sister Edith (*supra*) in producing the annual anthology *Wheels* and a collection called *Twentieth Century Harlequinade and other Poems* (1916); but it was his satirical and pacifist *The Winstonburg Line* in 1919 which first made a deep impression on the public. In 1926, the year in which he wrote the words for William Walton's *Belshazzar's Feast*, he published a novel, *Before the Bombardment*, which effectively evoked the impact on genteel Yorkshire society of the naval shelling of Scarborough in 1914. He was the author of several collections of satirical stories and works of travel and from 1951 to 1958 was a Trustee of the Tate Gallery. He was created a Companion of the British Empire in 1956 and a Companion of Honour two years later.

Between 1945 and 1950 Sir Osbert completed five volumes of autobiography; the fourth of these volumes, *Laughter in the Next Room* (1949), recalls his experience of Bloomsbury society in the aftermath of the First World War. He sought to convey his amusement at the so-called Bloomsbury accent, a quality of voice which appears to have originated with Lytton Strachey:* "The tones would convey with supreme efficacy the requisite degree of paradoxical interest, surprise, incredulity; in actual sound, analysed, they were unemphatic, save where emphasis was not to be expected; then there would be a sudden sickly stress, high where you would have presumed low, and the whole spoken sentence would run, as it were, at different speeds and on different gears and contain a good deal of expert but apparently meaningless syncopation". The book also contains the description of the "Bloomsbury junta in full session" at Shearman's* Armistice Night party. A later volume of reminiscence, *Tales my Father Taught Me* (1962) delineated more graphically Sir George's character.

On Sir Osbert Sitwell's death the baronetcy passed to his brother, Sacheverell (born at Scarborough in 1897), poet, biographer of Mozart and Liszt, and elegant interpreter of baroque art.

J. Pearson, *Façades* (London, 1978)

SMITH, (Lloyd) Logan Pearsall (1865–1946), essayist: born at Millville, New Jersey, the son of a Quaker glass manufacturer from Philadelphia. He was a brother of Alys Russell* and Mary Berenson* and an uncle of Ray Strachey* (born Rachel Costelloe) and Karin Stephen.* Pearsall Smith was educated at Harvard, but came to England as a young man, spending much of his time at Oxford and becoming naturalised in 1913, the year in which he became a founder-member of the Society for Pure English. Pearsall Smith has the misfortune to be best remembered for the pronouncement, "People say that life is the thing, but I prefer reading". He was an expert on idioms and published critical works on Sir Henry Wotton, Milton and the reading of Shakespeare as well as a collection of his own Songs and Sonnets. His liking for literary anecdotes led Lytton Strachey★ to describe him as "senile" at the age of fifty-one. *Trivia* in 1902 was followed by *More Trivia* in 1921 and *Afterthoughts* ten years later, the whole collection of aphorisms and essays being assembled in *All Trivia* (1934). He was tolerated by Old Bloomsbury, towards whom he was basically unsympathetic. Among his friends were Roger Fry★ and Philip Morrell,★ but he turned against Lady Ottoline Morrell,★ whom he held responsible for attracting Bertrand Russell★ away from his sister, Alys. Yet in his last months of life he even treated his sister harshly.

R. Gathorne-Hardy, *Recollections of Pearsall Smith* (London, 1949)

SMYTH, Ethel Mary (1858–1944), composer: born in Marylebone, the daughter of Major-General J. H. Smyth. She studied composition at Leipzig but it was in July 1893 that she first impressed the musical world in London, with a performance of her *Mass in D* at the Albert Hall. In 1908 she became an active suffragette, composed the *March of the Women*, and was imprisoned for two months in 1911 for her activities. Her German musical training showed up in the character of her best-known opera, *The Wreckers* (first performed at Leipzig in 1906 and in London in 1908); and even the light-hearted *The Boatswain's Mate* (première in London in 1916) would have had its first performance in Germany had not war intervened. In 1922 Ethel Smyth was created a Dame of the British Empire and soon afterwards began to write the first of six autobiographical volumes, faithfully conveying in print the egocentric militancy of her character. She frequented the Gower Street circle of Lady Ottoline Morrell★ in 1928 and sought out Virginia Woolf★ two years later, largely because she greatly admired her *A Room of One's Own*. They first met in the third week of February 1930. Although Virginia Woolf began by privately expressing amusement at this eccentric septuagenarian who had fallen in love with her, she was pleased to be told that Dame Ethel found in their friendship the delights she had known on first discovering the music of Brahms. They remained close confidantes for eleven years, Ethel sometimes writing two letters a day to

Virginia, but she had no contact with Bloomsbury as a whole. She died at Woking in May 1944.

C. St John, *Ethel Smyth* (London, 1959)

SOUVESTRE, Marie (c. 1830–1905), French schoolmistress: daughter of Emile Souvestre, Academician and writer. While still a young woman she started a girls' school, Les Ruches, at Fontainebleau, in partnership with Mlle Dussaut. In 1870 she moved the school, with only a few girls, to Florence to escape the Franco-Prussian War. There she met Lady Strachey★ for whom she conceived a great admiration. The two oldest Strachey girls, Elinor (Rendel★) and Dorothy (Bussy★) were sent to the school when it had returned to Fontainebleau; Dorothy developed an intense "crush" on Mlle Souvestre. The partnership broke up and Marie Souvestre started Allenswood School at South Fields, Wimbledon, soon after 1880; among her pupils was Eleanor Roosevelt. Dorothy Strachey helped with the English teaching, her younger sisters, Pernel★ and Marjorie★ attended the school, and the whole Strachey family often spent holidays there. The Souvestre influence was particularly great on Lytton Strachey;★ from her he acquired a love of French literature, and also a sharp and questioning approach to life. The witty, radical talk at Allenswood was a foretaste of Bloomsbury conversation.

SPENDER, Stephen Harold (1909–), poet and critic: born into a family much respected as liberal journalists. He spent his childhood in Hampstead, where he was educated at University College School, before going up to University College, Oxford. At the university he was one of several young poets—notably Cecil Day Lewis (1904–72), W. H. Auden (1907–73) and Louis MacNeice (1907–63)—who attracted the attention of Ottoline Morrell★ and the older generation of Bloomsbury. Through John Lehmann★ he met the Woolfs★★ and through Rosamond Lehmann★ he was a guest of Strachey★ at Ham Spray House at Christmas 1930. By then he had already published two volumes of verse and written a novel, which Virginia Woolf subsequently told him, emphatically, to "scrap". A sojourn in Germany—some of it spent near Berlin with Isherwood*—intensified his political awareness and he was, briefly, a member of the Communist Party. His autobiographical works show that he was too much of an individualist to conform to Marxist beliefs, but he was a propagandist for the Republican cause during the Spanish Civil War. In 1935 his first critical work—*The Destructive Element*—examined Yeats, Henry James* and Eliot* and stressed the need for political commitment. Eighteen years later *The Creative Element* modified his earlier views, emphasising the importance of the writer's independence and conscious creativity.

During the Second World War Spender taught for a term at Blundell's School, Tiverton, shared the editorship of *Horizon* with Cyril Connolly, and served for three years in the National Fire Service. For most of the 1950s and 1960s he combined the joint editorship of *Encounter* with teaching posts in five American universities and was Professor of English Literature at University College, London, from 1970 to 1977. His collected poems were published in 1954. He was made C.B.E. in 1962 and knighted in 1978.

S. Spender, *World within World* (London, 1951)

SPROTT, Walter John Herbert (1897–1971), psychologist: the son of a country solicitor, he was educated at Felsted School and Clare College, Cambridge. At the university he showed those qualities which merited election as an Apostle and friendship with Maynard Keynes,* who introduced him to Bloomsbury society in 1920 and took him on holiday in Algeria and Tunisia a year later. By 1922 he was a close companion of Lytton Strachey,* who always called him "Sebastian". He was with Strachey in Venice that summer and in later years joined him in the Dolomites and Holland, as well as acting as his amanuensis. Virginia Woolf* introduced Sprott to Ottoline Morrell* in March 1923 but in February 1925 firmly rejected his novel, submitted to the Hogarth Press. From 1922 to 1925 Sprott was a demonstrator at the Psychological Laboratory in Cambridge, collaborating occasionally with James Strachey.* The remaining forty years of Sprott's academic career were spent at Nottingham: as Lecturer in Psychology (1925), Reader in Philosophy (1928), Professor of Philosophy (1948–60), Public Orator (1948–64), Professor of

Psychology (1960–4), and subsequently Emeritus Professor. Sprott is said always to have spoken with a "Bloomsbury" intonation. He wrote several works on psychology and sociology as well as *Philosophy and Common Sense* (1949).

STEPHEN, Adrian Leslie (1883–1948), psychiatrist: youngest child of Leslie and Julia Stephen,** educated at Evelyn's Preparatory School, Hillingdon, and Westminster School. A small, delicate child at first, by eighteen he was six feet five inches tall. Later in life his sister Virginia (Woolf*) blamed herself for not pairing with him, instead of following the older Vanessa (Bell*) and Thoby.* She may well have remembered their St Ives holiday in 1892, when Adrian was not allowed to go "to the lighthouse" with the others. His mother's death in 1895, followed by his step-sister's marriage, left Adrian Stephen even more isolated; he was frightened of his father and fell short of his brother Thoby's success at school.

In 1902 he followed Thoby to Trinity College, Cambridge, where he deliberately ignored Thoby's set and made friends of his own, among them Horace Cole* with whom he embarked on several hoaxes. They deceived the Mayor of Cambridge into providing a civic welcome for the "Sultan of Zanzibar's uncle" in 1905, though Stephen's original idea was to impersonate a German detachment invading France from Alsace. The Zanzibar affair was a practice run for the great *Dreadnought* hoax of 1910. Adrian Stephen's combination of sarcastic humour and recklessness contributed to the success of the plot, of which he wrote an amusing account, *The Dreadnought Hoax* (Hogarth Press, 1936).

The short bursts of energy Stephen showed as a practical joker were not translated into sustained effort in everyday life. Like Thoby he studied Law, and was called to the bar in Lincoln's Inn in 1907, but had thoughts of medicine or the stage as an alternative. He and Virginia, left alone together after Thoby's death and Vanessa's marriage, were sharing 29 Fitzroy Square, where in the autumn of 1907 they revived their Thursday evening "At Homes", occasions sometimes regarded as the real beginning of the Bloomsbury group. Virginia was fond of her brother, but she found his lethargy depressing and reacted furiously to his frequent teasing. According to their nephew Quentin Bell* arguments often ended in the throwing of butter pats, and in 1911 they decided to invite friends to join them in a larger house, where they could lead separate lives. They took 38 Brunswick Square, with Keynes★ and Duncan Grant★ using the ground floor, Leonard Woolf★ at the top, and a floor each for the Stephens. When the Woolfs were married in August 1912, Adrian Stephen remained there, giving all-night card-parties and pursuing his attachment to Grant.

By the summer of 1914, however, he had fallen in love with Karin Costelloe (Stephen★) whom he persuaded to marry him in October. At the start of the war he announced his intention of enlisting, but in 1916 became a conscientious objector and worked on a dairy farm until a severe illness in 1917 affected his heart, and he was found a clerical post. In 1918 he had a wife and two daughters, Ann (*infra*) and Judith, but nothing left of his legal career. Karin had interested him in psychology, however, and he followed her lead in entering University College Hospital to gain the necessary medical qualification for the practice of psychiatry. His sister Virginia, convinced that this was just another false start, was proved wrong when he became a qualified doctor in 1926, aged forty-three. On the way Stephen was analysed himself, persevering in a process he found painful, and he and Karin separated for a while. Playing cards and sailing were in fact almost their only common interests outside their work, but both became successful psychiatrists.

Their home was now 50 Gordon Square, soon to be filled with patients and lodgers. During a dance there on 26 June 1920 a young man fell to his death from the flat roof, an incident that became a Bloomsbury legend and revealed Adrian's surprising nerve in a crisis. He saw the accident, went to the scene, and summoned and assisted the doctor, all quite calmly according to his sisters. The Stephens were very fond of parties, and gave the last true Bloomsbury fancy-dress affair, though in their new house in Regent's Park, on 28 January 1939. Virginia Woolf came as Cleopatra and T. S. Eliot★ as a strangely Strachey-like Crippen. In the Second World War Stephen served in the R.A.M.C. and in 1940 gave psychiatric treatment to survivors from Dunkirk; in June he supplied Leonard and Virginia Woolf with fatal doses of morphine in case of invasion. The following year he nearly died of pneumonia, but was able to resume his duties and left the army a Major. Although Adrian Stephen returned to private practice just after the war, his health never recovered and he died in 1948.

Quentin Bell, *Virginia Woolf* (London, 1972)

STEPHEN, Ann (1916–), doctor and teacher: older daughter of Adrian and Karin Stephen.** Educated at Isabel Fry's* Farmhouse School, King Alfred School, Golders Green, Frognal School, Hampstead, and Queen's College, Harley Street, she and her sister Judith (1918–72) were largely brought up by nurses at home in 50 Gordon Square. The life of Bloomsbury was known to the girls from servants' gossip, and both stayed with their aunts Vanessa Bell* and Virginia Woolf.* At Charleston Ann became friendly with her cousin Julian Bell.* The Stephens spent summers at "King's Head", their house on the Essex marshes near Thorpe-le-Soken, where they entertained their friends with cards and mud bathing. In winter 50 Gordon Square was open house for exciting games of "sardines", and there were always beds for benighted visitors. Later on Julian Bell's friend, Richard Llewellyn Davies, came to stay longer and he and Ann were married in 1938 when she came down from Cambridge; she was a scholar of Newnham College (1935–8).

From 1938 to 1942 Ann studied medicine at the Royal Free Hospital, London, Trinity College, Dublin, and Leeds and held several medical posts. In 1943 she was divorced from Llewellyn Davies and in 1945 married the biochemist Richard Synge (Nobel Prize Winner in 1952). The couple had seven children and Ann Synge worked as a translator from Swedish and Russian until 1965, when she trained as a teacher and taught in secondary schools until her retirement. She was a county councillor in Kincardineshire and an active peace campaigner.

STEPHEN, Caroline Emelia (1839–1909), author: was the only sister of Leslie Stephen* and was known to her nieces Vanessa (Bell*) and Virginia (Woolf*) as "Nun" or "the Quaker". After being disappointed in love as a young woman in the early 1860s, she found religious consolation within the Society of Friends. Her book *Quaker Strongholds* was published in 1891; she wrote pamphlets and a further edifying book, *Light Arising*, published a year before her death. She had been devoted to her brother Leslie's welfare and tried to keep house for him after his first wife's death but she found him too exacting and her health gave way within three weeks. For most of her life she lived in Cambridge, where she owned a house known as The Porch. She was fond of her nieces and helped Virginia recover from her mental breakdown by encouraging her to stay at The Porch in October and December 1904; as Adrian

Stephen* was still at Trinity College, Virginia was able to meet some of his friends. Towards the end of her life "the Quaker" disapproved of what she heard about Vanessa's Bloomsbury hospitality and was shocked by Adrian's involvement in the Sultan of Zanzibar hoax, which mocked Cambridge's civic dignitaries. Caroline Emelia died in Cambridge on 7 April 1909, Virginia writing an obituary which was published in *The Guardian* a fortnight later. She left Virginia a generous legacy of £2,500, but a mere £100 each to Vanessa and Adrian.

STEPHEN, Dorothea (1871–1965), author: the youngest child of Sir James Fitzjames Stephen (1829–94), Leslie Stephen's* brother. She had a powerful and somewhat aggressive personality. For much of her adult life she lived in India. Her book, *Indian Thought,* was published in 1918. Her cousins, Vanessa (Bell*) and Virginia (Woolf*), had found her intolerable when they were children and both resented her strictures on Vanessa's morals, made while she was in England during the winter of 1921–2, when she visited the Woolfs at Richmond.

STEPHEN, Julia Prinsep (1846–95), mother of Adrian and Thoby Stephen,** Vanessa (Bell*) and Virginia (Woolf*): born in Calcutta to Dr John Jackson, Surgeon to the East India Company, and his wife Maria, one of the famous and beautiful Pattle sisters. Julia, with her mother and her two older sisters, lived in England from 1848, finally settling in Brighton when Dr Jackson retired (1855). She became a notable beauty, much photographed by her aunt Julia Margaret Cameron, and painted by Watts and Burne-Jones. Julia shone also in the literary circle established by her aunt Sara Prinsep at Little Holland House, London. Here she met Thackeray's daughters, and Minny Thackeray's suitor, Leslie Stephen,* who felt some jealousy at Julia's engagement to the barrister Herbert Duckworth. The marriage lasted only from 1867 to 1870, when Duckworth died suddenly of a ruptured abscess, leaving his widow to bring up three small children, George,* Stella (Hills*) and the posthumous baby Gerald.*

Julia had remained friendly with Minny Thackeray after her marriage to Leslie Stephen, and when Minny died in 1875, she helped and advised the widower. In 1878 they were married,

Stephen moving himself and his daughter Laura* into Julia's house in Hyde Park Gate. Four more children were born to the Stephens; their marriage was happy, but very hard-working. Julia had to support her husband in his enormous literary labours, and soothe his nervous phobias. She was still the centre of an admiring circle of friends, including the writers Henry James,* George Meredith, and James Russell Lowell. After Lowell became U.S. Ambassador to Britain, he was a frequent visitor to the Stephens, and they dined at the Embassy once a fortnight. Many relatives were entertained at Hyde Park Gate and Julia's widowed mother lived there from 1887 to 1892. For three months every summer the family and guests transferred to Talland House, St Ives, Cornwall. Although Julia revelled in the summer playground and was often seen "bobbing about in the water in a large black hat", in St Ives as in London she devoted much time and energy to the poor and sick; a nursing fund was later set up in St Ives in her memory. Virginia Woolf provided a picture of these family holidays in *To the Lighthouse*, portraying her mother as Mrs Ramsay.

Even Julia's vitality was eventually exhausted by the claims of friends, relatives, children, and the needy, and perhaps most of all by her adoring and tyrannical husband. She died of influenza on 5 May 1895.

Elizabeth F. Boyd, *Bloomsbury Heritage* (London, 1976)
Quentin Bell, *Virginia Woolf* (London, 1972)

STEPHEN, Karin (1889–1953), psychologist, wife of Adrian Stephen:* born Catherine Elizabeth Conn Costelloe, younger daughter of Frank and Mary Costelloe (Berenson*). Her upbringing and education were similar to that of her sister Ray (Strachey*) with three differences: Ray was favoured by her mother and grandmother, Karin had ear trouble from her youth, and she was much the cleverer of the two. Her deafness was discovered in 1900, and she was operated on five times between 1905 and 1907, when she entered Newnham to read Moral Science. Cut off from much Cambridge life, she welcomed a year at Bryn Mawr College (1908–9) with her sister and mother, who thought she would find better lip-reading teachers in the U.S.A. Karin enjoyed the American lectures in philosophy and psychology; when she was back at Cambridge she benefited from the coaching of her uncle by marriage, Russell.* She was awarded a Double First, and in Part II of her Tripos (1911) became the first woman honoured by a distinction in philosophy.

In 1911 Karin was attracted by Oliver Strachey,* but was happy enough to have him marry her sister. She accompanied the couple to India in 1911–12, and visited Calcutta and Burma by herself. On her return she continued studying philosophy, and was elected to the Aristotelian society, to whom she read a paper, later expanded into a book, *The Misuse of Mind* (1922). In Florence in 1913 she avoided a lover of her mother's choosing by hurrying off to Munich and then returned to London to plunge eagerly into the Bloomsbury society of which she had already had a taste. Unlike her quieter sister, she loved the fancy-dress parties, such as the one she and Oliver attended as Karsavina and Nijinsky,* and became particularly fond of the Bells** and Duncan Grant.* However, Karin, with her stocky figure draped in purple or orange and her dog-like eagerness to be loved, did not attract Vanessa Bell or Virginia Woolf,* especially when their brother Adrian began to be interested in her.

Although not returning Adrian's love, she liked and respected him and they married in October 1914. Both were pacifists, so ignored the war and started married life in Cambridge, as Karin was now a Research Fellow at Newnham. After the birth of their daughter, Ann (Stephen*) in January 1916, Karin joined Adrian in the farm work he was obliged to do as a conscientious objector, until bad health earned him a desk job instead. In August 1918, while expecting their second child Judith, the Stephens stayed with the Woolfs at Asheham. Virginia's diary entries, then and later, reveal her irritation with Karin mixed with pity for her deafness. Karin was determined that both she and Adrian should be psychologists, even though it meant studying medicine for five years at University College Hospital, with Adrian retailing the lectures Karin could not hear. She passed her first examination brilliantly, but the strain broke up her marriage for a while. A drastic operation in 1925 greatly improved her hearing, though it left her face slightly lopsided for the rest of her life.

After qualifying she worked in a mental hospital in Baltimore (1927), then returned to Adrian and a post as clinical assistant at the Maudesley Hospital, London. Since the war they had lived at 50 Gordon Square, and they now bought an old, ramshackle inn, The King's Head, in the Essex Marshes near Thorpe-le-Soken. There they enjoyed sailing, not apparently with any great skill, and family holidays, but their daughters were mostly brought up by servants or relatives on whom they were dumped. Even Aunt Virginia learnt

to endure the sudden arrival of small Ann and Judith, and in fact
was rather fond of both.

Until the Second World War Karin wrote articles and lectured at
Cambridge, but when Adrian was stationed with the R.A.M.C. in
Scotland she took up work in a hospital near Glasgow. She became
interested in drugs and electric shock treatment for mental illness,
both of which she tried herself for depression following Adrian's
death in 1948. She gradually increased the amount of morphine
until she finally took an overdose.

Barbara Strachey, *Remarkable Relations* (London, 1980)

STEPHEN, Laura Makepeace (1870–1945), only child of Leslie
Stephen (*infra*) by his first wife, Minny: born in Kensington and
considered, even as an infant, mentally deficient. She spent much
of her early life at Hyde Park Gate, with her step-sisters and
step-brothers, but in her twenties she was sent to a succession of
"homes" and finally to an asylum at York. After going through
their father's letters soon after his death, her half-sister Virginia
(Woolf*) thought that Laura's mental disability had been the great
tragedy of his life.

STEPHEN, Leslie (1832–1904), biographer: born in 42 Hyde
Park Gate, Kensington, at a time when his father, Sir James
Stephen, was Colonial Under-Secretary of State, working to abolish
the slave trade. Leslie was educated at Eton and Trinity Hall,
Cambridge. Evangelical, muscular Christianity led him successively to ordination, a college Fellowship (in Mathematics),
philosophical doubts and, by the age of thirty-two, to professional
agnosticism. After ten years as a Cambridge don he settled in
London as a literary journalist and, in June 1867, married Harriet
("Minny") Thackeray, the elder daughter of W. M. Thackeray.
From 1871 to 1882 he edited *The Cornhill Magazine*, which his
wife's father had established in 1860. He was a distinguished Alpine
mountaineer, an interest reflected in his *The Playground of Europe*
(1871). Five years later came his major work, a *History of English
Thought in the 18th Century*. After the sudden death of "Minny" in
1875, on his forty-third birthday, he resumed an old friendship
with the widowed Julia Duckworth (see STEPHEN, Julia), whom

he married in March 1878. Minny's only child, Laura Stephen (*supra*), was mentally defective; Julia, in the first six years of their marriage, gave birth to Vanessa (Bell*), Thoby (*infra*), Virginia (Woolf*) and Adrian.*

In the summer of 1889 Leslie Stephen suffered a breakdown from the strain of being first Editor of the *Dictionary of National Biography* (1882–91), a compilation to which he contributed more than 380 entries. He remained an extraordinarily hard worker, sometimes completing articles of seven or eight thousand words at one sitting. For the last quarter of the nineteenth century he was accepted in London as a literary luminary, but experiments at educating his children at home were not entirely successful: he found it easier to stimulate intellectual curiosity than teach the skills of even his own subject, mathematics. By temperament and background he was spartan and ascetic, with no sense of colour or feeling for music, and with his daughters he was often irritable and impatient; natural affection and sympathetic understanding hardened into possessiveness if new friendships threatened to move him from the centre of their world. The moans and groans of self-pity intensified after the death of his second wife in May 1895. In his last years he wrote a biography of his brother, Sir James Fitzjames Stephen (1829–94), the historian of criminal law, and a study of the English Utilitarians. Leslie Stephen was created Knight Commander of the Bath in the Coronation Honours of July 1902; but intestinal cancer had already been diagnosed in April and his health was so poor that he received his insignia at home. He died, at 22 Hyde Park Gate, on 22 February 1904.

His impercipient treatment of both her mother and her step-sister, Stella Duckworth (Hills*) led Virginia Woolf to write harshly of her father in the earliest autobiographical fragments printed in *Moments of Being* (published in 1976) and he is recognisable as the self-centred Mr Ramsay of *To the Lighthouse*. From her letters, however, it is clear that Virginia loved him with an intensity he occasionally rebuffed.

Alan Bell, *Sir Leslie Stephen's Mausoleum Book* (Oxford, 1977)
N. Annan, *Leslie Stephen, His Thought and Character in Relation to his Time* (2nd edn, London, 1984)

STEPHEN, (Julian) Thoby (1880–1906), older son of Leslie and Julia Stephen:** educated at Evelyn's Preparatory School, Hillingdon and Clifton College. A large, confident child, he was the family favourite, and his sisters Vanessa (Bell*) and Virginia (Woolf*) were rivals for his affection. At school he succeeded academically and at games, and by the time he went up to Trinity College, Cambridge in 1899, he was a handsome young man of easy-going charm, nick-named "The Goth" for his height and fairness. Intellectuals accepted him as one of themselves, although he did not quite qualify as an Apostle and he was fond also of outdoor pursuits. His father and sisters, visiting him in the summer of 1900, were satisfied that he was doing very well at university, and in 1902 he was awarded a scholarship for his final year.

Most of all, perhaps, Thoby Stephen had a genius for friendship that kept in one group diverse characters like Lytton Strachey,* Clive Bell,* and Leonard Woolf.* When he came down from Cambridge and began reading for the bar in 1903, he wanted to keep in touch with his friends. After Leslie Stephen's death in 1904, he readily fell in with the plan of moving to 46 Gordon Square, and announced that he would be "At Home" on Thursday evenings, starting on 16 February 1905. Only one guest, the silent Saxon Sydney-Turner,* arrived for what can hardly have been a hilarious first Bloomsbury gathering, but others came later and the Stephen girls began to join them. Although he appreciated his sisters' quality, Thoby Stephen was conventional in social matters, and may not have meant to include them at first. However, they soon became an integral part of the circle and old friends of the Stephen family bewailed the effect on Vanessa and Virginia of sitting up until three in the morning without a chaperone, talking to Thoby's "unsuitable friends".

In June 1904 Thoby Stephen was called to the bar in the Inner Temple, and on 10 August he left with his brother Adrian* to ride through Montenegro and Albania and meet his sisters, accompanied by Violet Dickinson,* at Olympia in September. He returned to London before the rest of the party, and when the others reached Gordon Square they found him in bed with a fever. The illness, first diagnosed as malaria, proved to be typhoid, and Thoby Stephen died on 20 November 1906. For nearly a month Virginia pretended in letters to Violet Dickinson that he was recovering, probably because she could not face the fact that he was dead, while Vanessa agreed at last to marry Clive Bell. The legend of Thoby's potentially brilliant future stayed with Virginia all her life, and she expressed her feelings in two novels, *Jacob's Room* (1922) and *The Waves* (1931).

Quentin Bell, *Virginia Woolf* (London, 1972)

STRACHEY, Alix (1892–1973), psychologist, wife of James Strachey (*infra*): born Sargant-Florence in New Jersey, daughter of Henry Florence and his British wife, the painter Mary Sargant. Six weeks after Alix's birth her father drowned, and the family went to England, where in 1898 Mary built a country home, Lord's Wood, on Marlow Common. Alix, educated at Bedales School, spent a year at the Slade School of Art (1910–11) to please her mother. She was then allowed to follow her brother Philip to Cambridge, and read Mediaeval and Modern Languages at Newnham College (1911–14). She spent the summer of 1912 in a sanatorium, with an illness diagnosed as heart disease, but which was more like anorexia nervosa. The sturdy girl who was the only female in Bedales' first cricket eleven turned into the tall, thin "Red Indian" described by Virginia Woolf★ and others, and suffered from recurrent depression.

Alix had no idea what to do after university, so decided to stay with a college friend in Finland, but was trapped by the outbreak of war at her hosts' winter home in St Petersburg. Here she learnt to drive a car along the Nevsky Prospekt, and was ever after a keen motorist, and later motor-cyclist. In 1915 she was able to return home to share a Bloomsbury flat with her brother. She met most of the group, was a particular friend of Carrington,★ and after brief affairs with David Garnett★ and Harry Norton,★ began a steady pursuit of James Strachey. Such was the view of Virginia Woolf, who saw Alix as a drifting, despairing character, incapable of any sustained effort, in spite of her good brain. She certainly lasted only one day at the Hogarth Press in 1917, finding the work utterly boring, though she afterwards did some desultory research for Leonard Woolf.★ Alix met James at the 1917 Club and they found a common interest in the new science of psychology. In 1919 she leased 41 Gordon Square, where they could live together, and next year they were married to facilitate their journey to Vienna, as James wished to be analysed by Freud. After collapsing with palpitations at the Staatsoper, Alix decided to enter analysis as well, but had to break off in the winter of 1921–2 because of a severe attack of pleurisy. From September 1924 she stayed on her own in Berlin, then a great centre of psychology, to complete her analysis. She enjoyed the city's social life, especially dancing, and made new friends, but left after her analyst died at Christmas 1925.

The Stracheys were never again separated for long. They let the lower floors of 41 Gordon Square and lived at the top in great austerity; in later years they were said to eat in the kitchen next to the sink, so that they could put the dishes straight in to save time.

STRACHEY, JAMES BEAUMONT 167

The second floor was used as consulting-rooms for their patients, but their main task was to translate the whole of Freud's works. Alix wrote two other books, *The Unconscious Motives of War* (1957) and *The Psychology of Nationhood* (1960), and was psychologist to the London Clinic of Psycho-Analysis. After her husband's death in 1967 she lived alone at her old home, Lord's Wood.

Bloomsbury/Freud, The Letters of James and Alix Strachey, 1924–5, ed. P. Meisel and W. Kendrick (London, 1986)

STRACHEY, James Beaumont (1887–1967), psychologist: youngest child of Sir Richard and Lady Strachey,** born when they were aged seventy and forty-seven; his oldest sister's children called him "Uncle Baby". In 1898 he was sent to board at Hillbrow School, Rugby, but then went as a day-boy to St Paul's School, London. At both schools his cousin Duncan Grant* looked after him, and he was generally spoilt at home by his family. His brother Lytton* was his idol, and in 1905 he went up to Trinity College, Cambridge, in Lytton's old rooms, and was elected to the Apostles in his second term by Lytton's influence. "Little Strachey", as Cambridge called him, told his brother "I do no work and am mostly in trances", but did start learning German, again at Lytton's suggestion. He also emulated his brother's homosexuality, in an uncommitted way apart from his romantic yearning for Rupert Brooke,* who had been his friend since preparatory school. However in 1910 he began to take more interest in young women, including Noel Olivier* with whom he eventually had a long-lasting love affair. Music was perhaps his greatest enthusiasm, and after taking a Pass degree he drifted easily into musical and drama criticism for the *Spectator,* because the Editor was his cousin St Loe Strachey. He visited Moscow via Germany in 1914, and on the way grew the beard that increased his resemblance to Lytton, and in old age to Freud. In 1915 James Strachey was dismissed by his cousin because of his pacifism, and undertook relief work with the Quakers for the rest of the First World War.

James came to psychology by way of the Society for Psychical Research, which he had joined by 1912 when Freud wrote a paper for its *Proceedings.* In 1919, on the advice of the doyen of English psychologists, Ernest Jones, he began medical training at St Thomas's Hospital as a preliminary to becoming a psycho-analyst. James lasted just three weeks at St Thomas', caught influenza and returned to reviewing on the *Athenaeum*. However he had begun to go about with Alix Sargant-Florence (*supra*), who shared his interest in psychology and lack of ambition for anything else. She was the more persistent in their relationship, and induced him to live with her at 41 Gordon Square. In the infancy of psycho-analysis it was possible to qualify as a practitioner by being analysed, preferably by Freud himself, and James determined to go to Vienna for this purpose. Alix and he, now married, set out in September 1920; by June 1922 James' analysis was complete, and he was able to take patients of his own. Freud had already asked the Stracheys to translate one of his papers, and once settled in London again they embarked on the production of an English edition of all his work. Both Stracheys became active practitioners of psychiatry, and James attended international congresses, but they were never deflected from their main task, although James suffered greatly at his brother Lytton's death (1932). He and Alix had helped Lytton with the psychology in his last book, *Elizabeth and Essex* (1928), and it was dedicated to them.

Music was still James' chief leisure interest, and in 1934 he became a founder member of the Glyndebourne Opera, writing many of the programme notes still in use today. The Stracheys spent the war years (1939–45) at Alix's family home, Lord's Wood in Buckinghamshire, and retired there permanently in 1956. Volume 23, the last volume of the *Standard Edition* of Freud's works, was published in 1966. Although Alix had assisted throughout, James was overall editor and received the Schlegel-Tieck Prize for translation, but died in April 1967, before the presentation of the award. A final volume of indexes and bibliography was published in 1974 by Angela Richards, daughter of James' old love Noel Olivier.

Bloomsbury/Freud, The Letters of James and Alix Strachey, 1924–5, ed. P. Meisel and W. Kendrick (London, 1986)

STRACHEY, Jane Maria, Lady (1840–1928), Lytton Strachey's* mother: daughter of John Peter Grant, Lieutenant-governor of Bengal, born in a storm off the Cape of Good Hope during the voyage home from India. Jane went to school in London, spending holidays at Rothiemurchus, the family home in Scotland, or in Ireland. The Grants went back to India twice more, in 1851–4 and after the Mutiny in 1858, when John Peter Grant was President of the Council in Calcutta. That summer Jane met her father's colleague and friend, Major Richard Strachey,* and in January 1859 she became his second wife; she was eighteen to his forty-one.

At first the Stracheys' married life echoed the Grants', with Jane taking the family back to England for long periods after 1860. Although she enjoyed the social life of the British Raj, she lost two of her six babies born in India. In England her interests were literary and political; she met Browning, the Carlyles and George Eliot, and helped to circulate the first petition for votes for women. When Richard Strachey finally retired in 1872, the family settled in London, first in Stowey House, Clapham Common, where five more children arrived. Later they moved to 69 Lancaster Gate (1884); James (*supra*), the baby, was born there and the house was the centre of Strachey activities for the next twenty-four years.

Jane Strachey was a great traveller still. She had spent the winter of 1870–1 in Florence, where she met the teacher Marie Souvestre.* There were long trips to the U.S.A. with her husband (1877, 1884) and one final visit to India in 1878. At home her wide knowledge of French and English literature found expression in poetry readings, and anthologies. She edited her aunt's *Memoirs of a Highland Lady* and wrote verse, including "An International Song" for the International Alliance of Women's Suffrage Societies. She disliked housekeeping, claiming that her "ideal life would be to live entirely in boarding-houses", and left most of it to her daughters—even so the food often ran out. Absent-minded as she was, she managed to keep up with her ten children, writing once a week to each one, yet never interfering drastically with their lives. Lytton was her undoubted favourite.

In 1907 the Stracheys gave up Lancaster Gate, and moved to a smaller house in Hampstead. When Sir Richard died in February 1908, Lady Strachey was still in her vigorous sixties, joining in the united Women's Suffrage marches of 1907 and 1908, and writing songs and pamphlets for the movement. However, the headaches she had suffered from her youth became worse and her eyesight was affected; in 1917 she lost her left eye in an operation. In 1919 she began living at 51 Gordon Square with her daughters Marjorie* and Philippa,* and started to write her Memoirs. Although quite blind some years before her death, she enjoyed the company of the Bloomsburyites, and would sit on her balcony waving to them as they walked through the square. Virginia Woolf,* in her memorial tribute to Lady Strachey (*The Nation and the Athenaeum*, 22 December, 1928) described her gesture as "a vast maternal benediction. It was as if the Victorian age . . . were bestowing its blessing".

Elizabeth F. Boyd, *Bloomsbury Heritage* (London, 1976)

STRACHEY, Julia Frances (1901–79): born in Allahabad, India, daughter of Oliver Strachey⋆ and his first wife Ruby. A happy child at first, she felt rejected when suddenly sent to England in 1906 to live with her aunt Elinor Rendel, and was further depressed by the news of her parents' divorce. She made a lifelong friend, however, in Frances Marshall (Partridge⋆), whose presence relieved the misery of boarding-school life at Hindhead. In 1911 Oliver Strachey married again, and Julia was adopted by Alys Russell,⋆ the aunt of her stepmother Ray (Strachey⋆).

Alys, who lived with her brother Logan Pearsall Smith⋆ at Ford Place, Sussex, and later in Chelsea, was strict and economical, but happy to entertain Julia's friends and cousins. Julia became a boarder at Bedales School in 1915, and in the same year spent the first of many holidays at the Florentine villa of Ray's mother, Mary Berenson.⋆ After four more unsuccessful years at school, she entered Bedford College, London, to read Psychology, found that she had mistakenly enrolled in Physiology, and left after a term for the Slade School of Art.

When she finished at the Slade in 1921, Julia intended to take up commercial art, and began preparing drawings for an advertising agency, but devoted most of her time to parties and young men. She lived, intermittently, with her father at 42 Gordon Square, cheerfully mismanaging the house during her stepmother's frequent absences in the country. The drawings were eventually rejected, and in 1925 she was convalescing after a breakdown by staying with her aunt Dorothy (Bussy⋆) at Roquebrune in France. On returning to London she tried a new career, modelling, and met another member of "young Bloomsbury", the sculptor Stephen Tomlin.⋆ The couple became lovers and married in 1927. Their wedding at St Pancras church was described by Virginia Woolf,⋆ who was fond of Julia, in a letter to her sister as "a prosaic affair". For two years the marriage appeared happy, but Tomlin suffered from bouts of severe depression and drinking and both partners found relief in outside adventures. They eventually separated, though there was no divorce; Tomlin died in 1937.

Meanwhile Julia had begun to write seriously, and the Hogarth Press published her first novel, *Cheerful Weather for the Wedding*, in 1932, with a jacket designed by Duncan Grant.* She had a nominal job as receptionist for a photographer friend, but in 1939 began attending the St Denis Drama School, with the idea of becoming a dramatist. Here she met and fell in love with Lawrence Gowing, an art student and stage designer seventeen years younger than herself. They spent the years of the Second World War together in the country, near the Partridges at Ham Spray House.

After 1945 Julia worked as a publisher's reader for Secker and Warburg, and wrote her second novel, *The Man on the Pier* (1952). The Gowings were married in 1952 and lived in Newcastle, where Gowing was Professor of Fine Arts. On his appointment as Principal of Chelsea Art School in 1958, they moved south again, but were divorced in 1967. Julia led an increasingly solitary existence in London, though she visited Gowing and his new family, and kept up her friendship with Frances Partridge and a few others, often through rather embittered letters. Although she had published stories and sketches during and after the war, she wrote no other long work of fiction, but spent the rest of her life writing and re-writing her recollections (edited by Frances Partridge and published in 1983 as *Julia*).

STRACHEY, (Giles) Lytton (1880–1932), biographer and essayist: born at Stowey House, Clapham Common, London, the eleventh of the thirteen children of General Sir Richard Strachey* and his forty-year old wife Jane* (*née* Grant). The middle name honoured the child's godfather, the Earl of Lytton, a minor poet and sixth Viceroy of India. The boy, whose health was poor, was schooled briefly at crankily God-fearing Abbotsholme, on the edge of the Derbyshire Peak District, and for nine terms (1894–7) at Leamington College, but he was educated by his family and their friends, notably Marie Souvestre* at Allenswood, and by the literary figures whom Lady Strachey invited to her London home, 69 Lancaster Gate. In October 1897 he became a student at University College, Liverpool, studying Latin and Greek, Mathematics and English literature and history. The greatest influence upon him was the thirty-six-year-old Professor of English Literature, Walter Raleigh, ex-President of the Cambridge Union and already a biographer of Stevenson. Strachey visited Cambridge for the first time in Raleigh's company in May 1899 and he preferred the university to Oxford, where he had failed to obtain a scholarship at Christ Church or a place at Balliol. He accordingly went up to Trinity College, Cambridge, as an undergraduate in October 1899, with commendation from Raleigh as a student of remarkable distinction. Clive Bell★ records the Head Porter at Trinity drawing his attention to the long limpid freshman with pince-nez crossing the Great Court with the comment, "You wouldn't think he was a General's son".

As well as Bell, Strachey counted among his early friends at Trinity L. Woolf,★ T. Stephen,★ and S. Sydney-Turner;★ and he received academic encouragement from a Trinity man four years his senior, G. M. Trevelyan whose liking for long walks, earnestly talking history on top of a hearty breakfast, proved a taxing discipline. Physically Strachey remained frail, an erratic heart inclining him to hypochondria. Although Lytton was made a scholar of his college and won the Chancellor's Medal for verse in 1902 with an ode on Ely, he only gained second-class honours in both parts of his History Tripos. He flourished, however, in university reading clubs and *conversazioni*, notably the Midnight Society which, with Woolf, Bell, Thoby Stephen and Saxon-Turner, he founded in 1899–1900 and the *X* Society, a somewhat larger play-reading group. Graduates including Bertrand Russell,★ Desmond MacCarthy★ and E. M. Forster★ occasionally attended the Midnight Society's meetings, while James Strachey★ remembered coming up from St Paul's School for an *X* Society's reading of *Love for Love*. When, on the initiative of Ralph Hawtrey,★ Lytton was elected an Apostle (February 1902), the Midnight Society fell apart. Nine months later he became Secretary of the Apostles; their affairs and intellectual conceits shaped his world for at least another three years, probably longer.

As an Apostle Strachey came under the influence of G. E. Moore,★ whose *Principia Ethica* was published in the autumn of 1903. But Strachey and other young Apostles gave greater emphasis than Moore's philosopher colleagues to the last two chapters, with their delight in "the pleasures of human intercourse and the enjoyment of beautiful objects". They saw in Moore's assumption that it was impossible to define and analyse the Good a means of elevating aesthetics to a moral code. Strachey, his new friend Keynes,★ and his older associates exulted in a hitherto repressed homosexuality which, alongside an anti-religious rationalism, became fashionable among the aspiring intellectuals in Trinity and King's College, too.

For two and a half years Strachey concentrated on a thesis about Warren Hastings, hoping for election to a Trinity Fellowship. In this, in October 1905, he was disappointed. He returned to Lancaster Gate and sought to support himself in journalism, writing in particular for the *Spectator,* of which his cousin St Loe Strachey, was Editor. With another cousin, Duncan Grant,* Lytton convinced himself he was passionately in love that winter. He continued, however, to visit Cambridge as often as possible. As the passion of his Grant infatuation cooled, so Strachey became increasingly dependent on the friendship offered by Thoby Stephen, his brother Adrian* and their sisters at 46 Gordon Square, Bloomsbury, where Thursday evening salons revived memories of the Midnight Club and play-reading sessions at Trinity.

Strachey remained an intimate of Old Bloomsbury until it vanished in the First World War. He stayed occasionally with Clive and Vanessa Bell* but he never had a Bloomsbury home of his own, although Lady Strachey lived in Gordon Square after the war. Lytton kept rooms in Belsize Park Gardens, Hampstead, or leased country cottages when he wished to concentrate on his writing. So close was his friendship with Virginia Stephen (Woolf*) that in February 1909 he proposed marriage to her and to his consternation was accepted, although both of them changed their minds within a matter of hours. Virginia's cousin, H. A. L. Fisher,* commissioned Strachey's first book, *Landmarks in French Literature,* which the Home University Library published in 1912. From the autumn of 1910, there were new friendships: the valuable patronage of Lady Ottoline Morrell;* and the fascinating appeal of Henry Lamb,* the artist brother of his Trinity friend, Walter Lamb.* With £100 lent by Henry Norton,* Strachey settled down at a farmhouse at East Ilsley on the Berkshire Downs in the winter of 1912–13. There he planned the iconoclastic biographical essays which, appearing as *Eminent Victorians* in May 1918, made his literary reputation. After four years of world war a cynical reading public welcomed irreverent historical satire which deflated pretentious legends.

Strachey was a conscientious objector in the First World War; he was also declared medically grade C4 and was thus virtually unfit for any military service. His personal life was transformed after meeting the painter Dora Carrington* when she was staying with the Woolfs at Asheham in December 1915. Despite his homosexual proclivities Strachey became extremely fond of Carrington. Within two years they were living in the same house at Tidmarsh, Oxfordshire. Strachey, eager to emphasise his belief in tolerance over personal relationships, accepted Carrington's love affair with Mark Gertler★ and in 1921 recognised that it was natural for Carrington to marry an ex-officer to whom both she and Strachey himself were attracted, Ralph Partridge.★ When two years later Strachey bought the lease of Ham Spray House, south of Hungerford, husband and wife moved in with him, although Partridge spent much time in London from 1926 onwards.

It was at Mill House, Tidmarsh, rather than at Ham Spray that Strachey's most successful literary work was accomplished. *Eminent Victorians* was followed in 1921 by his elegantly written *Queen Victoria*, still intimately mischievous but by no means an unsympathetic portrait. A collection of essays, *Books and Characters*, dedicated to his friend Keynes, was also published while he was still at Tidmarsh. By October 1927, when he was working at Ham Spray on the Elizabethan age, his style was so popular that the *Daily Mail* paid him £500 for a single review of a biography of Edward VII. In that same year his friend Virginia Woolf thought herself fortunate to receive on her five novels English and American royalties totalling £545.

Elizabeth and Essex, published in 1928, was poor history salaciously written but interesting for its early use of Freudian speculation over the lasting consequences of Henry VIII's conduct on his daughter's pattern of behaviour. "It was a terribly exhausting book to write", he told Ottoline Morrell soon after it was published. His close friendships with Roger Senhouse★ and Philip Ritchie★ had sustained his creative energies while he was working on the book, but thereafter he wrote little, although he prepared *Portraits in Miniature* for publication in 1931. From 1929, too, he worked on a complete edition of *The Greville Memoirs*, a task completed six years after his death by Ralph and Frances Partridge and Roger Fulford.

Occasional attempts were made to interest Lytton Strachey in writing for the theatre or even the cinema. He often amused his guests at Ham Spray House with one-act entertainments. His sole attempt to grapple with the discipline imposed upon a dramatist was in 1912 when he wrote a tragic melodrama, *A Son of Heaven*, set in Peking during the Boxer Rising. He agreed that there should be two charity performances of the play at the Scala Theatre, London, in the summer of 1925. The set was designed by Duncan Grant, the programme by Vanessa Bell; incidental music was composed by William Walton; and most of the cast were amateurs from Cambridge or Bloomsbury, including John Sheppard,★ Professor Dennis Robertson, Ralph Partridge, Gerald Brenan★ and

Julia Strachey (*supra*). Lytton was troubled by a series of backstage intrigues and hurried off to the Dolomites with "Sebastian" Sprott* a few days before the performance. Many years after Strachey's death the play was broadcast by the B.B.C.

Although frequently tired by the journeys, he continued to travel extensively in 1930 and 1931: with Dadie Rylands* to Italy; as a guest of the Guinness family in Ireland; and to his beloved France. His health finally gave way at the end of November 1931; he was nursed through weeks of pain by Carrington, by his sister Philippa* and his brother James. The physicians were puzzled by his illness, suspecting paratyphoid. After his death—at Ham Spray House on 21 January 1932—it was discovered he had suffered from cancer of the stomach.

M. Holroyd, *Lytton Strachey, The Unknown Years, 1880–1910* (London, 1967) and *The Years of Achievement, 1910–1932* (London, 1968)

STRACHEY, Marjorie Colville (1882–1964), teacher, writer: born in London, daughter of Sir Richard and Lady Strachey**; nicknamed "Gumbo" in the family. Her brother Lytton (*supra*) was her great companion in their childhood; they collaborated on plays and verses, often in French, and corresponded regularly. Their education began together in 1886 at Hyde Park Kindergarten, and Marjorie's continued at Allenswood School, Royal Holloway College, and Somerville College, Oxford (1904–6), where she obtained a Class II degree in French. As a teacher of English literature, history and French to older children she was original and inspiring, and during her years in the state system she taught briefly in primary schools. A natural rebel, Marjorie also worked for women's suffrage, but found time to accompany Lytton on holiday and attend Bloomsbury parties. At these her sharp humour was expressed in rendering hymns or nursery rhymes so as to sound obscene without actually changing the words. Dancing was a great feature of her performance: Lytton reported that on one occasion in 1913 she danced naked, except for a miniature of the Prince Consort.

In January 1915 Marjorie confided to Vanessa Bell* and Virginia Woolf* the progress of her love affair with Colonel Josiah Wedgwood, a Liberal M.P. whom she met through the Morrells.** When eventually he obtained a divorce, however, he married his children's governess. Deteriorating eyesight and her mother's health forced Marjorie to stop teaching in state schools in 1919; she and her sister Philippa* moved into 51 Gordon Square to make a home for their mother until her death. From there Marjorie ran a private school for the children of Bloomsbury, moving for two summers to Charleston, where lessons took place out of doors. By 1936 she had a tiny country home of her own, in the grounds of her sister-in-law Ray Strachey's* "Mud House"; Ray's daughter Barbara recalled a hilarious visit to Bayreuth with her aunt about this time. After 1945 she also had a flat in Taviton Street, shared sometimes with Duncan Grant* and his friends. In 1960 she suffered a great shock when her niece, Janie Bussy,* died in an accident at 51 Gordon Square, and in the same year she lost her sister Dorothy (Bussy*) and brother Oliver (*infra*). She remained active in spite of arthritis until she entered a nursing-home shortly before her death in 1964.

Vanessa Bell (in 1908) and Grant (in 1909) both painted Marjorie Strachey; Grant's picture, *Le Crime et le Châtiment*, is in the Tate Gallery. Her books include two novels, the second, *The Counterfeiters* (1927), based on her Bloomsbury friends. *The Nightingale: a Life of Chopin* (1925), was very successful in the U.S.A. *Mazzini, Garibaldi and Cavour* (1937) is an example of her historical writing, and in later years she produced books on Church history without religion, the last being *Saints and Sinners of the Fourth Century* (1958).

STRACHEY, Oliver (1874–1960), railway official and cryptographer: son of Sir Richard Strachey.* Although a brilliant mathematician and gifted musician, he was idle. After Eton and Balliol College, Oxford—where he was sent down without a degree—he studied the piano in Vienna before following the family tradition and taking up a post with the Indian railways in 1897. He remained in India until 1911, marrying (and divorcing) Ruby Mayer, the daughter of a Swiss contractor; their child was Julia Strachey.*

While in India he exchanged letters on philosophy with Bertrand Russell.* It was at a weekend party of the Russells in March 1911 that Strachey met Ray Costelloe (Strachey*), whom he married quietly at Cambridge on 31 May. Only Lytton Strachey* and Ray's sister Karin (Stephen*) were present. The couple travelled out to

the Punjab before Oliver resigned from the Indian railways, his
final duty being to wait upon the Durbar train when it brought the
King-Emperor and his consort to Dinapore. Back in England in
1912, husband and wife collaborated on a book, *Keigwin's Rebellion*
(1916); they worked jointly in support of women's suffrage, and
regularly attended the Bloomsbury parties, from which Oliver
gained more pleasure than Ray. Their daughter, the author Barbara
Strachey, was born in 1912; their son Christopher (1916–74) was to
become Oxford's first Professor of Computation.

Oliver Strachey's own mathematical skills made him a gifted
cryptographer, both during and after the war. He was employed at
the War Office and at Cairo, surviving the torpedoing of the ship on
which he was sailing to Egypt. But he never became an
"establishment figure", joining Leonard Woolf★ as a founder-
member of the 1917 Club. While Ray Strachey preferred to live in
the country, Oliver stayed in their Gordon Square rooms, where he
was happy playing chess and the piano. He liked the Bloomsbury
milieu, and enjoyed the companionship of Inez Jenkins, an Oxford
graduate much despised by Virginia Woolf,★ until she married in
1923. While his wife was irritated by the adolescent Julia, Oliver
Strachey found her amusing and regarded her husband Stephen
Tomlin★ as a close friend; when Tomlin was dying in 1937, his
father-in-law was the only person whom he wished to see. In 1939
Oliver Strachey was retained after retirement age by the War office
and sent to Canada on a secret mission. He was there when his wife
died (1940) but returned home in 1943 after a heart attack, moving
into 51 Gordon Square with his surviving sisters, Philippa★ and
Marjorie (*supra*). From 1954 until his death in 1960 he was in a
nursing-home.

STRACHEY, (Joan) Pernel (1876–1951), university don: born in
London, the seventh child of Sir Richard and Lady Strachey.★ She
excelled in French and, after her schooling by Marie Souvestre,★
she needed only eight weeks coaching from her sister Dorothy
Bussy★ to pass the Cambridge entrance examination. She read
mediaeval and modern languages at Newnham College (1895–9).
Although the cocoa and cakes at 10 p.m. aspect of Newnham life
depressed her, she loved Cambridge itself and, after four years of
teaching at Royal Holloway College, London (1900–5), she was
pleased to return to Newnham for the rest of her academic life; she

was Vice-Principal, 1910–23, and Principal, 1923–41, and served on the governing body from 1943 until her death. Her other interests, music and women's rights, she shared with her favourite sister, Philippa (*infra*). She sang in the Cambridge Bach Choir. In Bloomsbury society her closest friends were probably Virginia and Leonard Woolf,★★ with whom she used to exchange visits. Her only publication was a poem on the Assumption of the Virgin Mary (1924).

STRACHEY, Philippa ("Pippa") (1872–1968), fifth child of Sir Richard and Lady Strachey★★: the first to be born in London. Her upbringing coincided with a period of family economy; she could not attend Marie Souvestre's★ school like her sisters and was unable to pass the Cambridge entrance examination.

Philippa enjoyed life in the Strachey home in Lancaster Gate, sharing dances and parties with her older sister Dorothy (Bussy★), and a love of music with her favourite sister Pernel (*supra*). She was the most athletic of the Stracheys, learning sailing and horse-driving, skating with Lytton, and starting the whole family, including her mother, on bicycling. Philippa's physical attraction and cheerfulness brought her many male friends, but her later love for Roger Fry★ was probably the most serious of her life, though the exact nature of their affair is unknown.

In 1900 she went to India to visit her favourite brother Ralph and attend her brother Oliver's★ wedding to Ruby Mayer. She stayed in Allahabad with her cousin, Sir Arthur Strachey, and journeyed as far as the Afghan frontier. Sir Arthur's sudden death the following year kept Philippa in India, helping his widow. She was bridesmaid at Ralph's marriage in October, and arrived home finally in March 1902, transformed by her experiences into a mature woman, the chief support of the Stracheys, not least when nursing the dying Lytton in 1932.

Philippa's overriding preoccupation outside her family was the campaign for women's suffrage. In 1907 she became Secretary of the London Society for Women's Suffrage and an organiser of the first great women's rally, the "Mud March", on 9 February 1907. On her retirement in 1951 she was made C.B.E. and appointed Honorary Secretary of the Millicent Fawcett Society.

Betty Askwith, *Two Victorian Families* (London, 1971)

STRACHEY, Ray, *née* Rachel Conn Costelloe (1887–1940), writer and suffragist: born in Westminster, elder daughter of Frank and Mary Costelloe (Berenson*) and sister of Karin Stephen.* The sisters were mainly brought up by a formidable Quaker grandmother, Hannah Whitall Smith. Ray blossomed academically at Kensington High School and became friendly with Lytton Strachey's* niece Ellie Rendel.* Ray and Karin went to Italy for their mother's wedding to Berenson in 1900; they often took their holidays in Florence, where Ray learned to drive as early as 1905.

After reading Mathematics at Newnham College, Cambridge (1905–8), she became a committed suffragist, joined the "Mud March" of February 1907 and accompanied the American suffragist, the Reverend Anna Shaw, on speaking tours of both the United States (1908) and England (1910). By then Mary Berenson had paid for the publication of Ray's first novel, *The World at Eighteen* (1907) and an allowance from the Berensons enabled her to divide her life between writing and suffrage work, finding time also to study electrical engineering at Oxford (1910). She attended Bloomsbury parties, although with little enjoyment, and met the Stephen family,* exchanging occasional visits with Virginia (Woolf*). Keynes* she had known since 1906, when he was one of two eligible young men chosen by her mother to escort her on an Italian motor tour.

In 1911 she joined a reading party organised by the Russells and met and liked Oliver Strachey,* newly back from India. As a jobless divorcé Oliver felt he had little to offer, but—as he reported to Karin—Ray proposed to him while boating on the Thames between Littlemore mental home and a sewage farm. To avoid ambitious plans for the wedding made by Ray's mother, the couple escaped to Cambridge for a quiet marriage on 31 May. After a visit to India they settled with her aunt, Alys Russell,* in Sussex where a daughter, Barbara, was born in 1912 and a son, Christopher, in 1916, the year in which Oliver and Ray completed their Indian history book, *Keigwin's Rebellion.*

Ray Strachey accepted great public responsibilities after 1916: Secretary of the National Union of Women's Suffrage Societies (to 1921); and Chairman of the Women's Service Bureau (to 1934). She helped check the wartime exploitation of women workers and saw the bill enfranchising women pass through Parliament. In 1918, 1922 and 1923 she stood unsuccessfully for Brentford and Chiswick as an Independent; briefly she was acting unpaid Political Secretary to Lady Astor. Ray Strachey was joint-founder of the League of Nations Union and Editor of the *Women's Leader,* persuading

Virginia Woolf to contribute an article in support of the Plumage Bill (1920) which restricted the import of exotic birds and feathers.

Although by 1920 Ray and Oliver leased 42 Gordon Square, she also owned "The Mud House" (made of compressed earth) at Fernhurst, where Marjorie Strachey* had a cottage in the grounds and the younger Stracheys enjoyed a swimming-pool, added in 1921. Public duties, including the establishment of a Women's Employment Federation (1935), occupied much of her time, but she continued to write books and articles and became a broadcaster. Her *A Quaker Grandmother* (1914) was followed by *The Cause* (1928), *Millicent Garrett Fawcett* (1932), and by two novels. She died on 16 July 1940 after an operation, content—as she told her mother before entering hospital—to have "enjoyed an interesting life".

Barbara Strachey, *Remarkable Relations* (London, 1980)

STRACHEY, General Sir Richard (1817–1908), father of Lytton Strachey*: born into a family connected on both sides with the British administration in India and educated at Addiscombe, a school which prepared for a military and engineering career. Strachey joined the East India Company Engineers in 1836 to specialise in railways, but after serving in the Sutlej campaign (1845–6) he was decorated and promoted to Major. During the 1850s he pursued his botanical interests on expeditions to Tibet which made his name among British scientists. As Secretary to the Government of the Central Provinces, Strachey saw active service again in the Indian Mutiny (1857–8), and worked closely with John Peter Grant, who held a similar post in Bengal. Strachey's first wife, Caroline Bowles, had died in childbirth in 1855, and in January 1859 he married Grant's daughter Jane (Strachey*).

By 1862 Richard Strachey, now Colonel, was Secretary to the Department of Public Works in Calcutta and Consulting Engineer for Railways. In 1865 he resigned from the service, but the failure of the Bank of Agra destroyed all his savings, and he was forced to sign on for another five years in 1866, becoming first Inspector-General of Irrigation next year. He virtually created India's canal and rail system (the railway bridge at Agra was named after him) and initiated financial reforms to stabilise the rupee. Strachey finally retired as a General in 1872 and settled in London, though he returned to India once more to be President of the Famine Commission in 1878.

Much of Strachey's retirement was spent in scientific research. With his wife he joined an American botanical survey of Colorado, Utah and Nevada, managing also to fit in some sight-seeing in Boston and Mexico and a visit to Brigham Young in Salt Lake City. He was President of the Royal Geographical Society (1880–90) and was awarded the Gold Medal of the Royal Society in 1897, the year in which he was knighted.

The Stracheys had ten surviving children, the youngest, James,* born when Sir Richard was seventy years old. The five oldest, Elinor (1860–1945) who married James Rendel, Richard (1861–1935), Ralph (1868–1923), Dorothy (Bussy*) and Philippa* were inevitably closer to their father than the younger ones. But Sir Richard was very kind to all his children's friends (as Leonard Woolf* recalled) and as generous as circumstances allowed; he had no pension until twenty years after retiring. From 1900 he suffered from chronic dysentery and increasing deafness, and in 1907 finally resigned his Indian railway chairmanships. The Stracheys moved to a smaller house in Hampstead, where Sir Richard died in February 1908.

Betty Askwith, *Two Victorian Families* (London, 1971)

SYDNEY-TURNER, Saxon Arnold (1880–1962), civil servant: born in Gloucester, the son of a doctor from Hove. He was educated at Westminster School, going up to Trinity College, Cambridge in 1899 and taking a Double First in the Classics Tripos (1902 and 1903). He was also a natural mathematician, who in London chose to travel by tram rather than by bus because the numbering of the tickets offered more scope for permutation. At Trinity he was a friend of Thoby Stephen,* who thought him a genius, and he was elected an Apostle in 1902, the same year as Woolf* and Lytton Strachey.* In 1904 he entered the Civil Service in the Estate Duty Office. On 16 February 1905 he became the first visitor to Thoby Stephen's Thursday Evenings at 46 Gordon Square. After eight conscientious years as a civil servant he was promoted and moved to the Treasury in 1913, where he remained until retirement after the Second World War ended. As a young man he wrote poetry, reputedly composed an opera, and was held in awe by his contemporaries for the twin profundities of his silence by day and of his talk after midnight. Virginia Woolf★ at times mocked his remarkable memory for what she regarded as useless facts.

"Saxon" participated in every social activity of Old Bloomsbury, and later of the Memoir Club; he dutifully followed his friends to Sussex or Dorset, Suffolk or Wiltshire; and in August 1909 he accompanied Adrian Stephen★ and Virginia to Bayreuth for the festival. From music he gained more pleasure than others in the Bloomsbury circle. He was respected as a Wagnerian and is known to have seen at least a hundred Tristans. For fifty years he was subject to attacks of sciatica and neuralgia and he became deeply devoted to Barbara Bagenal★ who nursed him. In old age he flourished in a legend of bachelor eccentricity, living in two rooms in Great Ormond Street with a stack of paintings by the Bloomsbury artists left undisplayed in the bedroom. He died in the second week of November 1962.

T

TOMLIN, Stephen ("Tommy") (1901–37), sculptor: youngest son of Lord Justice Tomlin. Although he went up to New College, Oxford as a Classics scholar in 1919, he spent only two terms there, and then studied sculpture. He met David Garnett★ when visiting his bookshop. The two founded a dining club called the "Cranium" in 1925, and Garnett introduced Tomlin to the Bloomsbury circle, where his great charm soon made him popular. Lytton Strachey★ and Carrington★ both found him attractive, and he often stayed with them at Ham Spray House. In 1926 he met Lytton's niece, Julia (Strachey★). The couple became lovers, spent the winter of 1926–7 together in Tomlin's studio in Paris, and married in the following July. Bloomsbury cautiously welcomed the match, but Lady Tomlin was greatly distressed.

At first the Tomlins were happy, dividing their time between Tomlin's little stone cottage at Swallowcliffe, Wiltshire, and a London studio. Gradually drinking and infidelity on his side led Julia also to take lovers, and by 1930 they had separated. Tomlin went often to Ham Spray alone, and Carrington came to depend on him greatly after Strachey's death in January 1932. He tried to dissuade her from killing herself, arranged for the Woolfs★★ to visit her on 10 March, and broke the news of her suicide to them the next day. When Julia wanted a divorce he threatened suicide himself, but in 1934 he agreed to a final separation and to get psychiatric help. He died suddenly on 5 January 1937, from pneumonia after having a tooth extracted.

Most famous of Tomlin's works are the bronze head of Lytton Strachey (1929), in the Tate Gallery, and the bust of Virginia Woolf (1931), in the National Portrait Gallery. The latter was unfinished because the subject would only allow six sittings. Tomlin also designed a window and wall sculptures at Ham Spray, and, in 1927, a pair of gates for Lincoln's Inn. These were presented by his father and are on the east side of New Square.

TREVELYAN, Robert Calverley (1872–1951), poet and play-wright: second son of Sir George Otto Trevelyan, O.M. (1838–1928), the Liberal politician, historian and biographer, and elder brother of G. M. Trevelyan, O.M. (1876–1962), the historian. Like most of his family he was educated at Harrow School and Trinity College, Cambridge, where he was elected an Apostle in 1893, a year after Russell.* He then shared a house with Roger Fry* in Beaufort Street, Chelsea, devoting himself to the writing of plays and verse. His first volume of poetry, *Mallow and Asphodel*, appeared in 1898 and was followed by *Polyphemus* three years later, with Fry illustrating the volume. Trevelyan once told Virginia Woolf* that he liked to write his poems recumbent on his stomach, with his legs in the air, so that the blood rushed to his head; and this is the impression which his early poems convey today. When he settled at Leigh Hill near Dorking in Surrey, Fry decorated the interior of the house for him and his Dutch wife, Bessie. Their son, Julian Otto Trevelyan (born February 1910), became a distin-guished painter.

"Bob Trevy", a great talker, joined G. E. Moore* for his Cornish and Devonian reading-parties from 1903 onwards, meeting there Lytton Strachey,* MacCarthy,* and Leonard Woolf.* By the summer of 1907 he was on the fringe of Bloomsbury but he did not become a close friend of the Woolfs until the First World War. He translated the Greek classics and continued to turn out volumes of his own verse: *The Foolishness of Solomon* (1915), *The Death of Man* (1919) and a collection of *Poems and Fables* which, in 1925, the Woolfs were glad to publish from the Hogarth Press. A play *Cecilia Gonzaga* appeared in 1903, followed two years later by *The Birth of Parsifal;* a curious two-act fable, *Pterodamazels*, pleased the London intelligentsia, including Katherine Mansfield* as well as Virginia Woolf. His critical study *Thamyris, or the Future of Poetry* was published in 1925. Trevelyan's *Three Plays* was published by the Hogarth Press in May 1931. His *The Bride of Dionysus* (1912) was a libretto for Sir Donald Tovey's one opera, eventually performed in Edinburgh seventeen years later.

Trevelyan was a dedicated and prolific writer. During the General Strike, six weeks before his fifty-fourth birthday, he cycled 28 miles from his Surrey home to Tavistock Square with two verse dramas for the Woolfs to read and assess. A legacy from his mother in 1928 gave Trevelyan the private income which was essential for him to continue his experiments in writing both verse and prose. His later works included a translation of the collected poems of the early nineteenth-century Neapolitan, Giacomo Leopardi (1941) and a collection of essays, *Windfalls* (1944).

Bloomsbury attitudes at times incensed Trevelyan; he was especially irritated by the derision with which the Woolfs treated news of the acceptance of a peerage by his pacifist and socialist friend, Clifford Allen, in January 1932. Four months later the Hogarth Press published his *Rimeless Numbers* which contained poetic *epistolae* addressed to such friends as Logan Pearsall Smith,* Arthur Waley* and MacCarthy; but in 1934 the Woolfs turned down a collection of his short stories. That summer he wrote the poem "To Virginia Woolf" which he included in his *Aftermath*, published by the Hogarth Press soon after her death. He died ten years later.

V

VAUGHAN, Emma (1874–1960), the youngest child of Henry Halford Vaughan and his wife Adeline, who was eldest sister of Julia Stephen.★ Until after the First World War, Emma Vaughan was a close friend of her cousin, Virginia Woolf,★ who nicknamed her "Toad" (alias "Todger", "Todkings" and "Toadlebinks"). Emma Vaughan studied music in Dresden and in October 1901 encouraged Virginia to take up bookbinding. The social conventions of Bloomsbury were not hers. During the First World War she showed moral courage in undertaking relief work for German prisoners-of-war.

VAUGHAN, (Dame) Janet Maria (1899–), pathologist: daughter of Madge Vaughan (*infra*), a niece of Emma Vaughan (*supra*) and a first cousin once removed of Vanessa Bell★ and Virginia Woolf.★ At the age of six Janet Vaughan was taken by her father, her nurse and Virginia to see the animals in Manchester zoo. She was educated at North Foreland Lodge school and Somerville College, Oxford, before becoming a medical student at University College Hospital, London, in the early 1920s and therefore living in Bloomsbury. Her independence of spirit, radical left sympathies, and desire to make a career for herself led to a rift with her father, William Vaughan, then Headmaster of Rugby. She became a specialist on diseases of the blood, her principal study, *The Anaemias*, first appearing in 1934 when, as Leverhulme Fellow of the Royal College of Physicians, she was the chief assistant in clinical pathology at the British Postgraduate Medical School, Hammersmith. She was a member of the wartime Royal Commission on Equal Pay and of several government committees, and from 1945 until 1967 she was

Principal of Somerville College, Oxford. There she entertained Dorothy Bussy,* and other Bloomsbury friends, when Gide received his honorary degree at Oxford. After receiving an O.B.E. in 1944 Janet Vaughan was made a Dame of the British Empire in 1957.

During her years at University College Hospital she spent many evenings with the Woolfs at their Tavistock Square home and they were impressed both by her professional skills and by the determination with which she supported the General Strike in 1926. When Virginia Woolf wrote *A Room of One's Own* (1929) some of her observations were based on conversations with Dr Janet Vaughan over her use of mincing-machines to produce Britain's first liver extract. Dame Janet's Bloomsbury links had been strengthened in 1930 by her marriage to David Gourlay (who died in 1963), a friend of Francis Birrell* and director of the Wayfarers Travel Agency which, as it was based in Bloomsbury, was patronised by the Woolfs and their friends.

VAUGHAN, Madge, *née* Margaret Symonds (1869–1925), author: a daughter of John Addington Symonds (1840–93), the poet, critic and historian of the Italian renaissance, who was a friend of Leslie Stephen.* She was educated largely in Switzerland but returned happily to England in the late 1880s. Much of the winter of 1889–90 she spent with the Stephen family at 22 Hyde Park Gate and she joined them in their Cornish holidays at a time when she was beginning a literary career of her own; her first book, *Days Spent on a Doge's Farm*, was published in 1893, and five years later she was co-author of a book on Perugia. As a sixteen-year-old, Virginia Stephen (Woolf*) experienced a deep and protracted passion for Madge, intensified by the elder woman's genuine appreciation of Virginia's literary talent. On 28 July 1898 Madge Symonds married the Stephens' cousin, William Wyamar Vaughan (1865–1938), brother of Emma and "Marny" (Margaret, *infra*), at All Saints Church, Ennismore Gardens, Kensington, with Vanessa (Bell*) as a bridesmaid.

For several years after her marriage Madge Vaughan (who wrote a number of unpublished novels) continued to exchange manuscripts with Virginia who, after her nervous breakdown in 1904, stayed with the Vaughans in Yorkshire at Giggleswick, where William was then headmaster. As a conventional schoolmaster he disapproved of his cousin's "bohemian" influence on his wife and was particularly irritated in 1910 by the *Dreadnought* hoax, staged when he was about to become Master of Wellington College, a school traditionally associated with the armed services. His wife, however, maintained a desultory correspondence with her Bloomsbury friends, despite William's hostility to what he believed that the group represented.

Madge Vaughan stayed at Charleston shortly after the birth of Angelica (Garnett★) and, in the spring of 1920, wished to rent the farmhouse for a three-week holiday. Vanessa Bell was angry when Cousin William—about to gain still further advancement, as Headmaster of Rugby—made it clear that he did not wish his family associated with such an "immoral" household. Virginia Woolf, who deplored (and exaggerated) Madge's "Victorian" subservience to her husband, refused to review her *A Child of the Alps* for *The Times Literary Supplement* in June 1920, but there was never a total breach between the old friends, Madge Vaughan visiting the Woolfs at Richmond a year after settling at Rugby. When her daughter Janet (*supra*) became a medical student in London, the Woolfs gave her their friendship.

Virginia Woolf's recollections of Margaret Symonds provided her with a model for Sally Beaton in *Mrs Dalloway*, which was published in May 1925. Unfortunately she never met her friend after the book appeared, for Madge Vaughan died in early November 1925; her husband's career still had six years to go as Headmaster of Rugby.

VAUGHAN, Margaret (1862–1929), voluntary social worker: second daughter of Henry Halford Vaughan and his wife, Adeline, and elder sister of Emma Vaughan.★ She was therefore a first cousin of Vanessa Bell★ and Virginia Woolf;★ they had been friendly with her in their childhood and always called her "Marny". When she was thirty-six and Virginia sixteen they learnt Greek together and in a Memoir Club paper Virginia later recalled how Jack Hills★ had first explained Plato to them a year later, while they were staying at Warboys in Hertfordshire. For most of her adult life Marny, a dutiful church-goer, undertook good work for the poor of Hoxton, in the East End of London. By the First World War she had little in common with her cousins. She shared a flat in Kensington Square Gardens with her sister, Emma. A visit by Marny to the Woolfs at Richmond on 8 December 1917 provided Virginia with material for a gently mocking conversation piece in a letter to her sister Vanessa (see *Letters of V. Woolf* (ed. Nicolson and Trautmann), Vol. II, no. 894).

VAUGHAN WILLIAMS, Adeline, *née* Fisher (1870–1951), a sister of H. A. L. Fisher★ and Admiral Sir William Fisher★ and therefore a first cousin of Vanessa Bell★ and Virginia Woolf.★ She married the composer Ralph Vaughan Williams in October 1897. Six years later she complained to Virginia that the younger Stephens neglected their Fisher relatives. There was little contact thereafter between the cousins. Virginia Woolf thought Vaughan Williams' music "dull" but she respected his personal charm and sympathised with his wife, who suffered for much of their married life from severe arthritis.

WALEY, Arthur David (1889–1966), translator, poet: born Arthur Schloss into a wealthy Jewish family, originally from Frankfurt, who changed their name to Waley at the start of the First World War. Educated at Rugby School and King's College, Cambridge, he was unfit for military service through partial blindness, though he was an expert skier and enthusiastic skater. In 1913 he was appointed Assistant Keeper of Oriental Prints and Drawings at the British Museum. From his rooms in 36 Endsleigh Street overlooking Gordon Square, Waley cycled to the museum daily, observing rather than joining in the activities of the Bloomsbury group. His first book, *A Hundred and Seventy Chinese Poems*, was a success in 1918, the year in which he met Beryl de Zoete, the dance critic and writer ten years his senior. She refused to marry him, and they lived together, intermittently, until her death. Beryl's exotic vitality made her the more conspicuous half of the couple, but neither were popular with Old Bloomsbury; the Bells** and Woolfs** thought Waley a bore, as he often was when he had nothing special to say. In 1929 he retired from the museum to devote himself entirely to writing; he produced twenty-two books of Chinese and Japanese translations and history, including a Chinese novel *Monkey* (1946), for which Duncan Grant* designed the jacket. His last book, *The Secret History of the Mongols*, appeared in 1963.

Honours were heaped on Waley after the Second World War; he became an Honorary Fellow of King's, Cambridge (1945) and an Honorary Lecturer in Chinese Poetry at the School of Oriental Studies, London University (1948). In 1952 he was made a C.B.E., and in 1956 a Companion of Honour. In addition he was awarded the Queens's Medal for Poetry (1953), and the Order of Merit of the Second Treasure from Japan (1959). Throughout these years Beryl de Zoete was dying from an incurable nervous disease, with Waley in constant attendance on her. Visitors to 50 Gordon Square, where the couple now lived in Clive Bell's old flat, included David Garnett* who gave a horrifying description of their existence. When Beryl died in 1962, Waley moved to Highgate with Alison Robinson, whom he first met in 1929; they were married in 1966, just before his death as a result of a car accident.

David Garnett, *Great Friends* (London, 1979)
Alison Waley, *A Half of Two Lives* (London, 1982)

WALPOLE, Hugh Seymour (1884–1941), novelist and critic: born in Auckland, New Zealand, the son of a clergyman who became Bishop of Edinburgh. He was educated at King's School, Canterbury, and Emmanuel College, Cambridge. After a brief spell of schoolmastering at Epsom College, he became a book reviewer and began writing novels: his third book, *Mr Perrin and Mr Traill* (1911), based on his teaching experiences, proved an outstanding success. Service with the Red Cross in Russia from 1915 to 1917 gave him material for *The Dark Forest* and the prize-winning *The Secret City* (1919) but he is best known for his Jeremy trilogy, his series of books based on a Cornish town and beginning with *The Cathedral* (1922), and from 1930 onwards the Herries chronicles, set in Cumberland. Walpole also completed studies of Conrad and Trollope and an anthology of Walter Scott, *The Waverley Pageant* (1932), which he dedicated to Virginia Woolf.*

He was created a C.B.E. for his work in Russia and received a knighthood in the Coronation honours of 1937. Despite his ability to write a succession of best-sellers, he thought his work was old-fashioned and constantly expressed admiration for the modern trends of Bloomsbury. From 1927 onwards he was a friend of Virginia Woolf—whose work he greatly admired—and of the Nicolsons.* Bloomsbury, envious of his success, occasionally mocked him, but he accepted Virginia Woolf's teasing with the meek modesty of an author who could not believe in his own good fortune. During the Second World War he continued to live at his flat in 90 Piccadilly, until the bombing forced him to seek refuge with his servant and his wife in Hampstead. He died nine weeks after Virginia Woolf.

R. Hart-Davis, *Hugh Walpole* (London, 1952)

WATERLOW, Sydney Philip Perigal (1878–1944), diplomat: born at New Barnet into a Hampshire family. He was educated at Eton and at Trinity College, Cambridge, where he was a brilliant classical scholar but, to his great disappointment, was not elected an Apostle. He entered the diplomatic service in 1900 and for a time served in Washington, marrying in 1902 the daughter of the great jurist, Sir Frederick Pollock. In 1905 he resigned from the diplomatic service because he wished to resume his academic studies. He returned to Cambridge, became a university extension lecturer, and published translations of Euripides. On this second sojourn in Cambridge he enjoyed the company of the younger intellectuals. In September 1910 he was with Clive and Vanessa Bell** at Studland in Dorset when Virginia Stephen (Woolf*) joined them, and throughout that winter Waterlow attached himself closely to the Bloomsbury group. Virginia Stephen saw him again at Cambridge in August 1911, discovering that he had by then left his wife. He was, however, still a married man when in November he proposed to Virginia and was rebuffed. His marriage ended in divorce in the spring of 1913.

Soon afterwards he married Margery Eckhard. In the First World War he re-joined the diplomatic service and at the Paris Peace Conference in 1919 he was an acting First Secretary; he was made a C.B.E. for his work. Waterlow was a member of the Memoir Club from its inception in the spring of 1920; and, although Virginia Woolf frequently ridiculed him, he maintained his Bloomsbury contacts while in London as Director of the Foreign Division of the Department for Overseas Trade (1922–4). From 1926 to 1929 he was abroad, as envoy extraordinary and minister at Bangkok and Addis Ababa. While on sick leave in London in 1930 he insisted on his right to attend Memoir Club meetings.

For most of the following decade he was in the Balkans, as Britain's envoy to Bulgaria until 1933 and then as British minister in Athens until the coming of the Second World War. His handling of the crisis over the restoration of the Greek monarchy in 1935 impressed the British government and he was duly knighted (K.C.M.G.). Sir Sydney spoke modern Greek, his interest in classical Greece enabling him to take an active role in the centenary celebrations of the Greek Archaeological Society in 1938, the year before his retirement. He was gratified to learn that his only son, John Waterlow, gained what had eluded him at Cambridge— election as an Apostle. In 1939 Sir Sydney settled at Oare in

Wiltshire where he was visited by the Woolfs and other survivors of Old Bloomsbury. He died in the first week of December 1944.

WELLESLEY, Dorothy Violet, *née* Ashton (1889–1956), poet: born into a wealthy Cheshire family, with the Earl of Scarborough as her stepfather. She married Lord Gerald Wellesley, the third son of the fourth Duke of Wellington, in 1914. Her first volume of poems was published in 1920; half a dozen more followed over the next thirty years, including the long *Genesis* in November 1926. Her poems lyricised endangered flora and fauna, and Bloomsbury did not take her too seriously. W. B. Yeats, however, thought highly of her work, including several poems in his *Oxford Book of Modern Verse* (1936). She was the recipient of his *Letters on Poetry,* which were published in 1940, a year after his death. Her own *Letters to Yeats* were also published posthumously, in 1958. She wrote a study of Sir George Goldie in Nigeria (1935) and an impressionistic autobiography, *Far Have I Travelled* (1952).

Lady Wellesley was a close friend of Vita Sackville-West,* whom she accompanied on her journey to Persia early in 1927 and on her preliminary visit to consider the purchase of Sissinghurst Castle in April 1930. Virginia Woolf* was, at times, jealous of "Dottie's" intimacy with "Vita". She did, however, edit the Living Poets series for the Hogarth Press and was a guest at Bloomsbury parties in the late 1920s and early 1930s. By then she was living apart from her husband and had purchased Penns-in-the-Rocks, Withyham, on the Sussex-Kent border. She commissioned Vanessa Bell* and Duncan Grant* to paint three large wall-panels for her dining-room and to design the furniture for her, a task undertaken mainly in the autumn of 1929 but not completed for another eighteen months; their achievement was praised and made their work more widely known. For the last thirteen years of her life Dorothy Wellesley was titular Duchess of Wellington. She died at Penns in July 1956.

WILBERFORCE, Octavia Mary (1888–1963), doctor: great-granddaughter of the reformer William Wilberforce. Eighth of nine children, and cast for the part of daughter at home, she struggled hard to become a doctor. When Virginia and Leonard Woolf** met her in 1937, she had practised medicine in Brighton for thirteen years, living with her friend Elizabeth Robins, an American actress who had known Virginia's mother. The Woolfs visited them to discuss the possible publication by the Hogarth Press of Elizabeth Robins' book on her brother. Virginia described Octavia as fresh and healthy-looking, without frills but kind, while Octavia admired Virginia's writing. She became friendly with the Woolfs, and during the winter of 1940–1 brought milk and cream to Monk's House from her own small farm.

On 24 March 1941 Virginia's diary indicates that she was contemplating writing about Octavia, but she was already in the grip of such serious depression that Leonard took her to Brighton on the 27th to consult the doctor professionally. Concealing her own illness, Octavia left her bed long enough to persuade her friend to have a thorough examination and found her in excellent physical health. She tried to reassure Virginia about her mental state, and wrote her a cheering note that evening, but when she rang up next day it was already too late; Virginia drowned herself on the morning of the 28th.

Leonard Woolf remained in contact with Octavia Wilberforce over the rest home for "tired professional women", for which Elizabeth Robins bequeathed her Sussex cottage in 1952. Woolf was on the governing board, while Octavia ran the home and the accompanying farm.

WOOLF, Leonard (1880–1969), author and political observer: born in London, the third of the nine children of Sidney Woolf, a barrister by profession and a nominally conformist orthodox Jew in religion. From St Paul's School Woolf went up to Trinity College, Cambridge, as a classicist in October 1899, the same term as Thoby Stephen,★ Lytton Strachey,★ Clive Bell★ and Saxon Sydney-Turner.★ Woolf gained a First in the first part of the Classical Tripos (1902) but a Second in the second part (1903), staying at Cambridge for a fifth year of more general studies. His mind, however, was shaped less by formal tuition than by the ideals accepted by the community in which he moved: he was influenced greatly by G. E. Moore,★ from whom he acquired a challenging intellectual scepticism and a belief in "personal affection and aesthetic enjoyments" as pre-eminently good qualities. So, too, did most of the Apostles, the society to which Woolf was elected in 1902. Friendship with Thoby Stephen introduced Woolf to his sisters, Virginia (Woolf★) and Vanessa (Bell★), and he dined with the Stephen family in the late autumn of 1904, on the eve of sailing for Colombo to take up a post with the Ceylon Civil Service.

He remained in Ceylon for seven years: at Jaffna, among the Tamils of the far north; as deputy to the Government Agent in Kandy (where his varied duties included witnessing floggings and hangings and arranging for the octogenarian Empress Eugénie to see Buddha's tooth); and as Assistant Government Agent in southern Hambantota, 1908–11, where he improved elementary schooling. He arrived home on leave on 11 June 1911, with "twinges of doubt in my imperial soul". By the autumn he was closely attached to Virginia Stephen, to whom he proposed marriage in the second week of the New Year. His resignation was accepted by the Colonial Office on 7 May, his proposal on 29 May. Virginia and Leonard Woolf were married at St Pancras Registry Office on 10 August 1912.

For twenty-nine years Leonard Woolf's devoted care and sense of family responsibility gave his wife the stability which enabled her to emerge from bouts of mental illness and find fulfilment in writing her novels and critical essays. His initiative in encouraging Virginia in 1916–17 to join him in founding the Hogarth Press was partly therapeutic, although he became passionately interested in the technical aspects of printing and managed the business side of the press from 1924 to 1939 while insisting that he would never be a full-time publisher. He saw himself as a professional writer whose deep concern with social problems made him active politically in the Fabian Society and the Labour Party.

Leonard Woolf wrote two novels: *The Village in the Jungle* (1913) emphasised the irrelevance of distant government policies to the struggle of a primitive community in Ceylon against pitiless and all-powerful nature; but *The Wise Virgins* (1914) was less successful, upsetting those members of his family who remained orthodox Jews. His journalism included the editorship of *The International Review* (1919) and of the international section of the *Contemporary Review* (1920–1), the literary editorship of *The Nation* from 1923 to 1930, and the joint editorship of the *Political Quarterly* from 1931 to 1959; he remained its Literary Editor well into his eighties. He wrote a series of *Stories from the East* (1921), some twelve books on contemporary history and politics, two collections of essays in literary criticism, and a dozen important pamphlets on matters ranging from India to international co-operative trade. Occasionally he was over-ambitious: his three volumes of political philosophy— *After the Deluge*, Vol. I (1931), Vol. II (1939) and his *Principia Politica* (1953)—sought to trace the interaction of "communal psychology" and historical events in a series of sweeping generalisations. But the books were always mentally stimulating and gracefully written.

During the First World War Woolf was exempt from conscription on medical grounds as "totally disabled", because he had inherited nervous trembling hands. Basically his politics were "anti-war" and he was a radical supporter of the Union of Democratic Control, like his friend "Goldie" Dickinson.★ He was also a convinced anti-imperialist, travelling up to Leeds in June 1917 for a convention which welcomed the (pre-Bolshevik) Russian Revolution and on 10 October becoming a founder committee member of the 1917 Club, set up four weeks before Lenin's seizure of power in Petrograd. Woolf was interested in the co-operative movement, painstakingly lecturing the Women's Co-operative Guild in the first winter of the war. But through his friendship with Beatrice and Sidney Webb, Woolf's refreshingly independent views drifted into the mainstream of Labour politics.

He was Secretary of two "Advisory Committees" of the Labour Party, on Imperial Questions and on International Questions. Yet although he helped mould Labour policy in the 1920s he only once stood for Parliament: he was Labour candidate for the Combined English Universities in 1922, finishing bottom of a poll headed by his wife's cousin, H. A. L. Fisher.★ Other proposed nominations he rejected, perhaps from reluctance to take on any task which was not in itself a partnership with Virginia. He continued, however, to sit on party committees and encourage local branches in the Lewes constituency as well as interesting himself in Labour Party theory; he was still seeking to define the nature of a moderate democratic socialist foreign policy in a Fabian Society pamphlet published as late as November 1947.

In *Who's Who* Woolf listed gardening as his sole recreation, and he cared deeply for the lawns, trees and flowers at Monk's House, his home in Sussex from 1919 until his death. When he was living at Richmond (1914–March 1924) he enjoyed riding on Wimbledon Common or in Richmond Park, for he was a good horseman; but Virginia wished to return to central London, and the Woolfs made 52 Tavistock Square their Bloomsbury home until moving their possessions to 37 Mecklenburgh Square on the eve of the Second World War. Leonard had plunged whole-heartedly into Blooms-bury society on his return from Ceylon: he joined Adrian Stephen,★ Sydney-Turner and Henry Lamb★ at Russian language classes from their common admiration for the Diaghilev★ "invasion"; and he was Secretary of the second Post-Impressionist exhibition (1912).

Preoccupation with the Hogarth Press intensified his affinity with literary Bloomsbury rather than with the artists, some of whom he found "exasperating". He was a founder-member of the Memoir Club and fully participated in the Bloomsbury fancy-dress parties. From his autobiography it is clear he especially liked good conversation; significantly, of Lytton Strachey, he wrote that "his talk was profounder, wittier, more interesting and original than his writing". Woolf had the gift of lifting his wife's spirits by the inquisitive mood in which he encouraged her to accompany him on journeys to Europe, notably to France, Italy and Greece, but even across Hitler's Germany and, in the spring of 1934, to Ireland.

After his wife's death in 1941 he continued to make Rodmell his main home, living frugally (as always). He added, however, a large conservatory to Monk's House, for he became especially interested in the more exotic plants which needed warmth and attention. Every honour that was offered to him was refused, except one—a Doctorate of Letters at the new University of Sussex, the foundation of which he warmly supported. He died at Monk's House in August 1969; and his ashes, like those of his wife, were scattered beneath an elm tree in the garden, beside what had once been his bowling lawn.

Woolf's autobiography (5 vols) *Sowing, 1880–1904* (London, 1960); *Growing, 1904–1911* (London, 1961); *Beginning Again, 1911–1918* (London, 1964); *Downhill All The Way, 1919–1939* (London, 1967); *The Journey Not the Arrival Matters, 1939–1969* (London, 1969)
Duncan Wilson, *Leonard Woolf, A Political Biography* (London, 1978)

WOOLF, Philip Sidney (1889–1962), youngest brother of Leonard Woolf (*supra*): born in London and hoped originally to be a painter. He was commissioned in the Royal Hussars and, at the end of November 1917, was wounded at Cambrai by the same shell that killed his brother Cecil (a Fellow of Trinity College, Cambridge, born 1887). While convalescent Philip brought some of Cecil's poems to Leonard and Virginia Woolf,** who printed them as the second publication of the Hogarth Press. After training on a farm in Oxfordshire and visiting India, Philip served from 1922 to 1952 as estate manager for his kinsman, James de Rothschild, at Waddesdon Manor, Buckinghamshire. He married Marjorie

Lowndes in 1922, and between 1924 and 1939 his brother and sister-in-law occasionally visited their house at Upper Winchendon. Her diary entries suggest that Virginia Woolf treated Philip, his wife and their three children with aloof condescension.

WOOLF, (Adeline) Virginia (1882–1941), novelist, essayist, biographer and critic: born at 22 Hyde Park Gate, Kensington, in west London, the third of the four children of Leslie and Julia Stephen.** She was never baptised but her secular sponsor ("Godpapa") was the Harvard satirist, poet and essayist, James Russell Lowell who, at the time of her birth, was U.S. Minister in London. Neither Virginia nor her elder sister Vanessa (Bell*) had any formal schooling; they were educated by their parents, with private tuition in music, drawing, dancing and similar social accomplishments. At nine she was writing for a weekly family gazette, the *Hyde Park News;* and, according to her sister Vanessa, she was still a young girl when she received her first rejection slip, for a story submitted to the weekly, *Tit-Bits.*

In so small a world, family events dominated her life: the migration each summer until her thirteenth year to St Ives in Cornwall, where Leslie Stephen leased Talland House; visits to family friends or relatives; the eccentricities of eminent guests, such as Henry James.* Virginia was also influenced by the presence in the household of two much older step-brothers, George and Gerald Duckworth,** both of whom—George in particular—sexually interfered with her occasionally between the ages of six and twenty-two. Possibly in later letters and an autobiographical fragment she exaggerated these molestations but the experience continued to trouble an overwrought mind, contributing to her personal frigidity and inner uncertainties about herself. When her mother died, in May 1895, she had the first of several breakdowns, hearing hallucinatory voices, and for some twenty months she had no lessons. In July 1897 her much loved half-sister, Stella Duckworth (Hills*) died, a hundred days after her marriage to Jack Hills.* This bereavement did not wound Virginia so deeply as her sister and elder brother had feared, probably because she soon thereafter developed a romantic attachment to her cousin, Madge Vaughan.* By November Virginia was attending classes in Greek and History at King's College, London; she attached herself to the college intermittently over the following three years, before starting private Greek lessons in 1902 with Janet Case,* who became a close confidante.

When Thoby Stephen* was up at Cambridge both sisters went to the Trinity May Ball of 1900, where Virginia later remembered meeting for the first time Clive Bell* and Hawtrey.* She was launched in London "society" by her half-brother George in 1903, but was not impressed. After her father's death in February 1904 she spent a month in Pembrokeshire with Vanessa and their half-brother Gerald, and the sisters were in Italy for most of the spring, escorted back to London by George. On 10 May, the day following their return, Virginia had a second nervous breakdown. "All that summer she was mad", her nephew and biographer, Quentin Bell,* roundly declares. She certainly suffered from hallucinations and was reluctant to eat; and when, with three nurses in attendance, she went to stay with her friend Violet Dickinson* near Welwyn, she made a gesture of suicide by throwing herself from a ground-floor window. But she recovered speedily when Thoby arranged for the family to move from Hyde Park Gate, with its sad associations, to 46 Gordon Square and when George married and virtually went out of his step-sisters' lives. By the end of the year she had written an article (on Haworth) and a book review for *The Guardian*, a Protestant weekly. Soon afterwards she began teaching evening classes at Morley College, south London.

In 1905–6 she shared, with Vanessa, the pleasures of acting as hostess for the Thursday evenings which were the nucleus of Old Bloomsbury and in February 1905 she began reviewing for *The Times Literary Supplement*. This happy period was ended by a trip to Greece and Turkey in the autumn of 1906 with her brothers Thoby and Adrian Stephen,* her sister and Violet Dickinson, on which Thoby contracted typhoid. His death, three weeks after his sisters' return to England, was soon followed by Vanessa's marriage to Clive Bell, forcing Virginia and her surviving brother, Adrian, to move to 29 Fitzroy Square, where in October 1907 they sought to re-establish the Thursday evenings. At the same time Virginia began writing her first novel, which appeared as *The Voyage Out* in 1915.

With a legacy of £2,500 from her father's sister, Caroline Stephen,* she was able to accompany her brother, Adrian, and Sydney-Turner* to the Bayreuth Festival in August 1909 and she was encouraged by Adrian to take part in the *Dreadnought* hoax of February 1910, disguised as Ras Mendax, with face blackened and bewhiskered. A month later she was close to nervous collapse and spent some seven weeks that summer in Burley House, a private mental asylum at Twickenham, but she seemed fully restored to health by Christmas and rented a house at Firle, near Lewes, where she spent much of the summer of 1911. In late November she moved to 38 Brunswick Square, Bloomsbury, sharing the house with Adrian, Maynard Keynes* and Grant.*

She received proposals of marriage from Lytton Strachey* (briefly accepted in a post-St Valentine's Day euphoria in 1909), Hilton Young (*infra*) and Walter Lamb,* flirted outrageously with her brother-in-law Clive Bell and maintained a platonic friendship with Rupert Brooke.* On 11 January 1912 Thoby's old friend Leonard Woolf* proposed to her, the offer troubling her so deeply that she had another attack of mental illness and was forced to return to Burley House for a fortnight in February. In June, however, she accepted Woolf: they were married on 10 August, spending some of their honeymoon at Holford in Somerset before going on to France, Spain and Italy for six weeks. By July 1913 she was deeply depressed, another fortnight at Burley House doing nothing to improve her condition. On 9 September she took an overdose of veronal, while at 38 Brunswick Square, and her life was only saved by the prompt action of Geoffrey Keynes* in fetching a stomach-pump from his hospital. For the following five months nurses were in close attendance on her.

Her recovery was slow. She was once more at Burley House in late March 1915, her mental breakdown coinciding with the publication by her half-brother Gerald Duckworth of her first book. Interest in the Hogarth Press, in her new home at Richmond and long periods of rest at Asheham, in Sussex, sustained her and enabled her to begin work on a second novel, *Night and Day*, published by Duckworth in October 1919, a few weeks after the Woolfs moved into Monk's House, Rodmell. In 1922–3 she developed the techniques of impressionist narration, first clearly defined in *Jacob's Room* (published by the Hogarth Press in October 1922) but standing out as her main contribution to stream-of-consciousness "modernism" in the early pages of *Mrs Dalloway* (published May 1925). At the same time she was recognised as a literary critic (*The Common Reader*, 1925, with a second series in 1932) and respected for her attacks on the realism of such popular novelists as Arnold Bennett. During these years she spent most of the working week in Tavistock Square, Bloomsbury, but much of her creative writing was done at Rodmell. *To the Lighthouse* (May 1927) and *The Waves* (October 1931) were her principal novels, the completion and appearance of each of them accompanied by weeks of mental anguish and nervous exhaustion.

A Room of One's Own (October 1929) and *Three Guineas* (June 1938) were major essays in feminism. *Flush* (October 1933) is a fantasy incarnation of the author as Elizabeth Barrett Browning's dog, a work which Leonard Woolf refused to take seriously. He also underestimated *Orlando* (October 1928), an imaginative biographical essay in bi-sexual reincarnation through four centuries of an aristocratic figure, which was inspired by Virginia Woolf's personal devotion to Vita Sackville-West.★ Both *Flush* and *Orlando* reveal more of his wife's flights of imaginative fancy than Leonard Woolf perceived.

In October 1934 the publication of Virginia Woolf's *Walter Sickert, A Conversation* showed the understanding which she could bring to the creative mind of an artist, and it was followed within two months by an invitation to write a biography of Roger Fry,★ who had been her friend since before the First World War. She worked intermittently on this task for five years, but throughout most of the spring and summer of 1936 she was suffering from nervous depression, lacking confidence in her longest novel, *The Years*, published after much rewriting in March 1937. The book was more conventionally "factual" than her earlier novels, a modernised form of family chronicle, tracing the impact of six decades on the children of a Victorian household. For *Between the Acts*, her final novel, the setting was a country house and a village pageant, but the treatment of rural life through several centuries was, once more, impressionistic and experimental. The writing of the book was not finished until the last week in February 1941, leaving the author again despondent. Significantly the acutely sensitive producer of the pageant in the novel moans, in the end, that her artistry has been in vain, "a failure".

Virginia Woolf remained active in the social and literary life of London throughout the 1930s although she spent little time in Bloomsbury after the spring of 1939. The Woolfs moved the Hogarth Press, and their London flat, from Tavistock Square to a house in Mecklenburgh Square a fortnight before the outbreak of war. Virginia's half-share in the Hogarth Press had already been sold to John Lehmann★ in 1938, but she read manuscripts and gave advice to the press until the last months of her life. She seems to have found existence on the Sussex coast during the Battle of Britain oddly exhilarating, rather than a menacing experience; there are several references in her letters to playing bowls on the lawn at Rodmell while German aircraft were overhead. She was saddened by the bombing of London—Mecklenburgh Square and Tavistock Square as well as the City—but she remained personally courageous. By mid-March 1941, however, she was convinced that she was going mad, hearing voices again, and afraid that the art of writing had left her with the completion of *Between the Acts*. Consultation with Octavia Wilberforce★ in Brighton on 27 March failed to reassure her. Next morning she drowned herself in the Sussex Ouse, about half a mile from Monk's House, having filled the pockets of her coat with stones. Her body was found in the river three weeks later; after cremation the ashes were scattered beneath the trees of her garden.

Leonard Woolf subsequently edited many of his wife's essays in literary criticism, finally collecting them in four volumes published by the Hogarth Press in 1966–7. Ten years later the Hogarth Press also published the two versions (1923 and 1935) of Virginia Woolf's only play, *Freshwater*, a comedy about her great-aunt, the Victorian photographer Julia Cameron, never given a public performance.

Q. Bell, *Virginia Woolf* (2 vols, London, 1972)

V. Bell, *Notes on Virginia's Childhood*, ed. R. J. Schaubeck (New York, 1974)

V. Woolf, *Moments of Being; Unpublished Autobiographical Writings*, ed. J. Schulkind (London, 1976)

The Letters of Virginia Woolf, ed. N. Nicolson and J. Trautmann (6 vols, London, 1975–80)

The Diary of Virginia Woolf, ed. A. Olivier Bell and A. McNeillie (5 vols, London, 1977–84)

S. Trombley: *"All that Summer She was Mad"* (London, 1981)

See, too, the literary approach in L. Gordon, *Virginia Woolf, A Writer's Life* (Oxford, 1984)

YOUNG, Edward Hilton (1879–1960), raised to the peerage as Baron Kennett in 1935, politician and poet: born in London, the third son of Sir George Young (Bart), a mountaineering friend of Leslie Stephen;* the Young boys and the Stephen children occasionally played together in Kensington Gardens. He was educated at Marlborough, Eton and University College, London, before going up to Trinity College, Cambridge, where he became President of the Union (1900) and gained first-class honours in Natural Science. In 1904, the year in which he was called to the bar, he became a regular visitor at the Stephens' home in Bloomsbury and was an early member of the Thursday Club. Desmond MacCarthy* dubbed him "the Sphinx without a Secret" while to Vanessa Bell* he seemed "like an elephant in a china shop". Lytton Strachey,* although finding him pompous, recognised his kindness of heart—not least in allowing Lytton generous use of his weekend cottage near Marlborough. There was a long flirtation between Hilton Young and Virginia Stephen (*supra*): he proposed marriage to her while punting at Cambridge in May 1909, only to be told—not very convincingly—that she could marry no one except Lytton.

Much of Hilton Young's work in these pre-war years was undertaken for the Liberal Party, but he was also a journalist, becoming assistant editor of *The Economist* in 1910 and completing a study of *National Finance*, long accepted as a basic textbook in economics. By 1915, when this book was published, Hilton Young was commissioned in the Royal Naval Volunteer Reserve, subsequently helping to evacuate the Serb Government from Albania to Corfu and winning the Distinguished Service Cross in 1917 as Commander of a battery of naval guns along the tiny segment of Belgian coast not under German occupation. In March

1918 Virginia Woolf met him for the first time in many years while visiting her friend "Ka" Cox★ (whom she believed Young might marry): Virginia noted in her diary that he seemed "a perfect type of naval officer"; she "thought him kind & trusty & a little romantic". Seven weeks later he was aboard H.M.S. *Vindictive* in the raid on Zeebrugge Mole, where he was wounded and lost an arm. His heroism at Zeebrugge won him a bar to the D.S.C.

He was returned as a Liberal M.P. for Norwich at an unopposed by-election in 1915, moving politically to the right and in 1926 joining the Conservatives after the General Strike. In 1922 he married the widow of the polar explorer, Captain Scott, and drifted away from his Bloomsbury friends. From 1929 to 1935 he was Conservative M.P. for Sevenoaks and, as Minister of Health in Ramsay Macdonald's national government of 1931, he promoted some of the earliest projects in town and country planning. Lord Kennett had never taken much interest in narrowly Party politics; and, after going to the Lords, he was happy to write verses and collaborate with his stepson—the naturalist and artist, Peter Scott—in producing a book, *A Bird in the Bush* (1936). Both as an M.P. and as a peer he served on British delegations to important conferences abroad.

What's What: a Glossary

ACADÉMIE JULIAN: famous art school in the Rue de Faubourg St Denis, Paris, renowned for its independence and artistic initiative; founded by Rudolphe Julian (1839–1907) in 1860.

APOSTLES: name commonly given to the Cambridge Conversazione Society, founded in 1820 by George Tomlinson and his friends at the university, who sought to discover and follow the virtuous life. *The* Society—as it is sometimes called—was a self-perpetuating and nominally secret fraternity who selected likely candidates ("embryos") mainly from two colleges, King's and Trinity. If the intellectual and personal qualities of an embryo were found, after observation, to satisfy the fraternity he was elected an Apostle. Senior members were "Angels"; they might return to Cambridge from London for the Society's meetings and were expected to assist brother Apostles after election. Meetings were held on Saturday evenings in the Secretary's rooms; an Apostle would read a paper, which would then be discussed. Normally no more than three embryos were elected each year. Apostles prominent in pre-1814 Bloomsbury were: R. Fry (elected 1887), D. MacCarthy (1896), E. M. Forster (1901), L. Strachey (1902), S. Sydney-Turner (1902), L. Woolf (1902), J. M. Keynes (1903), J. Strachey (1906), H. J. Norton (1906), and G. Shove (1909). Five of the twenty-one Apostles elected between 1892 and 1904 were later awarded the O.M.: Russell, Moore, Trevelyan, Forster and Keynes.

"DREADNOUGHT" HOAX: H.M.S. *Dreadnought* was the first all-big-gun battleship in the world; when she was launched and commissioned in 1906 she was faster than any capital ship afloat and her guns had a greater range than those of any rival. In 1910 she was the flagship of Admiral Sir William May, Commander-in-chief Home Fleet. On 10 February 1910, while anchored at Portland, *Dreadnought* was visited and inspected by "the Emperor of Abyssinia" and his suite of three "Abyssinians", together with an interpreter and a man from the Foreign Office. This hoax was perpetrated by Adrian Stephen and Horace Cole, with the assistance of Duncan Grant, Virginia Stephen and two Cambridge friends. Cole later revealed details of the hoax to the press and questions were asked in Parliament. Much indignation was felt by Commander W. W. Fisher (a first cousin of the Stephens) who, as Flag Commander of the fleet, was fooled by the hoaxers. The commanding officer of H.M.S. *Dreadnought*, Captain H. W. Richmond, became Master of Downing College, Cambridge (1936–46), after retiring from the Royal Navy as an Admiral, a knight and a naval historian.

FABIAN SOCIETY: established in January 1884 to encourage the discussion of socialist ideals among British intellectuals and to examine ways of applying socialist principles to the British system. In 1900 the Fabian Society became a constituent element of the newly established Labour Representation Committee (renamed Labour Party in 1906). It believed, not in revolution, but in the gradual achievement of a socialist Britain through democratic means. The society was strong in Cambridge University only after 1906, influencing in particular Rupert Brooke and James Strachey. Leonard Woolf was the main Bloomsbury Fabian.

FRIDAY CLUB: group founded by Vanessa Stephen (Bell) in 1905 for discussion of painting and the fine arts in general. The first formal meeting appears to have been at 46 Gordon Square on 13 October 1905. An exhibition followed in November, the first of several which continued until 1914 and, from 1910 onwards, attracted good press notices. The club drew on a wider range of Vanessa Stephen's acquaintances than the Thursday Evenings (q.v.), bringing together former students from several different London art schools as well as her Bloomsbury relatives and friends.

HOGARTH PRESS: begun in March 1917 by Leonard Woolf to provide his wife with a therapeutic interest. The name was taken from the Woolfs' home at that time, in Richmond. The first printing was done on a small hand-press, the Woolfs buying a mechanical press before they undertook the production of works by Katherine Mansfield and T. S. Eliot. The press was moved to 52 Tavistock Square in 1924, to 37 Mecklenburgh Square in 1939 and, after the bombing of 1940, to Letchworth. R. Partridge (1920–3), G. Rylands (1924), A. Davidson (1924–7), J. Lehmann (1931–2 and 1938–46) all sought to work with Woolf, but found him a difficult colleague. Chatto and Windus absorbed Hogarth in 1946.

LONDON ARTISTS' ASSOCIATION: an enterprise established in 1926, largely on the initiative of Maynard Keynes, by which certain artists would be guaranteed a salary offset by the sale of their work at regular exhibitions, held particularly before Christmas. Membership of the association, which flourished until the eve of the Second World War, was not limited to painters and it therefore helped revive some of the decorative work of the Omega Workshops (q.v.).

LONDON GROUP: an association of British painters established in November 1913, with Sickert as its principal luminary. It included the Camden Town group (fl. 1911–12) of Sickert's followers and also the vorticists associated with Wyndham Lewis and other secessionists from the Omega Workshops (q.v.).

MEMOIR CLUB: an inner post-war Bloomsbury group which sprang from the proposed Novel Club, an abortive idea put forward by Molly MacCarthy in 1918 in the vain hope of encouraging her husband to write fiction. In the following winter this group was transformed into a Memoir Club, with Molly MacCarthy serving as "secretary and drudge" until January 1946. The first meeting was at 25 Wellington Square, Chelsea, on Thursday, 4 March 1920, postponed from the previous Friday. Members of the club were expected to write and deliver short papers of personal recollections. The rules insisted that no one should take offence at their content and papers were not to be mentioned outside the meeting. Some versions were, however, later published. The founder members were the original Bloomsbury group; new members were elected unanimously but by secret ballot. Between 1920 and 1931 the club met in conclave on a hundred occasions; meetings became fewer thereafter but the Memoir Club survived until the 1960s, electing members who had been only children when it was established.

NEW ENGLISH ART CLUB (N.E.A.C.): society of British artists existing since 1885 when painters who found their inspiration in contemporary France became exasperated by the traditionalism of the Royal Academy. In late Edwardian England the N.E.A.C. was considered conservative, progressive artists seceding into smaller bodies, notably the London Group (q.v.).

1917 CLUB: club founded in October 1917 (before Lenin's Bolshevik Revolution) which met at 4 Gerrard Street, Soho, and brought together Bloomsbury figures (e.g. the Woolfs and Barbara Bagenal) and democratic socialists (Ramsay Macdonald, J. Wedgwood, and many others). The first general meeting was on 19 December 1917.

OMEGA WORKSHOPS: a project conceived by Roger Fry for encouraging young painters to bring their artistic skills to interior decoration, particularly in the design and colouring of bowls, vases, tables, chairs, soft furnishings, rugs and curtains. The Omega Workshops, which owed something in inspiration to the Wiener Werkstatte (Vienna, 1903) and the Atelier Martine (Paris, 1911), became a registered company in May 1913 and opened at 33 Fitzroy Square, Bloomsbury, on 8 July 1913. Among artists who, for a small weekly wage, worked part-time for the Omega were Vanessa Bell, Duncan Grant, Wyndham Lewis, Frederick Etchells and Mark Gertler. Omega exhibitions were held from October 1913 until November 1918 but the project suffered from wartime prejudices. Although Omega closed down in June 1919 its traditions influenced and brightened decorative work for the following two decades.

POST-IMPRESSIONIST EXHIBITIONS: Roger Fry organised two London exhibitions to make the English public aware of the changes in French art in the period 1890–1910. The first exhibition, "Manet and the Post-Impressionists" was held at the Grafton Galleries, London (8 November 1910–15 January 1911) with paintings by Cézanne, Van Gogh, Gauguin, Picasso, Derain and Matisse causing a great sensation. The second Post-Impressionist exhibition opened at the Grafton Galleries in November 1912 and included works by British and Russian artists as well as the French. The term "Post-Impressionism" embraced representatives of several continental traditions: Neo-Impressionists such as Seurat and Pissarro; cubism; the Fauves; Gauguin and the Pont-Aven school, etc.

THURSDAY EVENINGS: "At Homes" started by Thoby Stephen at 46 Gordon Square on 16 February 1905 and revived by Adrian and Virginia Stephen at 29 Fitzroy Square in the late autumn of 1907. These gatherings of friends became the core of pre-war "Old Bloomsbury".

Where's Where:
A Guide to the Homes

In Bloomsbury

Bedford Square, 44: Philip and Ottoline Morrell, 1905–15.

Bernard Street, 48: Roger Fry and Helen Anrep, 1926–34.

Brunswick Square, 27: E. M. Forster, 1929–39.

——, 38: Virginia and Adrian Stephen, Duncan Grant, Maynard Keynes, Leonard Woolf intermittently 1911–13; Geoffrey Keynes, 1913.

Fitzroy Square, 21: Duncan Grant and Maynard Keynes, 1909–11.

——, 29: Virginia and Adrian Stephen, 1907–11.

——, 33: Omega Workshops, 1913–19.

Fitzroy Street, 8: Vanessa Bell and Duncan Grant's studios, 1929–40.

Gordon Square, 41: James and Alix Strachey, post-1919, and Ralph Partridge and Frances Marshall 1926–30.

——, 42: Oliver, Ray and Julia Strachey, post-1920.

——, 46: Thoby, Adrian, Vanessa and Virginia Stephen, 1904–7; Clive and Vanessa Bell, 1907–16; Maynard Keynes from 1916 and Lydia (Lopokova) from 1925; absorbed into Birkbeck College in the 1960s.

——, 50: Adrian and Karin Stephen, early 1920s–1939; Clive Bell, succeeded c. 1951–2 by Arthur Waley, to 1962.

——, 51: Lady Strachey and her family, 1919; absorbed by London University in the early 1960s.

Gower Street, 3: Maynard Keynes, Gerald Shove and John Sheppard 1914–16; Middleton Murry and Katherine Mansfield; Brett and Carrington, 1916–17.

——, 10: Philip and Ottoline Morrell, 1928–38.

Great James Street, 16: Nonesuch Press, David Garnett, Ralph Partridge and Frances Marshall, 1930–2.

Mecklenburgh Square, 37: Leonard and Virginia Woolf and the Hogarth Press, 1939–40.

Tavistock Square, 52: Leonard and Virginia Woolf and the Hogarth Press, 1924–39; site now part of the Tavistock Hotel.

Taviton Street, 19: Frances Birrell and David Garnett Bookshop, 1919–23.

Elsewhere in London

Kensington, 22 Hyde Park Gate: home of the Stephen family, 1878–1904.

Bayswater, 69 Lancaster Gate: home of the Strachey family, 1884–1907.

Richmond, Hogarth House, Paradise Road: home of Leonard and Virginia Woolf, 1915–24.

Chelsea, 25 Wellington Square: home of the MacCarthys, 1910–40.

Chelsea, 15 The Vale: home of Ethel Sands, 1913–37.

In Sussex

Asheham House, Firle: 4 miles south-east of Lewes on B2109, leased by Vanessa Bell and Virgina Stephen 1912–14 and until 1917 by the Woolfs; now over-shadowed by a cement works.

Charleston, Firle: Farmhouse 6 miles east of Lewes, south of the A27. Home of Vanessa Bell and her family, of Duncan Grant and their friends from 1916 to 1978. Restored by the Charleston Trust and opened to the public in the summer of 1986.

Rodmell, Monk's House: 3 miles south of Lewes and 6 miles north of Newhaven, on A275. Home of Virginia and Leonard Woolf from 1919. Now National Trust.

Tilton: Farmhouse 900 yards east of Charleston (q.v.), country home of Maynard and Lydia Keynes from 1925.

West Wittering, Eleanor House: cottage 8 miles south-west of Chichester, leased by St John and Mary Hutchinson before First World War and sub-let to Vanessa Bell in 1915.

Elsewhere in England

Berkshire, Mill House, Tidmarsh: 1 mile south of Pangbourne, home of Lytton Strachey and Carrington, 1917–24.

Cornwall, Talland House, St Ives: House in Talland Road overlooking the bay, leased by Leslie Stephen for the summer, 1882–94; later converted into holiday apartments.

Kent, Sissinghurst Castle: restored Elizabethan manor, 2 miles north of Cranbrook, home of Vita Sackville-West and Harold Nicolson from 1930; now National Trust.

Oxfordshire, Garsington Manor: 5 miles south-east of Oxford, home of Philip and Lady Ottoline Morrell, 1915–27.

Suffolk, Green Farm, Ampton: 5 miles north of Bury St Edmunds, country home of Desmond and Molly MacCarthy, 1906–10.

Suffolk, Wissett Lodge, Wissett: Farmhouse off the A144, 2 miles west of Halesworth, home of Duncan Grant and David Garnett, March–September 1916.

Surrey, Durbins, near Guildford: built by Roger Fry, 1909; his home until 1917.

Surrey, The Cearne, Limpsfield Chart: village off the B269, 6 miles south-east of Godstone on the M25, home of Edward and Constance Garnett, 1896–1946.

Surrey, West Hackhurst, Abinger Hammer: off the A25, 5 miles south-west of Dorking, home of E. M. Forster, 1902–45.

Wiltshire, Ham Spray House: 1 mile east of Ham village and 5 miles south of Hungerford, home of Lytton Strachey and Carrington, 1924–32, with share held by Ralph Partridge who lived there with Frances Partridge, 1932–60.

Wiltshire, The Lacket, Lockeridge: cottage 3 miles south-west of Marlborough. It was owned by Hilton Young who leased it to Lytton Strachey, 1913–15.

In France

Cassis, "La Bergère": converted farmhouse, above the small port of Cassis, 17 miles east of Marseilles, rented by Vanessa Bell and Duncan Grant, 1927–37, and visited by many of their Bloomsbury friends.

Offranville, "Chateau Auppegard": for over thirty years from the early 1920s the home of Ethel Sands, some 5 miles south of Dieppe.

Roquebrune, "La Souco": villa on high ground some 3 miles west of Menton, overlooking the Corniche; home of the Bussy family 1903–54, apart from the years 1940–5.

St Rémy-en-Provence: small town some 13 miles south-east of Avignon, where Roger Fry was part-owner of a farmhouse, 1931–4.

Bibliographical Note

We have cited books of particular relevance to a specific person under the appropriate entry so as to suggest material which may be read for fuller treatment of a subject. Some works, however, we have found of such value that we feel they should also be cited separately. Unless otherwise indicated they were published in London.

Anscombe, Isabelle, *Omega and After, Bloomsbury and the Decorative Arts* (1981)

Askwith, B. E., *Two Victorian Families* (1971)

Bell, Clive, *Old Friends, Personal Recollections* (1956)

Bell, Julian, *Essays, Poems and Letters*, edited by Quentin Bell (1938)

Bell, Quentin, *Bloomsbury* (1968)

——, *Virginia Woolf, A Biography*, 2 vols (1972)

Bell, Vanessa, *Notes on Virginia's Childhood*, edited by R. J. Schaubeck (New York, 1974)

Boyd, Elizabeth F., *Bloomsbury Heritage* (1976)

Brenan, Gerald, *South from Granada* (1957)

——, *A Life of One's Own* (1962)

——, *A Personal Record* (1974)

Buckle, Richard, *Diaghilev* (1979)

Carrington, Dora, *Letters and Extracts from her Diary*, edited by David Garnett (1970)

Carrington, Noel, *Carrington* (rev. edition, 1980)

Clements, K., *Henry Lamb, the Artist and his Friends* (Bristol, 1985)

Edel, Leon, *Bloomsbury, House of Lions* (Philadelphia, 1979)

Fry, Roger, *Letters of Roger Fry*, edited by Denys Sutton, 2 vols (1972)

Gadd, David,   *The Loving Friends* (1974)

Garnett, Angelica,   *Deceived with Kindness* (1984)

Garnett, David,   *The Golden Echo* (1954)

——,   *The Flowers of the Forest* (1956)

——,   *The Familiar Faces* (1962)

——,   *Great Friends* (1979)

Gertler, Mark,   *Selected Letters of Mark Gertler*, edited by Noel Carrington (1965)

Gide, André and Bussy, Dorothy,   *Selected Letters*, edited by R. Tedeschi (1983)

Glendinning, Victoria,   *Vita* (1983)

Gordon, L.,   *Virginia Woolf, A Writer's Life* (Oxford 1984)

Heilbrun, C.,   *The Garnett Family* (1961)

Holroyd, Michael,   *Lytton Strachey* (1971)

——,   *Lytton Strachey and the Bloomsbury Group* (1971)

Keynes, Milo (ed.),   *Essays on John Maynard Keynes* (Cambridge, 1975)

——,   *Lydia Lopokova* (1983)

Lehmann, John,   *Virginia Woolf and her World* (1975)

Levy, Paul,   *Moore: G. E. Moore and the Cambridge Apostles* (1979)

MacCarthy, Desmond,   *Memories* (1953)

Noble, Joan R. (ed.),   *Recollections of Virginia Woolf* (1972)

Partridge, Frances,   *A Pacifist's War* (1978)

——,   *Memories* (1981)

——,   *Julia* (1983)

——,   *Everything to Lose* (1985)

Shone, Richard,   *Bloomsbury Portraits* (Oxford, 1976)

Skidelsky, Robert,   *John Maynard Keynes; Hopes Betrayed 1883–1920* (1984))

Spalding, Frances,   *Roger Fry, Art and Life* (1980)

——,   *Vanessa Bell* (1983)

Strachey, Barbara,   *Remarkable Relations* (1980)

——,   *The Strachey Line* (1985)

Strachey, James & Alix,   *Bloomsbury/Freud, The Letters of James and Alix Strachey, 1924–5*, edited by P. Meisel and W. Kendrick (1986)

Trombley, S.,   *All that Summer She was Mad* (1981)

Woodeson, John,   *Mark Gertler* (1972)

Woolf, Leonard,   *Sowing, 1880–1904* (1960)

——,   *Growing, 1904–1911* (1961)

——,   *Beginning Again, 1911–1918* (1964)

——,   *Downhill All the Way, 1919–1939* (1967)

——, *The Journey Not The Arrival Matters, 1939–1969* (1969)

Woolf, Virginia, *Moments of Being, Unpublished Autobiographical Writings*, edited by J. Schulkind (1976)

——, *The Letters of Virginia Woolf*, edited by Nigel Nicolson and Joanne Trautmann, 6 vols (1975–80)

——, *The Diary of Virginia Woolf*, edited by A. Olivier Bell and A. McNeillie, 5 vols (1977–84)